THE LONG AND
THE SHORT OF IT

THE LONG AND THE SHORT OF IT

THE AUTOBIOGRAPHY OF BRITAIN'S GREATEST AMATEUR GOLFER

GARY WOLSTENHOLME MBE

JB

N BLAKE

Published by John Blake Publishing Ltd,
3 Bramber Court, 2 Bramber Road,
London W14 9PB, England

www.johnblakepublishing.co.uk

First edition, published 2010

ISBN: 978 1 84358 256 4

British Library Cataloguing-in-Publication Data:
A catalogue record for this book is available from the British Library.

Design by www.envydesign.co.uk

Printed in the UK by CPI William Clowes Beccles NR34 7TL

1 3 5 7 9 10 8 6 4 2

Papers used by John Blake Publishing are natural, recyclable products
made from wood grown in sustainable forests. The manufacturing processes conform
to the environmental regulations of the country of origin.

Every attempt has been made to contact the relevant copyright-holders, but some were
unobtainable. We would be grateful if the appropriate people could contact us.

I dedicate this to my mum, Joan – it is a small way of showing my undying love and appreciation for everything she has done for me. Without her help, support and love, I am sure that I would never be in the position of having an autobiography published.

I hope that this book might also inspire other players to go on and represent their country as I did, despite any impediments that might stand in their way.

ACKNOWLEDGEMENTS

There are a great many people that I would like to thank: Peter Allison, and all the staff at Yes! Golf; Peter and Jackie Alliss; Cecil Bloice; Alan Brindley; John Hayes, Matthew Hayes and everyone at Champions UK; Ray and Chandra Chaudhuri; my ghostwriter, Derek Clements; Richard Clifford and family, and all at SKCIN; Neil Cook, and all at Golfsmith UK; Cumbria Golf Union; Mike Curley; Graham Curtin, and all at the excellent Carus Green Golf Club, near Kendal; Ryan Done; Tony Donovan, and everyone at Age Concern Leicestershire & Rutland; everyone at The English Golf Union; Simon Fletcher; Eric Herd and all at Farmfoods; Gloucestershire Golf Union; David Grecic; Eddie Hammond; Cliff Heath; Nick Hibbs; Robin Higgins and Team Nutrition; Sam Holmes; Lt Col. Don Jeffery OBE; Karsten Ping UK, and all who work there; Mike Kelly; Leicestershire and Rutland Golf Union; Malcolm and Sari Lewis; John Lovett; Peter McEvoy; Julian Morley and all at Truvis; Brian Mudge; everyone at Myerscough College; Northampton University; Jeff Paton and all at the Golf Club of Georgia; Andrea Peacock; Jon Plaxton; David Powell;

David and Jennifer Prentice; Dr Harry and Pat Proctor; The R&A and all who work there; Pam Richardson; David Ridley; Silverdale Golf Club; Ron Smith; Nikki Spence; Peter Thompson;Willie Thorne; Roger and Ann Vicary, and all at Kilworth Springs Golf Club; Martin Wild; John and Barbara Wrigley; and finally all of the clubs where I'm an Honorary Member: Berkhamsted; Bristol & Clifton; County Sligo Rosses Point; Golf Club of Georgia; Grange-over-Sands; Heysham; Morecambe; Scarborough North Cliff; The Berkshire; The Leicestershire; The Old Giggleswickian Golf Society; and, last but not least, Trevose. Apologies in advance for anyone that I might have missed in these acknowledgments!

CONTENTS

FOREWORD

My first memories of Gary are looking at him lying in a baby's cot, aged about six weeks. His father Guy and I had been friends since 1946, when we started our National Service together. If my memory serves me right, he was only two or three places behind me in the queue to sign on, and when I was asked if I would like to be a gunner, my mind flashed back to those far-off days of the Battle of Britain and bombing raids on occupied Europe. Sadly it was not to be, I was off and into the RAF Regiment.

Little did I think that with the passing of the years Gary would be writing a book on his life in golf. And what a remarkable life it has been, competing at the very highest level in Amateur Golf; certainly holding a position in the top ten finest Amateurs this country has ever produced.

Now, after conquering most of those fields, he's moving into the 'paid ranks', beginning a new career at the age of fifty. As his godfather I can only wish him well, and urge him to keep playing the game as he has been for the past 25 years. He will, I'm sure, be an asset to the European Senior Tour and I hope it won't be too long before I see the name 'G. Wolstenholme' and an image of him holding on high the winner's trophy with, in the other hand, a well deserved cheque!

Gary has always had a reputation for being outspoken, and whilst reading passages from this book, I can almost hear him saying the words that appear in print.

There's no prouder person in the world at the moment than his mother, Joan, who has been a wonderful supporter of her son through the good and not-so-good days. But I, for one, think there are many more good ones ahead.

Enjoy!

Peter Alliss

CHAPTER ONE
END OF AN ERA

'I am sorry Gary, but we are not going to be picking you for the England team to play in the Home Internationals at the end of the year.' As Anthony Abraham, the chairman of selectors at the English Golf Union (the EGU), uttered those fateful words to me over the phone one June day in 2008, I realised that my England career was over. After representing my country on 218 occasions, I was being 'put out to grass' – excuse the pun. I don't suppose I should have been too surprised that there wasn't any great fanfare goodbye. When I won my 100th cap England did nothing to mark it; what's more they also even ignored my reaching 150 caps. When I played for England for the 200th time it was in a match against Spain at Royal Ashdown Forest. I played well all week, went out in the top singles match and was even interviewed on Sky Television, who did a biopic of my career to mark the milestone achievement, and, lo and behold, the EGU presented me with a cut-glass decanter. I was very grateful, but nearly fainted!

I made up my mind that if 2008 was to mark the end of my England career, it might as well be the end of my time in amateur golf too. I was shattered. Yes, I was 47 and I had far more good golf behind me than I probably had to look forward to, but I was still one of the best players in Britain at the time. I even finished the season that year seventh on the EGU Order of Merit. It was mid season and I only had months to turn it around. So that's what I did, finishing second in the South of England championship and winning the Lee Westwood Trophy with four sub-70 rounds in what turned out to be my last ever amateur competition.

My international demise had all begun earlier that year in May when I had played poorly for England in an international match against France at Frilford Heath. But everybody, surely, is entitled to an off day or two. Besides, I had all sorts of issues in my life at that time, not the least of which was that I had recently given up my job, put my house on the market, and decided to move back to my beloved Morecambe Bay, where I had spent my childhood years. These changes turned out to be pretty traumatic.

I'd had a bit of a spat with my then coach David Ridley, who happened to be the lead national coach, at the 2007 European Men's Team Championships at Glasgow Gailes – something and nothing really – and, after that, I had always felt that there was a slightly uncomfortable edge in and around the England setup. It seemed that my clash with David had perhaps been the catalyst for change and, from that moment onwards, they were thinking that it was time to bring down the curtain on my amateur representative career. It had been made abundantly clear to me that the EGU wanted to focus on players under the age of twenty-five. If you were older than that it seemed you might as well forget about being able to represent your country, even though the vast majority of young golfers only saw the England team – and the opportunities it provided them with – as a stepping-stone to professional golf. Regretfully to me, it seems that this is something the EGU now actively encourage with little or no real feel as to what the history of amateur golf provides, just regarding it as a breeding ground for the Tours of the future.

I don't think they even considered that, with all the years of experience I had under my belt, I would be a good person to help those same young players, to point them in the right direction and to make them aware of the potential challenges they might face. I desperately wanted to give something back. Even today, if they asked me to help them out, I would of course say yes, although I doubt whether it will ever happen now.

Much of the respect I'd had for the amateur bodies who control the game diminished when the England and Great Britain and Ireland selectors discarded me. I hadn't always been the most popular player around. A bit like Marmite, you either loved me or you didn't, and, as you will discover, I had often struggled to sit there and say nothing if I felt things were wrong within the amateur game. However I still don't believe that I deserved to be discarded like an old pair of slippers. It is, of course, their game; it is their bat and ball. I accept that, but after giving them twenty years or so of my life and making some pretty huge sacrifices during this time, that when the end did eventually come, I envisaged it arriving in a slightly more dignified manner, with a thanks and good luck message. In the end it was just a phone call one Tuesday afternoon.

I had hoped that I might have been able to decide for

3

myself when it was time to call it a day. Instead, here I was feeling that I had been shoved out before my time, a bit like retiring Red Rum after just two Grand National wins. First and foremost, however, I am a pragmatist, and crying over spilt milk is not my way. What's more it is a waste of time as half the people you're playing against don't care, and the other half are glad you're out of the equation.

In one way or another I owe amateur golf for much of what I have achieved today, and for that I will be eternally grateful. It has given me the opportunity to visit some truly amazing places across the globe, allowed me to play on the best courses in the world and introduced me to amazing people from all walks of life. It also presented me with a chance to establish a huge amount of credibility for myself, both physically and spiritually. I used to receive lots of letters from people who were looking for advice. I guess they figured that, because of everything I had achieved in amateur golf in the way that I did, I was in a position to help them, and I tried my level best to reply to every letter I ever got.

People would stop me in supermarkets when I was trying to choose between peas or carrots for tea and ask: 'Hello there. Aren't you Gary Wolstenholme? How does my son (or daughter) become a good golfer?' There may have been times when I just wanted to get on with my shopping, but I never did. I always took time out to listen to their story and then I would try to give the best possible advice. Without fail, I always went away from the conversation with a smile on my face, thinking what a funny life I led.

Through golf I even received an MBE in the 2007 New Year's Honours List – something that came as a huge surprise. I collected it in May 2007 at Buckingham Palace from the Queen herself. What a day and what a truly special honour that was, both for me and for my mum, who came with me.

I had never really particularly wanted to play golf professionally, but suddenly I took the decision on a September day in 2008. At breakfast I was an amateur of some repute, and by teatime I was a budding professional, beginning a new career at the bottom of the ladder all over again. Talk about being a sucker for punishment.

The Royal and Ancient Golf Club (R&A) couldn't find any further use for my services and the EGU had essentially said: 'Bye, you're no longer good enough.' It was their loss, not mine, and I really believe that. However, I had no job and no way to make a decent living other than through golf. The only thing I had ever been able to do really successfully in my life was to play this game that I love so very much. I had other talents, of course, but wasn't 'qualified' for anything other than being a notable golfing personality.

What was I going to do? Some friends figured that with my fiftieth birthday coming along in 2010, perhaps it was time to be selfish for a change and put my ambitions first, but initially I wasn't so sure. However eventually we decided that the only sensible thing for me to do was to turn pro as soon as was possible and try to get ready for the European Seniors Tour where, with a bit of luck, I would be made to (a) feel as though I had some worth and (b) have the opportunity, for the first time in my life, to earn some proper money through playing golf.

And so here I am, hoping that it is all going to turn out okay for me and that in a few years from now I will trot off into the sunset with my bag of gold over my shoulder. I still smile at that thought. Making a career change of this magnitude at my time of life is huge of course and carries no guarantee of success, but I am filled with a genuine excitement and now believe that I have made the right choice. So watch this space.

CHAPTER TWO

BORN WITH A CLUB IN MY HAND

I was born with a love of sport and, in particular of golf, in my blood. My paternal grandfather was Harry Wolstenholme, who had six children, one of whom was Guy, my father, who was born on March 8, 1931. Harry was a disciplinarian and an avid golf lover. Fortunately for me, as it turned out, it seems he had a soft spot for Dad. Even so, on one occasion, the young Guy had been pitching golf balls at home in the back garden and accidentally knocked one through the French windows, shattering the glass. As a result, Harry banned him from playing golf for a month, a lesson well learnt because during his best years Dad's chipping became formidable.

My grandfather loved golf with a passion and revelled in the success that Dad would achieve in amateur golf. Harry lived until he was ninety-three. He had worked for a chemical firm, Geigy Chemicals, in Glasgow and on one harrowing occasion was involved in rescuing a number of work colleagues after some dangerous chemicals had leaked out into the atmosphere. Harry put his life on the line that day to ensure that people were led to safety but ended up inhaling some of the toxic gas himself. It affected his lungs for the rest of his life. He was later awarded the OBE for his bravery that day. When he was told that he was being honoured, Harry said in typical fashion that he was far too busy to attend Buckingham Palace, and the Lord Provost of Glasgow had to go to his workplace to present him with his OBE.

He was one of the most unassuming people you could ever wish to meet. Even into his late eighties he used to play nine holes of golf and walk two miles to the library and back pretty much every day, so he kept himself pretty fit. I used to visit my grandfather in his flat in Morecambe and enjoyed my time with him greatly. His eyesight eventually failed, though, and he started tripping over things – something that came as an awful shock to the system for him – so he had to stop playing his beloved golf, as well as taking his walks to the library. He ended up moving to Nottingham, but died shortly afterwards.

My father was Guy Wolstenholme, who became particularly well known after he finished sixth in The Open at St Andrews in 1960 while still an amateur. It was the Centenary Open, which was won by the Australian golfer, Kel Nagle, after the heavens had opened and had done their very best to wash away the Old Course. Water cascaded down the steps of the R&A clubhouse like a waterfall and the Valley of Sin in front of the 18th green quickly filled up with water. It was the era when Arnold Palmer, who had been taking the game by storm in America and had built up a huge legion of fans who loved his swashbuckling style of play, came over to Scotland to take part in The Open and, pretty much single-handedly, breathed life back into the Championship. Until Palmer turned up, The Open was struggling, but suddenly it became the major that everybody wanted to win. And, of course, my father was now very much a part of it, and got to meet this wonderful American golfer among others on numerous occasions throughout his career.

Despite the rain, the course dried out and the tournament was completed. Dad finished with a final round of 68 and recorded the lowest four-round total in relation to par for an amateur (283, five-under par) until Justin Rose came along and wrote his place in the history books at the 1998 Open, when he finished tied for fourth on six-under par as a seventeen-year-old amateur.

I am not sure how much enjoyment Mum got from my father's play in The Open back in 1960 though because she had other things on her mind at the time, namely the imminent arrival of yours truly.

Dad was a very fine amateur golfer, winning both the English strokeplay and matchplay championships, the latter on two occasions. He won a host of other top titles, too, including the Berkshire Trophy three times, as well as the German amateur championship. And he also played in the 1957 and 1959 Walker Cup matches for Great Britain and Ireland against the USA, as well as competing in the Eisenhower Trophy and the Commonwealth Trophy. Most of Dad's siblings had tried golf and he had a brother, Chip, who was also a first-class golfer. There is a famous family story about the brothers playing an eighteen-hole match at Kirby Muxloe in Leicestershire a day or so after Dad had won the English Amateur Championship, and Chip beat my father 3&2. It was a great way to be brought back down to earth – not that grandfather Harry would have allowed Dad to get too big for his boots anyway.

Like the rest of his family, Dad was born and bred in

Leicester and was largely responsible for putting Leicestershire on the amateur golfing map. There were not many great courses in the county, and there were even fewer great players. Until one Guy Bertram Wolstenholme came along, that is. To give you some idea of just how few top amateurs came out of the county, after Dad, I was the next Leicestershire golfer to be capped by England. That has all changed in recent years however, and I would like to think I may have had something to do with inspiring a new generation of golfers from Leicestershire international players.

Dad was regarded as one of the best amateur golfers of his generation and played for England fifty times. He never won The Amateur Championship, although he did once reach the semi-finals in 1959 at Royal St. Georges, losing to Bill Hyndman, the great American amateur. Hyndman was fairly typical of many of the golfers of that era. There was not a huge amount of money to be made from playing the game as a professional, and the sport was full of career amateurs – many of whom came from wealthy families and could afford to spend their days on the golf course, funded by trust funds or from salaries paid to them by the family company.

Dad was never really in that position. He had to work, and it made what he achieved in the amateur game all the more satisfying, because many of the men he was taking on and beating were effectively professional in everything but name. In this country there were some great competitive amateurs, including the likes of Charlie Green, who was employed by a distillery and spent his life playing golf entertaining clients, and who dominated the amateur game in Scotland for many years; the prodigious Sir Michael Bonallack had the support of a family haulage business; and Joe Carr, the legendary Irish International, was also sufficiently financially well placed to be able to concentrate solely on just his golf, without having any money worries.

Dad had worked in the knitwear and textile industry in Leicester for a man called Pip Howe in those early years, and the two of them forged a good relationship that allowed Dad to take time off to compete with the cream of British talent of those days. It was a sad occasion for my father when Howe died in the late 1950s. Other potential bosses in the area could see no real benefit in employing somebody who was looking to take days off to go and play golf, even though Dad was effectively working as an ambassador for anyone who might employ him. If only they could have seen it: he could get them free publicity and also provide them with the opportunity to bask in his glory.

After Pip Howe's death, therefore, my father had little choice but to head south for work and ended up in London. With the help of Gerald Micklem and Raymond Oppenhiemer (who were movers and shakers in golfing circles in that era) he joined Sunningdale Golf Club and certainly fell on his feet, when a member helped him to land himself a job selling Bentleys. Then, as now, these were sought-after luxury cars and every time he sold one he received a nice commission payment and would give Mum extra money towards the housekeeping.

In those days, independently wealthy individuals, especially those based in the London area, chose to support the better amateur golfers of their generation, contributing towards their playing expenses and allowing them to play in all the big tournaments. My father was lucky enough to have benefactors such as this towards the end of his amateur career. In return, they may have asked Dad to play a round with one of their clients, or to play 'money games' with them; if that was what it took, then that is what he, and many others like him, would do. Besides, it wasn't that much of a hardship, because it usually involved playing on the finest golf courses in the land, and he was doing the thing that he wanted to do.

The 1950s and '60s were halcyon days for amateur golf. There was a whole host of great, great players. Apart from Bonallack and Green there was Joe Carr, mentioned above, who is arguably the finest amateur golfer Ireland has ever produced. Dr David Marsh was another notable in those great days too. A good story Mum told me was when Dad and she were giving David a lift up to the Walker Cup in 1959 at Muirfield. Dad opened the boot to let David put his kit away. David gasped at the amount of kit Dad had brought with him. Four pairs of golf shoes, six dozen balls etc. Dad looked at David, and asked, 'Where's all your kit?' David looked at his bag and holdall, and said, 'That's it.' There was simply one pair of shoes, a set of clubs and a dozen balls. They certainly lived in different circles in those days. David and Dad became great friends, and even now I enjoy the opportunity to chat with David about those memorable times. Nowadays, these guys would turn twenty and become professional, but the 50s and 60s were very different times. There is no doubt in my mind that these superb players could all have competed with the best professionals of their era, but it hasn't always been like that. Indeed, in the 1970s and '80s, the difference in ability between the top amateurs and tour professionals was marked, and was proved by how many joined the paid ranks and failed to make the grade.

That all began to change again in the 1990s when the amateur bodies were transformed from being run from the back of someone's house into the professional organisations they are today, with young amateur golfers being groomed for stardom from a very early age. Indeed, now the gap has narrowed still further and we are seeing amateur golfers winning professional tournaments – for example Shane Lowry, Pablo Martin, Ryo Ishikawa and Danny Lee have all done just that in recent times.

I am sure my father had no particular plans to turn professional, but after having gone close to winning The Open in 1960, that's exactly what he decided to do. The Royal and Ancient had changed the rules that year, making it possible for amateur golfers to go straight into the paid ranks – prior to that, they would have had to serve an apprenticeship, earning next to no money while working in a shop, learning how to repair clubs and giving lessons to members, etc. Don't get me wrong, there is nothing wrong with that, but it is not the path that somebody in their late twenties or early thirties would ever have dreamt of following prior to chasing a dream of winning majors. Suddenly, however, the R&A changed things, and it meant that my father and players like him, who had competed and won at the highest levels of the amateur game, were allowed to turn pro, compete in tournaments and win prize money, albeit that, initially, they couldn't earn such remuneration for the first six months.

Dad decided to take the plunge, even though by then he was already twenty-nine years old. Apart from the changes in the rules, it was also quite likely that he realised Palmer's arrival on the scene was leading to a golf boom, and he wanted to be part of it. For those of you who are too young to remember, just think of the huge upsurge of interest in golf that accompanied Tiger Woods when he first burst onto the professional scene. That's exactly the way it was with Palmer, Jack Nicklaus and Gary Player. And it is to their credit that they maintained a clean-cut image throughout their career, with Palmer even agreeing to stop smoking on the golf course when it was pointed out that putting a cigarette in his mouth was not setting the right example.

Dad got a job as an assistant professional at St George's Hill Golf Club, although all he was really interested in was playing in tournaments, and he, my mother and their baby son (me) moved into a flat in Virginia Water in Surrey, not far from the magnificent Wentworth and Sunningdale golf clubs.

It is fair to say that he never made significant amounts of money as a tour pro, but it also has to be remembered that in those days not many players did. Although, as I've already said, the R&A had changed the rules for new professionals, for reasons best known to themselves they decreed that a professional could not win prize money during the first six months of his career. As luck would have it, my father won one of the first events in which he competed as a pro and they gave him a set of leather luggage instead of the prize money he would have won, which, in hindsight, was probably worth more than the first prize would have been. They were Corinthian days indeed, and he made up his money by competing in pro-ams and exhibition matches, as well as through a little bit of gambling on and off the course.

Dad won five European Tour tournaments. Today, that would almost certainly have made him a millionaire. He won the British PGA Close championship, the Kenya Open, the Danish Open and the Dutch Open, as well as the Jeyes tournament in Dublin, by what was then a record winning margin of 12 shots. So you can see that he was a very good player. He would also go on to enjoy considerable success in Australia, but more of that later.

My mother is Joan, and she has been, and remains, my rock, the constant in my life, the woman who has been there for me through thick and thin. She was born and bred in Caton, near Lancaster. Her father was Tom Hustler, who was a successful entrepreneur, and I do mean successful. He had a Rolls Royce and at one time he owned a house that contained a cinema – this was in the days when even some towns didn't have a cinema.

He owned two huge mansions during his life St. Wilfred's and Pengarth, with massive paintings hanging on the walls, and among other things he helped turn Lancaster Golf Club into a good eighteen-hole course after the Second World War. During that period, huge swathes of land were set aside for farming, so the course was in a real mess, hence the need to reconstitute it. He was also a very useful golfer in his own right – good enough to compete in the English Amateur Championship – and it was through going along to one of those tournaments with him that Mum met the man who would eventually become my father.

Because Tom was so wealthy, he was a star attraction, and Joan stood out too because she was an attractive girl. How could the young Guy Wolstenholme not be bowled over by it all? I am sure that he must have thought to himself: 'Mmm, there's a bit of a catch here!'

Joan loved sport, and taught me in later life how to play cricket, tennis and badminton. It was Mum and my grandparents, Tom and Eleanor, who really encouraged me to play golf. Dad was never especially keen for me to take up the game. I am sure that he had his reasons. I am guessing that chief among them would be the fact that he did not want me to enter a profession where there is such an unpredictable earning potential. I suppose every father would want their child to avoid the mistakes they felt they had made. Dad only ever gave me one golf lesson, and that was when I was sixteen. I had an aunt, Margy, who married a Lancashire county player called Clive Middleton, so golf was part and parcel of my life from a young age, whether my father liked it or not. Looking back on it now, I suppose it was inevitable that it would become the focus of my life at some stage, but that certainly was not the case through my early years and into my teens.

When Mum and Dad got married, Mum's parents gave them a house in Grange-over-Sands in Cumbria, where they lived until Dad turned professional; at that point, my grandparents bought the house back and gave my parents the money to buy the flat in Virginia Water. Remaining in the northwest of England was not an option because back then Manchester airport was tiny and it meant that if Dad was playing in a tournament in Europe he would have to drive all the way to London. It was just too much for him to do if he wanted to compete effectively. In short, it was easier to travel around the world starting from Surrey.

On August 21, 1960, not long after they had moved, I was born at Frimley Maternity Hospital near Egham. Unfortunately the marital problems began a few years later. Dad was away a lot and Mum was left to cope on her own with a young child, without her family around to help. It was a pretty lonely experience, being so far from her beloved Lancashire. Today's top pros take their families all over the world with them, but that wasn't an option back then. Apart from anything else, and I can't stress this enough, the prize money was poor and appearance payment wasn't even a twinkle in Mark McCormack's eye, which meant that if a player travelled to, say, Kenya and then missed the cut, it meant not only that he wouldn't pick up any prize money, but that he would also still have to pay his expenses for the rest of the week – and that is why so many of them gambled in those days. It was anything but a glamorous life, but it was certainly an adventure, and there were plenty of interesting characters on the pro golf circuit in those days, including Peter Alliss, Dave Thomas, Hugh Lewis, Lionel Platts, Hedley Muscroft and Simon Hobday, to name but a few.

In the early 1960s, Alliss, Thomas, Bernard Hunt and Neil Coles were the players who were dominating the game and all of them, plus other similar characters, had turned professional as soon as they could. Yes, they had probably played junior golf (Peter Alliss and my father played for the England Boys team together), but they got into the paid ranks as fast as their legs could carry them. The amateurs who were joining the ones who were paid weren't as battle-hardened as these established pros and many of them disappeared without trace, although Dad never really fell into that category.

To save money, Dad used to drive to the ferry ports, catch a boat and then motor across Europe to reach his tournament destination. He would share the car with a fellow player in order to cut the costs, but it was hard work driving across the likes of Holland, Belgium, France, Germany and Italy. Just imagine arriving at a tournament venue having driven hundreds of miles, then having to find somewhere to stay (it had to be somewhere cheap) and trying to motivate yourself to go out and have a practise round before the tournament began, perhaps only playing two of these, missing the cut and then being faced with either turning the car round and heading back to the ferry port or driving on to the next venue, knowing that if you missed the cut again you probably would barely be able to afford the petrol to get home. I am not saying that happened to my father particularly, but there were many golfers, young and experienced alike, who fought a constant battle to balance the books, all dreaming of that one week when they might finally make it. In that respect, perhaps not much has really changed.

When they played events on the Safari Tour, as it was known, they had no option but to fly. The tournaments were played in countries such as Kenya, Egypt, Rhodesia (now Zimbabwe), Mozambique and South Africa, and the respective governments were pleased to see the players. They wanted to encourage the growth of the game, and there was no better way of doing it than by having GB&I's (Great Britain and Ireland's) finest golfers on display to help promote what their country had to offer. As an additional bonus, high-powered businessmen were desperate to play in the pro-ams that took place before the tournaments began, and it was during those that plenty of serious business deals were brokered – deals that simply wouldn't have taken place had it not been for the tournaments.

It was pretty tough for the players, but it was an adventure. The flights took much longer in those days, and then the guys had to take their lives in their hands when they clambered into the local taxis, complete with all their luggage and golf clubs. Back then, it wasn't unusual to find that a player's clubs would get lost in transit and would either turn up a day or two late, or not at all, so they had to beg, borrow or steal golf clubs just to play. It is safe to say that, despite the best efforts of the tournament organisers to ensure that the players were as comfortable as possible, the hotels were not always the best. In addition, you have to throw in stifling heat, mosquitoes (and worse) and, of course, the food. On top of that, some of the courses were not always quite as well groomed as they were used to at home. The tour professionals, however, knew they had to follow the sun if they were to make any kind of a living, and if that meant heading to Europe, Africa, South America and the Far East, then so be it.

If players were really lucky, they would be offered accommodation at the homes of club members. It was only the likes of Bob Charles, Peter Thomson or Gary Player, however, who found themselves being put up in five-star hotels.

So if the prize money was poor and there was no appearance payment, how did golfers such as my dad survive? The truth is that most of them were pretty useful gamblers, turning their hands to anything from backgammon to bridge or poker. They would also bet on the golf course. Dad was lucky enough to be given the opportunity to fly out to Australia, New Zealand and Japan to play in tournaments there. He was sought after because he could play a decent hand at bridge, coax music from the piano and was also good company at the dinner table.

His ability on the piano was legendary and he was a naturally entertaining man so, wherever he went, he was often the centre of attention. He made people laugh just by being himself. In those days, there was a piano in many houses and he would sit down and play for hours. He was self-taught and didn't learn to read music until much later in life, but he could listen to a tune and within an hour or so he would have worked it out and could play it note perfect. I can imagine that when the players had come off the course, thousands of miles from home, Guy Wolstenholme Esq was popular, as he helped them keep their minds off the families they had left back at home. Music must have relieved his own homesickness too.

He was good at networking and went out of his way to get to know the right people, such as Peter Thomson and Peter Alliss, who is my godfather. He got to know all the most influential people in the game from the Far East to Europe, and that helped him get into the right tournaments as well as the right accommodation most of the time.

Mum, meanwhile, was stuck at home with a young child. She was only twenty when they first got married, and being left on her own was not what she had in mind for herself, so it was inevitable that it would put a strain on their relationship. It was a big problem for her. I don't want you to get the impression that Dad abandoned her, because that wasn't the case at all, and she did go with him sometimes, but to the likes of the south of France, most definitely not to Africa or the Far East. And it only happened if somebody else was taking their wife with them and suggested that Dad do the same.

However, as a result of all his travels, my father fell in love with Australia and he came home and tried to persuade Mum to go and live there with him, but she refused. If she felt lonely in England, just imagine how she would have felt in Australia while he was away playing golf. At least while we lived at Virginia Water she could talk to her parents on the phone and go and see them occasionally. But this was Australia. Dad had made up his mind. He loved the warmer climate and was determined that he was going to settle in

Melbourne, near his great friend Peter Thomson, the five-time Open champion, with or without his wife and son.

Mum and Dad eventually split up in 1964 when I was just four years old, and I vividly remember an occasion when, as a toddler, I crawled into the living room and they were sitting on either side of the coffee table, deep in discussion, and the subject was their future life together or, rather, the lack of it. I can remember it like it was yesterday, the two of them looking at each other so seriously, talking about splitting up and going their separate ways: Dad to Australia and Mum back home to Grange-over-Sands.

Divorce proceedings were started and Mum and I moved back up north to Grange-over-Sands to live with Tom and Eleanor Hustler, my maternal grandparents. The house was easily big enough for the four of us and it was a great town for me as a young boy. I suppose you would describe it as a 'sheltered' town, where we all felt safe and secure. For those of you who don't know it, it is an Edwardian resort set between the famous Lakeland Fells and Morecambe Bay. It was originally transformed by the advent of the Furness Railway, which helped to attract wealthy merchants who had grand houses built, many of which are now hotels. The town features a traffic-free promenade, ornamental gardens, a duck pond, golf courses, brass-band concerts and vantage points for bird watching, and many of the shop fronts still retain their Edwardian appearance.

I went to Charney Hall, a private prep school in the town, when I was seven, and all was well in my world, apart from the fact that my father wasn't on the scene; but I was lucky enough to have my grandfather instead. Mum was matron at Charney Hall, which I can only describe as being a bit like a holiday camp for boys. From an educational point of view, it was a disaster for me. At a young age Mum decided to get me every communicable disease going – measles, chickenpox, etc. You name it and I'd had it. The moment she heard that somebody's son or daughter had picked up, say, chickenpox, I would be taken round to the house to make sure I caught it too. Her theory was that the quicker you caught all these things the better, because they were always far more virulent if you caught them later in life. It was a great theory, and I can fully understand why she did it, but the downside was that I always seemed to be off school, so I was permanently playing catch-up with the other kids when I eventually recovered. It wasn't until I was much older that I learnt that I had a mild form of dyslexia, so I am sure that didn't help either.

Mum was a great parent, though she never encouraged me to read books, so I was almost totally illiterate by the time I went to school and I struggled as a result. But I was pretty sharp as I used to watch a lot of television, educational productions such as *The World About Us* and similarly edifying programmes. I was also a great communicator for my age and could hold a sensible conversation with anyone. We were one of the first families in the area to have a colour TV and I was fascinated by documentaries, so I picked up a great deal of knowledge while I was recovering from my various ailments. I was transfixed. In those days, BBC2 hardly showed any programmes – there would be a test card and then a documentary or education programme would come on for about twenty minutes, and I watched them all. I learnt about the world that way. I remember once arguing with a teacher who insisted that pineapples grew on trees, and I said that they didn't, that they grew on the ground. I knew that I was correct because I had seen it on TV, but that didn't stop the teacher punishing me for arguing.

They finally closed Charney Hall when the number of pupils fell to less than forty-five. Bullying was part and parcel of school life in those days, an aspect of the growing up process I guess and although I had never seen or experienced anything like it before, it is amazing how quickly you learn to accept it and adapt. It was a wake-up call for a seven-year-old though. I really enjoyed school life, as all of a sudden I had loads of new friends. I was an only child and there was nobody of my own age at home, so I enjoyed the social side of school, and sports in particular.

It is hard to believe now, but back then I was allowed to roam around the town in the holidays with little to worry about, and I took full advantage of everything it had to offer, including a fabulous outdoor swimming pool and municipal putting green on the front at Grange. In those days there was no crime to speak of in the town or the surrounding area that I knew of. Everything felt so safe. Mum had an active social scene in which lots of people played tennis, squash and badminton, so I was introduced to those wonderful games at an early age, and got to try my hand at most of them.

Although it was Mum who first encouraged me and taught me sports, I picked up most games by watching other people, especially those who were the best. I learnt chess that way, watching a few games, working out what each piece did. Mind you, my style of play was very attacking, so games often didn't last for very long – a 'crash and burn' style I suppose you could call it.

Mum played a little bit of golf in the early days but she stopped because she found it very frustrating. She had been used to sports that were 'reaction' games such as tennis, so the idea of hitting a stationary object often infuriated her, particularly when the ball didn't go where she wanted it to. Mum much preferred sports where she had to react; all that she ever wanted to do when playing golf was to try to hit the golf ball as hard and as far as she possibly could, and anybody who has ever played the game to any kind of standard will tell you that isn't the best thing to do. It requires timing and patience and good course management. So it was no great hardship for her to hang up her clubs for good and focus on tennis and badminton. I do remember, however, that Mum could hit a golf ball a long way.

It was mainly my grandparents who encouraged me to play golf, but by the mid-1960s Grandad Tom no longer played because he had a bad hip, so my grandmother used to take me to Grange Fell Golf Club, which was the first course I ever played. Neither of them ever pushed me though, and I was so keen to try my hand at everything else that I never really stuck with golf to the exclusion of other sports at that stage. I had three little cut-down clubs – a five wood, a seven iron and a putter. As you will learn later, the five wood was to play quite a part in my amateur career.

I had my first lesson at Grange Fell – how things have changed, because they no longer have a pro and haven't had one for at least thirty-five years. There was no practise ground, so he used to give lessons down the first fairway, and we would simply move to the side if anybody wanted to tee off. I remember that once I reached a certain ability I received my first proper set of golf clubs – a matched set of Dunlop Junior Blue Flash clubs. I got them for Christmas in 1967, when I was seven, and I can still see vividly in my mind's eye the red-and-black bag and head covers for the woods leaning against the window seat in the house on that crisp Christmas morning.

You read about the likes of Tiger Woods spending his entire childhood beating golf balls, but I was too interested in other childhood games ever to contemplate doing anything like that. I was able to entertain myself, and would do so for hours on end. I was perfectly happy making my own fun, in my own company. To be honest, I've never needed to be surrounded by lots of people.

Being such a solitary individual probably helped me with my golf in later years. When I was older, I was quite happy to play nine holes on my own, or to spend a couple of hours on the practise ground. It didn't bother me that I didn't have company. Some people will not play golf unless they have somebody to play with, but I have never been too worried on that score. Golf is a pretty individual sport anyway, apart from those rare occasions when you are playing in a team.

We lived in Grange-over-Sands until I was about ten years old, when my grandparents sold the house and we moved to Keighley in Yorkshire, where Grandad had a textile bobbin business. I played a little bit of golf while we were there, and I still have the letter I received in 1975 saying that my application to become a junior member of Keighley Golf Club had been rejected because they were full. I did eventually get in the following year, though.

When we lived in Keighley I went to Catterall Hall prep school and later attended Giggleswick public school in Settle in west Yorkshire. These were very different establishments. Now it was serious education and I had to work hard to try and catch up with my fellow pupils, which was easier said than done because they were miles ahead of me academically. I picked up things slowly but surely. I was pretty worldly-wise for my age and quickly realised that if you did certain things well you wouldn't get bullied by the senior boys, so I learnt to do what I had to do in order to get by. Children can be pretty mean and vindictive, so it paid to know what was what, or else to learn very quickly.

During the holidays I would occasionally pick up a golf club when encouraged to do so and, although I could hit the ball pretty well, I bobbed along with a twenty-four handicap for years as, in those days, I didn't get the chance to play many competitions and I had no great desire to reduce it. One game at Keighley sticks in my mind, though that occasion could have finished my golf career before it ever began. It was during the school holidays, and I teed off at the first hole, following an elderly couple – they weren't very good, to put it mildly – and I soon found myself right up behind them waiting on every single shot. While I was standing on the third hole I heard a golf ball thud onto the fairway behind me and realised that there was a fourball on the tee behind me and, as a junior playing on my own, I was expected to stand to the side and let them play through. After they hade done so, another fourball appeared and again I had to make way. After thirty-five more minutes of this happening I left the course in tears of anger and frustration because of one of golf's more eccentric rules of the day: if you are playing on your own, you have no standing, particularly as a junior. In those days we were also taught that children should be seen and not heard. That incident could have put me off golf, and I am certain that it must have driven many promising youngsters out of the game.

During this time I would only see Dad once a year, when he came back to Britain for about eight weeks to play some European Tour events. Although they were long since divorced, there was still a spark between my parents and in 1973 they tried to make the relationship work again. By this time Dad was settled in Melbourne and he persuaded Mum to join him there. They had been divorced for eight years and, apart from that brief spell in Virginia Water, my mother had spent all of her life in the north of England. It was a huge step for her to take, a genuine leap of faith.

I was duly installed at Melbourne Grammar, which, as you can imagine, was a hell of a culture shock. There was one huge bonus to the move, however, and that was the fact that I enjoyed what was surely the longest summer holiday break that any child has ever had. I had just finished the summer break in England when we headed Down Under, and went more or less straight into another in Australia.

The holiday couldn't last forever, of course, and eventually I had to walk through the gates of Melbourne Grammar. I have to say that it transformed me. I was given extra tuition to help me catch up, particularly in English – try to get your head around a boy from England being given extra tuition in English in an Australian school! I slowly caught up though and when I started reading I realised that I couldn't get enough of it. The first book I ever read, from cover to cover, was *Lord of the Rings*. It may have taken me the best part of six months, but I did it.

There were 3,000 pupils at Melbourne Grammar and it was by far the biggest school I had ever attended. In my year alone they fielded six cricket teams each weekend, and they were all of a pretty decent standard. In Australia there was never any chance of a pupil being given a game simply in order to make up the numbers; they played to win, even back then.

I was the third-youngest boy in the entire school. I was

also English, which meant that I was picked on by certain people. I took it, day after day until, finally, something in me snapped. We used to have lockers where we kept our kit, textbooks and some personal belongings, and the first thing that happened was that some bright spark decided to wrap some wire round mine, making it almost impossible to get into. I managed to get rid of that and the next thing I discovered was that when I came to open the padlock on my locker, somebody had filled it with plaster of Paris, which meant I had to cut off the loops that held the lock on.

I then of course found myself in a position where it was impossible to lock the door, and I would come back to my locker after being in class and discover that the entire contents had been tipped out. Sometimes they would do it in front of me and stand back and watch me picking everything up. There would always be a few of them laughing at the joke, which made it pretty hard to sort things out amicably, and eventually I just lost it. I was a big lad of over six feet and around 14 stone, and I battered one kid, made a mess of another, and the others just ran away. It was 'handbags at dawn' in reality, but nobody ever bothered me after that. I admit that I lost the plot but, in my defence, this type of thing had been going on for weeks on end, and I'd just reached the point where I'd had enough.

Mum knew there was something going on in my life, but I kept it bottled up. I had friends, but they weren't the sort of kids who could have helped me out of this corner. When you're being picked on you tend to find friends among those who never get involved if things get sticky, so I could hardly go to any of them and say: 'Right lads, I need you to help me sort this out.' Besides, if I had done that it would have made me no better than they were. And losing my cool in one explosive moment was probably far more effective anyway. I learnt a valuable lesson that day – there are times when you just have to stand up for yourself.

Peer pressure can be a terrible thing. If, as a youngster, you are good looking or you excel at sport, you will find yourself at the top of the 'food chain', with everybody wanting to be your friend, and all the best looking girls wanting to go out with you. Sadly, if you are small, spotty, with no real personality or have two left feet, the chances are that school can be a pretty miserable experience. Tragically, you hear about children committing suicide over things like this. I can understand how it happens.

Having exorcised my own demons, I found that I was finally accepted. Apart from the fact that the bullying stopped completely, I did pretty well at sport. I especially enjoyed cricket and recall a match against a rival school played on their ground. I always had a good arm, and the ball had been hit past me for a boundary off the last ball of the over, and I threw it back, not realising that the umpire was giving one of the batsmen his guard position. The umpire, who was one of the senior pupils from the opposing school, was completely focused on what he was doing and as I looked up I realised that the ball was heading in his direction, so I shouted: 'Fore!' Since we were playing cricket, it wasn't the greatest surprise in the world that nobody moved, and the ball hit him square on top of the head and knocked him clean out. Everybody looked at me in disbelief, as if I were some kind of idiot. Even though it was an accident, I was mortified. For a second or two I think everyone thought that I had killed him. He was taken to hospital where, thankfully, he made a full recovery. Mum made me write a letter of apology. In my defence, it was a great throw and it would have hit the stumps square-on had his head not got in the way.

While we were in Melbourne, I remember Dad would spend hours practising on the piano. If he had wanted to, I'm sure he could have made a living from it. We lived in a first-floor flat on Marne Street off Toorak Road and I will never be able to work out how the removal men got my father's grand piano into the building, but they did, and he really loved playing. It was how he forgot about golf, his stress-buster I suppose.

Dad loved Australia and the Australians seemed to adopt their entertaining Pommy readily. He also enjoyed a good measure of success there as a golfer, particularly later in life. At that time, back in the 60's, everybody was predicting that Australia was going to be where golf's next boom was going to occur. It certainly had, and still has, some quite wonderful golf courses, not least Royal Melbourne and the other such establishments on Melbourne's legendary 'sand belt'. But it is on the other side of the world and, even today, the amount of time it takes to fly there and the time difference means that it will never host more than a handful of world-class golf tournaments every year.

There are those who believe with a passion that Australia should host a major and while there is no doubt that the crowds would turn out in their thousands, the harsh reality is that the time difference means that the European and American television networks wouldn't be interested, and if you can't get them hooked then you are fishing with a rod that has no bait.

For the record, Dad won the Victoria Open four times (1971, 1976, 1978, 1980), the South Australian Open in 1971 and the Australian Senior Masters in 1981. While

Mum and I were with him he was going through a really rough patch on the course. He struggled for form and, as a result, he wasn't making much money, and his confidence ebbed away. Any of you who have ever played the game will know that without confidence you have no real chance of playing well. Thankfully he was earning a bit of money through work he did for the legendary Australian golfer Peter Thomson, who had a thriving course design business. Dad was responsible for the Bali Handara course in Indonesia, where he was in charge of a workforce of about 3,000 local women, a Russian steamroller and 20 tons of dynamite but, with those tools, he managed to produce a golf course to which Thomson was happy to put his name. Dad got to and from the course on a Honda motorbike, and even picked up malaria for his pains.

He used to come and watch me playing cricket at school, and was happy that I was turning into a decent all-rounder. But still, he would not outwardly encourage me to play golf. I played a little bit more as I got older though, and I was probably turning into the best twenty-four handicapper in the world. In my entire life I only ever played a handful of times with Dad, and one of them was at a municipal course in Melbourne. Mum had pushed him to take me out and he walked fifty yards in front of me for the entire round, which was sad as we had rarely spent time together. But he was still, and always will be, a hero of mine. We had various discussions, where he would tell me that if I wanted to concentrate on sport he would far rather I became a cricketer, but that he would actually prefer it if I became a dentist or a doctor. With my educational background that was always a forlorn hope!

I had a wicked temper on the course as a youngster and

if the game wasn't going well I could be pretty explosive. On one occasion I played at the local municipal course with Mum as my caddy and we joined up with three strangers. Let's just say that I got a bit hot under the collar and stormed off the eighteenth green without thanking them for the game and leaving my poor mother to apologise for my behaviour. That never happened again.

I am glad to be able to say, though, that I have some very fond memories of my father during those days in Melbourne. He had a true love for music, sports (cricket in particular) and red wine. He was quite capable of drinking an entire bottle in a sitting if he was in the mood. When he used to play on the European Tour with a number of Australian professionals, they would often buy a shipment of various wines and have it shipped back to Australia. Dad's share could be at least 200 bottles, which he would proceed to consume with one and all. When he was a little merry, I would often get a lecture, usually while I was trying to watch my favourite TV show. His favourite subjects were grasses and course design, the state of Australian politics, my schooling and the England cricket team, and he would walk into the living room with his glass of wine in his hand, go to lean on the mantelpiece and sometimes miss, which was very funny. It was all gentle, slapstick fun. Or he would start playing the piano and, inevitably, he would hit a bum note, stop and play the whole thing again, over and over until he finally got it right. Mum and I still laugh about those good times even today.

One night he was watching some programme on TV with his feet up on a stool and I was trying everything to get a response, but there was nothing. I tied his shoelaces together. Nothing. I rolled up his trousers legs – no response. I couldn't believe my luck. I tied his legs together with a dressing-gown cord. Still nothing. I was in fits. With his arms tied to the chair by the arms of my dressing gown, I then placed some underpants on his head. And still he didn't react. By this stage I was wetting myself with laughter, as the scene was so surreal. Eventually he held up his hand – or rather he tried to – and said: 'Right, that's enough.' He attempted to get up, but, of course, he couldn't, and that just made me laugh even more.

In the mornings I would bound into Mum and Dad's bedroom, jump into bed with them and would sometimes start playing 'hunt the hair' on his chest; Dad didn't have many hairs on his chest, and whenever I found one I would yank it out, much to his annoyance. It was all harmless stuff, but it was fun and he was always happy to go along with it. In hindsight I realise I must have been a dreadful child.

Inevitably, the differences between my parents surfaced again. To make matters worse, the family back home would regularly send us tapes and everybody always seemed to be in tears by the end of it. Mum would then make a tape to send back to England, and she, too, would be in tears. She made it clear that she was missing her parents a great deal and that she wanted to visit them once a year. Dad put his foot down and said there was no way he could afford to do that. If he had said that he would see what he could do, but that it might have to wait until the state of his finances made it possible, Mum might well have accepted it, but that wasn't how it worked out.

She was very close to her parents and was homesick, so she told Dad that she was going to take me back to England. And that's precisely what she did. They had stuck it out together for eighteen months, but this time the split was final.

We returned to Keighley, went back to live with my grandparents and I went to Giggleswick school, where I remained for two years. Going back into the English system was easier for me because Australia was academically a year ahead in some subjects, so finally I wasn't playing catch-up all the time. It was such a relief. I began to do well in physics and chemistry and more than held my own in English, although maths was the usual nightmare.

It was a public school, paid for by my father, so it gave me opportunities that I might not otherwise have had. Sport is an important aspect of public-school life and I embraced it with a passion, playing cricket and rugby in particular, but also just about everything else that was available. I was a reasonable runner up to 400m, so quite enjoyed athletics, and I found a way to get round the cross-country courses, usually by sprinting for a while, then walking, then sprinting again.

Unfortunately, Dad's money ran out and after a couple of years I had to leave Giggleswick and move to Heversham Grammar, which was in Cumbria. Mum was matron at the school and had been living and working there for a while – she would come back to Keighley at weekends, but it was far from ideal, so it actually helped when Dad could no longer afford the fees at Giggleswick because it made sense for me to join my mother in Cumbria, and there was a house with the job, so it was perfect.

I made the move in 1977 and I was put straight into the lower-sixth form. I had enjoyed rugby while at school, or so I thought, until the day we faced a team from Barrow who decided it was more fun to play the game not with the ball, but with their opponents' heads instead. Basically it was an opportunity for them to have a legalised brawl. One member of our team, an Irish lad, was carried off twice, and came back on both times. He was as hard as nails, but he was eventually dragged off by our coach because he started running with the ball in the wrong direction, although we almost had to tie him down to prevent him going back onto the pitch! Today, he would have been taken to hospital and the school would probably have been sued. Funnily enough, we won 25–23 with the last kick of the game.

I got caught at the bottom of a maul during the game and boots and fists were coming at me from all directions until somebody caught my knee with a metal stud and almost ruptured the tendon. I was carried off, was on crutches for a week or two and while I was recovering I thought to myself: 'Why would anyone want to carry on playing this crazy game? Rugby is meant to be a game of skill, where you take the ball and try to evade your opponent and either score a try or set one up. I don't want to keep playing a game where the opposition just want to knock six bells out of me and my team-mates! I've had enough.'

And I never played rugby again. The other thing that struck me was that many of the local Cumbria fourteen- and fifteen-year-old lads we were playing in those days seemed to have stubble and were all built like brick outhouses. I don't know what their parents reared them on, but those lads all seemed to mature way, way ahead of schedule. And when they walked onto a rugby pitch they meant business, so I was quite comfortable with my decision to go into early retirement.

Next I discovered field hockey, and took to it like a duck to water. Anybody who tries to tell you that it's a girl's game has never played it. Field hockey is a wonderful sport, requiring a great deal of skill and dexterity if it is to be played at a decent level. I was quick, I hit the ball hard and I possessed pretty good stick skills. I had excellent peripheral vision too, which allowed me to deliver the ball out wide to our players very easily and very effectively. I had started off as a striker, but I was moved into midfield because the powers-that-be recognised that I had the ability to set up chances for the rest of the team.

I just about held my own academically at Heversham, but the problem was that if anybody ever asked me if I fancied a game of anything, no matter what I was occupied with, or what I was supposed to be doing, I would always say: 'Yes, of course I'll play.' As a result, my schoolwork suffered yet again and I suppose it would be fair to say that I never quite fulfilled my academic potential. I think I got more detention for not doing my homework properly than the rest of school put together.

Now I should say that at this point in my life, aged about seventeen, I did not have the foggiest idea what I wanted to do with the rest of my life. I particularly remember an interview, the one and only session I ever had with my careers 'advisor', at the end of which we had agreed that I would apply for a job as a trainee cameraman at the BBC. Why? You are not going to believe this, but I swear that it's true – it was just because I told him that I enjoyed watching television. Careers advice in those days was, to put it mildly, not very high tech.

CHAPTER THREE
SECOND BEST

D ad might well have been an absent parent, but he still jumped in with two feet given the opportunity and told me that I should leave school. A-levels wouldn't get me a job but a degree in a relevant subject might, or so he reckoned. Thus I ended up at Carlisle Technical College on an OND business studies course. I got a grant and managed to stick at it for a year. By this time, aged eighteen, I had joined Silverdale Golf Club and had my first official golf handicap of twenty-three. I couldn't afford the membership, so Mum helped me pay for it.

I admit here and now that I was probably the world's best twenty-three handicapper, but everybody has to start somewhere. I wish that I'd had some proper coaching and played some national competitions during that time because I imagine I would have won quite a bit, but I didn't have the money and Mum couldn't afford it either. In those days there was no junior golf development programme, so you were very much left to your own devices, which meant that boys who had wealthy parents always had an edge right from the start because they were used to getting top coaching and playing in tournaments at a very early age, and were able to hone their competitive skills while still very young.

I started playing in medals and various other club competitions and managed to cut my handicap to fourteen in my first year. I finally realised that not only did I enjoy playing golf, but that I also had an aptitude for it. I began to practise and, as I did so, I continued to improve.

What can I say about Carlisle Tech? It was an interesting educational process, and I was able to come home at weekends and spend time with Mum and go out and play golf. I learnt the basics about the business world, I suppose, but it was not hugely stimulating and after twelve months, Dad said: 'Listen, there is no point in having a degree because there's loads of people on the dole with degrees. I'll get you a job ... in Leicester.'

So I went to meet a guy called Lars Helgusson, who was in charge of Corah Knitwear, which, at the time, was a big knitwear company that had more than £1 million-worth of stock held for Marks & Spencer at any one time. Lars was a friend of a man called Ron Smith, who was in turn a friend of my dad, so it really was a case of landing a job through a friend of a friend. Ron was a member at Kirby Muxloe Golf Club, where my father had been based while he was an amateur. When he turned pro and moved to Australia he would come back every so often and bring the likes of Peter Thomson and Greg Norman with him and they would play high-profile exhibition matches at the course.

I wasn't offered a job straight away at Corah, so I went back up north, returned to college and even thought about completing the course, but there was never any question of that because Dad had made his mind up. Sure enough, I was eventually offered a job in the 'seconds' department. I can't even remember the job title, but I think it may have been 'trainee manager'. I wasn't particularly interested in the job, although I have to admit that I learnt quite a bit about the trade. I would often find myself looking at these so-called seconds and thinking: 'There's nothing wrong with these.' They would end up being sold on market stalls for knockdown prices.

I frequently used to ask myself what I was doing. I was stuck in Leicester, where I didn't really know anybody, and although I guess I should have been thankful that I had a job, you will not be hugely surprised to learn that the wages were not great. It was 1979, I was nineteen years old, I was earning about £60 a week and I was sharing a flat with a couple of cousins. The textile business was going through hell at the time and, after I had been there for six months, the company made 250 people redundant, including yours truly – last in first out. I cannot say that I was surprised to be shown the door because, although I had been given a job, there wasn't the work to justify keeping me on even if things had been going well. If I am honest, I wasn't very good at the work either.

So here I was, unemployed, with no A-levels and no business studies degree either. Some good advice then. Thanks Dad.

I had been put up for membership at Kirby Muxloe Golf Club and was accepted about four months after I arrived in the town – at almost exactly the same time that I lost my job. By now, my handicap was down to nine, but they told me that they wouldn't accept my handicap and that I would have to submit three cards to get a new one. I did that, and ended up playing off seven. I then played in the club championship and shot rounds of 72 and 81 and found that I had been cut by another two strokes, so suddenly I was playing off five. Remember that roughly eighteen months earlier my handicap had been twenty-three. I had well and truly found golf by that stage and had been bitten by the bug.

I spent the summer on the dole playing golf and then found a job in a sports shop, Pacemaker Sports, in Leicester. To this day, I have no idea why I didn't go home when I lost my 'high-flying' job with Corah. It made no sense to remain in Leicester, but I did stay there. If the work at Corah had been mind-numbing, then the job in the sports shop was even worse. 'Good morning madam, how may I help you?' was one of my habitual greetings.

Standing around waiting for customers on a dreary February afternoon, hoping for a sale, having taken minus £6.50 after a refund that morning, did make me wonder where I was going with it all. I did stick it though for the best part of two years. When I left in 1982, I had another six months off, which once again coincided with the golf season, and I worked really hard on my game and before long a letter arrived to tell me that I had been picked to play for the county team, thanks in the main to a local amateur golfing legend named Eddie Hammond, who took me under his wing. By now, I was playing off two or three.

Eddie was a huge influence on me. He was a Glaswegian who had played for Rangers before breaking both his legs. He had a short spell with Motherwell and, after hanging up his boots, he moved to the Midlands, where he worked for Rolls Royce. He had always been a first-class golfer and when he came to England he found his niche pretty quickly.

He was a big strong man with a very unorthodox golf swing, and I count myself very fortunate that he helped me progress through the county golf scene. He was a hugely influential individual in Leicestershire golf and it was Eddie who made suitable noises in the ears of the right people to get me into the second team, where I played for about a year. I revelled in it and was almost unbeatable. We played in eight-man teams, with foursomes followed by singles, and my mentor in that team was a guy called Alan Harrison, who was a good deal older than me. He was a perfect foursomes partner and, like Eddie Hammond, he looked out for me.

We played in the Anglia League, which meant we faced Norfolk, Suffolk, Cambridgeshire, Northamptonshire and Lincolnshire. There would be two or three away games, and a couple of friendlies early in the season as well as the regular Leicestershire county competitions.

Somebody would drive us to away matches and accommodation, food and drink were paid for, but we had to pay for everything else ourselves. We also used to have to sit down for formal dinners where everybody had to wear a blazer, shirt and tie, so one of the first things I had to do was to get hold of a jacket. Fortunately, somebody said that I could borrow one, and they never asked for it back. I was thankful because I couldn't afford to buy one. When you had played a set number of matches you would receive a county second-team tie, which was great because that was when you felt that you belonged. To be honest, though, I was chomping at the bit to be chosen for the first team.

From that point on, I never really looked back, but even then I never did things the easy way. I didn't have a car, which meant that I had to get the bus to the golf course, and it used to take an hour from my flat in Leicester to Kirby. The last bus home would leave at 10.15pm in the summer and I was usually on it and would be getting home late at night. There were no decent practise facilities at Kirby Muxloe in those days, so I used to have to go out onto the course and beat balls, but you couldn't do that during the day when the course was busy.

I would spend hours chipping and putting to the seventh and eighth greens, with the result that I developed a wonderful short game – I was never a long hitter, so I needed to be good around the greens, and I was. Throughout my amateur career I have consistently proved to myself and to my opponents that you don't have to hit the ball miles in order to be successful, which is just as well really.

I was always the last person off the course, calling it a day only when it became too dark to see where the ball was landing. And when I was finished I would rake every bunker, replace every divot and repair every pitch mark. The green keeper must have come round every morning, looked at those fairways and greens and thought to himself: 'I haven't done that, and if I haven't done it, who on earth has?'

As much as I loved it, I realised that I had to leave Kirby Muxloe and move to somewhere closer to where I lived, so applied for membership at the Leicestershire Golf Club, which didn't make me terribly popular with some of the members at Kirby, who had helped to get me into the club in the first place. I had no choice though. Apart from the logistics involved, the Leicestershire was, and is, a better golf course, with superior facilities. For a start, it has a proper practise ground.

Kirby Muxloe was relatively easy to score on. I remember shooting a round of 64 in a medal and had nine birdies and an eagle, as well as a triple-bogey and a couple of other dropped shots. They refused to regard it as a course record because there was a hole which was sometimes played as a par three and at other times it was played from a different tee as a par four and on that particular day we were playing the hole as a par three, which to my mind was more difficult.

This was the sort of golf that had got me into the county team. I was enjoying my golf enormously, but I always struggled to afford it and this caused all sorts of issues in different ways. We travelled to Purdis Heath Golf Club near Ipswich to play Suffolk one time and before we teed off for the practise round somebody announced that we were going to be playing for money and that we were each expected to put up £5 per head, but I didn't have £5. After scraping together every last penny I believe that I had something like £2.85 with me. I didn't think we would need anything because I knew that our meals and drinks were going to be paid for by the county. I was on the dole at this point and everything was a bit tight. I have never earned much so it's just as well that I don't have expensive tastes, but back in those days I lived a hand-to-mouth existence. I never went out for meals or anything flash unless somebody else was paying.

On this particular day at Purdis Heath, I had seven birdies and an eagle and won everybody's money, but I don't have any idea at all what I would have said or done if I'd had a stinker of a round. I believe that Lee Trevino often used to take part in money-matches without a cent in his pocket – he said that it made him hungry and that it honed his competitive edge. I am sure he was also pretty nimble on his feet too. Trevino was a self-confessed hustler, but that was never my style. Believe me when I tell you that I had a very uncomfortable afternoon on that golf course in Suffolk until I realised that I had won.

This sort of thing happened quite a lot though, and I hated it because I didn't have the cash to lose. Yet it didn't half make me concentrate. Everybody else would be totally relaxed about it all because it didn't matter to them if they lost a fiver, but I would be grinding away from the very first shot. Incredibly, though, I hardly ever lost, although the boot ended up on the other foot with the assistant professional at the Leicestershire who, at one point, owed me £2,300. We used to have chipping and putting competitions through the summer and I was almost unbeatable. It was always double or quits and, inevitably, he finally won one contest and we both promptly agreed that it was probably a good idea that we quit gambling for those sorts of stakes in future.

I loved tests-of-skill contests from a very early stage. If somebody told me that I couldn't pitch a golf ball into a bucket I would be determined to prove them wrong and I would go away and master the shot until I could do it. Or if somebody said it was impossible to pitch a ball over a specific object from a set distance I would revel in trying to do that very thing. I had a Wilson Staff sand wedge that I used for every shot around the green, whether it be high floaters or pitch and runs. I could make that club talk, until eventually it lost its voice because I wore it out. And that used to happen with all my sand wedges – I would hit so many shots with them, both in competition and on the practise ground, that I would wear them out and have to replace them.

It also helped that I was a world-class putter. I could hole out from anywhere. Oh yes, and I was very, very competitive. Early on I used to hit the ball a reasonable distance, but I started looking at how the best golfers won, and I am talking here about professionals as well as amateurs, and I came to the conclusion that the only way to succeed was by hitting fairways and greens. What was the point of hitting the ball 300 yards off the tee if you were going to be playing your second shot from the middle of a forest? 'The woods are full of big hitters,' an old friend of mine would always say to me. Why would you want to risk giving it a big heave-ho if there was a lake running down the right-hand side of the fairway? This was not the way I decided I wanted to play the game, so I worked incredibly hard at keeping the ball straight with my driver, with the result that I hit lots of fairways but became shorter and shorter off the tee. In the end it was ridiculous: I was barely hitting my driver 220 yards, but I decided to live with it because I could guarantee that I could find the middle of the greens from the fairway. It did, however, mean that I was being out-driven by fifty-plus yards on a regular basis. In matchplay particularly this worked in my favour however, as I annoyed one opponent after another by beating them in this way. They'd outdrive me by miles, but then I'd apply the pressure by hitting green after green, and, more often than not, hole the putt too.

I sometimes struggled to reach long par fours in two shots, but I always knew that I could bank on my short game to save my par more often than not and sometimes I would chip in for the sort of birdie that really hurts your opponent, no matter what level you are playing at. They finished up having to hole putts to avoid losing the hole, whereas minutes before they thought they had it in the bag.

It may surprise you to learn that through these early

years I never had any proper formal coaching, although at various times I had a few lessons from a number of professionals who pointed me in the right direction. I survived on good tips more than anything, which was okay as far it lasted. When you are hitting the ball straight the last thing you would ever want to do is to go to a coach and risk having him destroy your game, all for the sake of trying to find an extra twenty or thirty yards off the tee. The other thing is that the longer you play, the better understanding you have of your own swing too, so if ever things did start to go slightly awry, I would always pretty much know what to focus on to put it right; a sixth sense if you will, acquired through shear hard practice.

I was out of work for six months after my job at Pacemaker Sports came to an end and, eventually, I realised that I was going to have to find employment, so I managed to get taken on by Black's Camping and Leisure. It was another shop job and, once again, it was none too taxing and I stuck at that for about a year or so, but by now it was 1984, I was playing off scratch, was getting lots of local newspaper coverage and, to be honest, all that I wanted to do was play golf.

I was taking on and beating all of the very best players in the county. In fact, it quickly became obvious to me that, apart from a guy called Alan Martinez, there really wasn't anybody else in Leicestershire who could beat me, certainly not on a regular basis. There was a tournament called the Leicestershire Silver Fox, which was played at a beautiful golf course called Willesley Park in Ashby-de-la-Zouch; I always did well in it because the venue suited me down to the ground, as it was tree-lined and required pinpoint accuracy. I won it in 1984, 1985 and in 1989.

My first national competition, however, was the Brabazon Trophy in 1983 played at Woburn. I had to pre-qualify and did so by a shot with a round of 81. I found myself drawn in the qualifier with amateur legends Reg Glading and Michael Bonallack. Some people may have found this inspiring, but it heaped a load of extra pressure on me in my first really big competition. Glading and Bonallack were both contemporaries of my father, and there is no doubt in my mind that somebody had a little bit of good-natured mischief in mind when the draw was made.

Bonallack had a horrendous time. His daughter was carrying his clubs and it was obvious that he no longer played much. I beat him comfortably. I finished way ahead of Glading too, who was also long past his best. Some golfers have a photographic memory of the rounds of golf they have played, but I have never been like that. In the main draw I was out, rather amazingly, with Alan Martinez, my county colleague, and a quiet kid called David Gilford, who would go on to make a nice living for himself as a professional and played in the Ryder Cup when Nick Faldo famously partnered him and apparently didn't speak to him for virtually the whole round. They used to call Gilford the 'Cashmere Insert' because although it always appeared that he hit the ball very gently, it was actually quite powerful. I didn't pull up any trees at the Brabazon that year, but it was nice to get my first national tournament under my belt.

I travelled to Woburn on a young person's railcard because it was the cheapest way of getting there, walked into town carrying my holdall and my golf clubs, and went into a butcher's shop to ask for directions to the golf club. The butcher said: 'Funnily enough, I am going up there to deliver some meat, so I can give you a lift.' Thus I arrived at

47

Woburn, one of the most famous golf clubs in England, in the back of a meat van. My digs were a mile-and-a-half away and I walked to and from the golf course every day, setting the pattern for a large section of my amateur career.

I will never forget Richard Boxall, who is now a Sky TV commentator and golf analyst, walking into the golf club reception area to register for the tournament and asking for the location of the nearest decent hotel. He wasn't interested in a room in somebody's house, or a bed and breakfast or a youth hostel. Boxall's father was a scrap-metal dealer and Richard always wore plenty of bling. He even had his own car, for goodness sake. When I heard him asking to be directed to a good hotel I was in awe of him, assuming that he was one of the favourites that year. Indeed he was, and could well have become one of Britain's best. He certainly seemed to be on the road to superstardom until that fateful moment at The Open Championship at Royal Birkdale in 1991, when he hit a drive mid round and broke his leg – he was in agony. He was never quite the same player after that.

There was another player competing in that year's Brabazon Trophy I remember: Steve Bottomley, who had been given a practise bag full of brand new Titleist balls. A Yorkshire lad, Steve liked to show off and wanted everybody to know that when he went down to the driving range he was hitting new golf balls – the rest of us were happy to use whatever we could get our hands on, and I was next to him, practising with my old balls. Peter McEvoy was conspicuously on his own at the other end of the range, hitting golf balls towards us, and Bottomley said: 'Look at McEvoy, he obviously thinks that he is better than the rest of us.'

McEvoy wasn't stupid, though. His golf balls were

landing in a different part of the range to everybody else's, so there was no chance of them getting mixed up with ours. Bottomley continued to make this huge fuss over these fabulous Titleist balls, as well as all the other new kit he had from the company. As he was hitting away merrily and talking to various people between shots, golfers were wandering down the range to retrieve their balls – or so Bottomley thought. It was only when he was finished and went to retrieve his Titleists that he discovered there were only about ten or fifteen of them left because the other boys had picked them up and put them in their bags. He was livid, but it was pretty funny. Peter McEvoy, of course, didn't lose any.

Alan Martinez and I were sharing our B&B with a young Austrian player who was a skiing instructor during the winter and played golf when the snow melted. He was representing the Austrian Golf Federation and being paid loads of money for the privilege. This player sported a very fetching coloured headband to keep his long hair out of his eyes which, as you can imagine, raised more than a few eyebrows with the EGU hierarchy when he teed off in the first round. Every night that week I had the same food – vegetable soup, fish and chips, and apple pie and ice cream. It was the cheapest option, but as it happens, I still like that choice, so it was no real hardship.

I missed the cut that year, got a lift to the station and returned to Leicester on the train. My first experience of the Brabazon Trophy was over. At this stage, Alan Martinez was a better player than me no doubt, but that was about to change. At the county tournaments he had been winning as a matter of course, but he now knew that he had to be at his best if he was to beat me, which he did in the final of that year's county matchplay tournament on the final green at Londcliffe. It was a game, however, that I should have won. He knew it, I knew it, and everybody who followed the final knew it, but it turned out to be the moment when the balance of power in Leicestershire county golf shifted from Alan to me. He still won things, of course, but not nearly as regularly.

Every year we would play events such as the Eastern Counties Foursomes at Hunstanton and it was a great experience on a long, difficult golf course. Leicestershire had some decent players, although we were never one of the strongest counties, but playing for them in tournaments like this and the Midlands qualifier for the English County Finals each year helped shape me further. As my confidence in my own ability started to grow I began to play in more regional and national tournaments. There was the English Amateur Championship one year at Woodhall Spa and although I didn't win, I knocked out the favourite, beating Andrew Sherbourne in the first round, one up. I chipped and putted him off the course and he hated every minute of it. To this day, I really don't think he's forgiven me. At the time he was one of England's best golfers and big things were expected of him. It was certainly never in the script that he would lose to some relative unknown. All of a sudden people started to sit up and take interest in me; yes they knew the name, but that was only because of my father. Sadly, however, I lost in the next round and that was that.

By this stage I had been promoted to the county first team. In the foursomes I was partnered with Eddie Hammond, at his request, and we were virtually unbeatable. I had the accuracy and short game skills that made me such a popular partner and he had the power and the gift of the gab. Eddie could talk the hind legs off a donkey and he would grind our opponents down. I used to smile to myself because Eddie was able to talk some very, very good players out of their game: people of the calibre of Peter McEvoy, Andrew Carman and Paul Broadhurst.

I played in a county match against Peter McEvoy when he was representing Warwickshire, and quickly realised the standard I had to reach if I was ever going to achieve anything in the amateur game – you would never describe Peter as a really big hitter, but he could hit his three iron as far as I did my driver.

There were quite a few characters in those days, such as Tony Allen, Andrew Carman, Bobby Eggo and James Cook, and then there was Paul Downes. Unusually at the time, he went to college in America and, although not a big hitter, was expected to do great things by those in the know. As it turned out, he may not have done much on the golf course, but he certainly made up for it with his ability as a gambler. He finished up buying a series of old people's homes with the money he had won through his gambling ability. Paul won the British poker championship during the 1980s, and you don't do that unless you know what you are doing. He also once won a house. It wasn't all plain sailing, of course, and he once reputedly had an arm broken because of a gambling debt. They asked him which arm he wanted them to break. He thought it through, then chose the left.

He was a great competitor on the golf course and very difficult to beat. I liked him and enjoyed his company. I bumped into him at the Brabazon one year at Hollinwell and discovered that he had managed to persuade a few fellow competitors to play poker with him. Oh dear. Inevitably, he cleaned them out. I refused to play cards with him because I couldn't afford to lose and, besides, he was just too good.

I used to play the odd game of brag with players and one time I was sitting there with three aces, thinking that I had an unbeatable hand. It got to the point where there were three of us left. The aforementioned Steve Bottomley who had Jack, Queen, King, which he, in turn, thought was unbeatable. Eventually the pot grew to £70 and I was about to start borrowing some money when Freddie George, an England colleague at the time sitting opposite, said: 'Enough! That's enough. I can't take any more of your money. You cannot beat me.' With that, he put his cards down, face up – he had a prial of threes (the best hand in the game). Relief doesn't even begin to cover the emotions I felt right there. I could, and would, have lost hundreds on that hand of cards. It taught me that there is no such thing as a certainty in life, unless of course you're blessed with a prial of threes.

CHAPTER FOUR

GOING TO WORK ON AN EGG

You may wonder why, playing off scratch – which I achieved by the age of twenty-three – I didn't think about turning professional. Honestly, the thought never entered my head at the time. Not once. I wasn't the home-grown boy come good, so there was never any question of anybody in Leicestershire taking me to one side and giving me a bucketful of money to keep me going while I tried to make a go of it. Perhaps if I had remained in the north of England things would have worked out differently, but the question of turning pro never came up.

My grandfather, who at one time was in a position to have helped me out, had lost all his money by this time. I mentioned earlier that he was a something of entrepreneur, who took a few risks, and I guess he took one poor risk too many when he went into the textile business in Keighley and it swallowed up all his savings. He also had another couple of deals go sour, buying and selling at absolutely the wrong time. For somebody who'd had everything, it was such a shame to see it all slip away.

When he died his estate had diminished considerably and there was very little left. This was a man who had bought huge mansions for cash, and who had driven a Rolls Royce when only the very wealthiest people in the land could afford to do so. He built prefab houses during the Second World War that are still being lived in today. His old age, and that of my grandmother, should have been seen out in comfort, but that was not to be.

Through all this, Mum remained the constant in my life. She would always try to help me out whenever she was in a position to do so, and she always insisted that I come home for Christmas, when I would be well fed and watered, and she would always send me back down south with plenty of provisions. Why didn't I just stay with her? It was not as if I had anything to keep me in Leicester except my golf. By now, in my mid-twenties, I was living as a boarder in an elderly couple's house on East Park Road in the centre of Leicester. It was not an ideal situation. There was no high-powered job and there was no real girlfriend. Even if I'd met somebody I had been attracted to, I wouldn't have been able to take her back to my digs. Besides, how many girls of that age would want a boyfriend who worked in a shop (sometimes) and who played golf every weekend (always)? I was hardly what you would describe as a prize catch, was I?

It was a pretty difficult existence, but I adapted. Why didn't I move? Well, it was convenient for the golf club – it was only a two-mile walk to the Leicestershire and I needed to be within walking distance of it because although I'd passed my driving test by then, there was no question of my being able to afford to buy and run a car. I say that it was 'only' a two-mile walk, but it was all uphill going to the club and it was still a fair trek when you also had a set of golf clubs slung over your shoulder. It was quite remarkable how often I would be walking along and a member would pass, toot the horn, wave to me, and then drive on by. It made no difference what the weather was like. It seemed that it never entered their heads to ask whether I might want a lift. I walked everywhere in those days, even into Leicester, playing all sorts of games in my mind to pass the time. One of my favourites was to see whether I could walk all the way into the city and back without standing on a crack between the paving stones.

And that brings me to my OCD, or obsessive-compulsive disorder. I have never been officially diagnosed, but I am pretty sure that if I don't suffer from the full-blown condition then I most definitely have a variation of it. Everything has to be in its place in my life. Speaking of pavements, I hate it when I stand on the cracks even now when I'm walking along. I get really upset if a caddy puts a golf club back in the wrong place in my bag – there are an equal number of slots in a bag and there are fourteen clubs, so I don't think putting each one back where it belongs amounts to rocket science. I don't like mess or things to be out of kilter either. I am obsessive about arriving at any destination or meeting on time, so I always leave ridiculously early to ensure I am not late.

The golf balls in my bag all have to be marked the same way. I am not that obsessive about the number, but I don't like playing with two's or four's for some reason. My head covers have to match the colour of my bag, and my clothes must be spotlessly clean, immaculately pressed and they all need to match. When I travel, my toiletries are always neatly lined up, and I will never just throw change on to the top of a bedside table – it has to be in tidy piles. I pay meticulous attention to detail in everything that I do. I am certain that it has helped me in my golf career over the years, as it is a game in which you need to be well organised. Preparation is everything.

Back to my walking days. As I said, I walked everywhere, and I was fast. I have long legs and most people struggle to keep up with me, even now. I am the same on the golf course, too. I like to hit my shot and get to the ball without any fuss. It used to take me twenty minutes to walk from my digs into Leicester city centre, and I am sure that it would have taken most other people at least twice that length of time. I kid you not when I tell you that I think I could have been an Olympic-standard walker. I just switch off while I am doing it and contemplate other things; it was my 'thinking time'.

I lived in Leicestershire for nine years during my first stint in the county and although there were quite a few people I called good friends, none were ever soul mates. As far as the county team was concerned, I enjoyed the company of the guys I played with and I always made sure that I gave one hundred per cent on the course. I was, and still am, a perfectionist on the golf course, which means that I get frustrated with myself from time to time. But I would never get upset with a team-mate who played a poor shot that put me in trouble, unless the shot he had played was just plain stupid. The thing with golf is that everybody who plays the game knows that it is possible to hit a bad shot at any time, and nobody deliberately hits a ball into the rough or a hazard. However, there are times when discretion is the better part of valour and it is best to play safe; for example, on some occasions it makes sense to leave the driver in the bag and hit an iron to make sure you finish in the fairway.

It is all about applying common sense, and sometimes my partner would go his own way for a career shot and when it didn't come off I would be the one left with the task of playing the ball from an often-impossible lie.

I figured that by the latter stages of my amateur career I could virtually guarantee Leicestershire two points before a ball was struck in any inter-county match. I always felt I was good enough to win my singles match against anybody, and if I had a good foursomes partner the chances were that we would win our match too. Foursomes is where you play alternate shots, and I would rarely put my partner into genuine trouble. I was lucky in that I usually had good partners, but sometimes I would have to go out and play with somebody and I would be groaning inside. Sweat would ooze from every pore on my body – truly, that is how hard I tried. And when I was partnered with somebody who was all over the place, it simply made me try all the harder. What really used to frustrate me though was being partnered with somebody who wasn't trying. It is an honour to represent a team, no matter at what level – I believed it then and I believe it now – and the very least you owe the people who put their faith in your ability is a commitment to keep trying, right to the bitter end. Leicestershire wasn't a strong county because we only had twenty-odd clubs, so it was inevitable that, from time to time, we would have to field players who weren't quite good enough. I had no problem with that, but not trying? That is just unforgivable, and we had a great bunch of triers in our team like myself and in particular David Gibson.

No matter how I might have been feeling inside, I never once bad-mouthed any partner, either outright or behind their back, but it didn't stop me fuming if we lost. I just hate losing, full stop, and for that matter I can't stand playing badly either. It pushed me to practise harder, but to some people it was completely incomprehensible that I could get so upset over a lost game or a misplaced shot, but it was this that kept driving me on and made me who I became as a competitor.

I played in an England match at Woodhall Spa with a guy called John Lupton, who blamed me after we had been beaten, even though he missed two very short putts and had missed almost every fairway. What made matters worse was that John made his views known to other people and the chairman of selectors walked up and had a go at me. Fortunately, David Gibson, my Leicestershire county colleague, had watched me that day and said afterwards: 'If I had played with you we would have won 7&6. That defeat was not your fault. You did everything you could to win the game.' Which was absolutely true.

CHAPTER FIVE

THE UNKINDEST CUT OF ALL

L ike most people, I have regrets, and among those is that I never lived in one place all my life so as to acquire a regional identity. I believe that if I had, I may well have settled down with somebody and got married. However, would I then have achieved what I have? Who knows? The longest I ever stayed in any one place was at Kilworth Springs Golf Club, in Leicestershire, where I remained for eleven years.

Dad didn't seem to need roots, either. Like me, he had played golf all over Great Britain as an amateur and when he turned professional he was quite happy to fly off all over Europe and the rest of the world following the sun. He had few regrets about heading to Australia either, except, perhaps, for the fact that golf Down Under never really took off as he had expected it to. But then he thought that he had spotted his golden opportunity to cash in when he turned fifty and realised there was good money to be made on the US Seniors Tour. So he managed to land himself a job as a teaching professional in Charlotte, North Carolina, and if everything had gone according to plan I may well have joined him in the USA, turned professional, become a teaching pro myself, and settled down with a house full of kids. But it wasn't to be. Fate took a hand once more.

In late 1983 Dad sold his house in Melbourne and bought a plot of land in Charlotte, on which he planned to build his new home, and he envisaged living the good life on the US Seniors Tour, which was then still in its infancy. He played in a pro-am with Bob Hope and was building up a good reputation Stateside. Best of all, he had rediscovered his game. Before leaving Australia he had beaten Arnold Palmer in a playoff to win the Victorian Open, and he had also beaten Gary Player in another such competition to win the same tournament again. Not long after he turned fifty he had half a season on the Seniors Tour and had cleared more than $100,000 in prize money, which was a fortune to him.

Just before he was due to leave Australia for good, he hadn't been feeling too well so he went to see a doctor and was diagnosed with cancer. He underwent an operation more or less immediately and they told him they thought they had caught it early enough and that he was going to be fine. Within three months he was playing again, but I thought: 'This can't be right. He's had a major operation and been through a course of chemotherapy, so surely he needs more time to recuperate.'

He seemed to be fine and was actually playing pretty well again, using a buggy under a medical exemption, until he had a relapse, and this time they told him that his body was now riddled with cancer and that there was little or nothing they could do. He was told that he could live for five years if he remained in Australia and underwent the necessary treatment, or he could have perhaps eighteen months without medical intervention.

Dad had been given a colostomy bag and made the decision that he didn't want any further medical treatment, so basically he came home to Britain to die. He was a shell of his former self and spent his last months visiting all his friends, effectively saying goodbye to them all. It was heartbreaking to witness. He had remarried in about 1976, to Robyn, some six months or so after Mum and I had returned from Australia. This was a bit of a shock at the time, I can tell you, but he and Mum were divorced and he felt that he had given their relationship his best shot. His second wife was from New Zealand and she was a nurse, so at least she was able to take care of him, but my Dad was a walking skeleton by then. He was a fighter though, still had the wry sense of humour which had always made him so popular.

I believe he was proud of me, because I'd turned out to be a decent, rounded young man. He also seemed to accept that I was going to play golf at a reasonable level, but said: 'Please don't turn pro as golf can be such a cruel game.' I came back to visit him after I'd won the Leicestershire Fox trophy in the August. He asked how I'd played. After I'd said that I'd shot rounds of 68 and 74, he replied in his inimitable style: 'Well, what happened in the 74?'

Everybody made a fuss of him and he asked relatives in Nottingham if he and his young family (he had two young boys by then, James and Myles, with him too) could stay with them for a short time. He remained with them for almost five months until eventually they told him: 'Listen Guy, we are really sorry, but our children are finding this all very upsetting. You are going to have to find somewhere else to stay.' It was all just very, very tragic, but it wasn't fair to ask young children to watch somebody waste away in front of their eyes, and it didn't help that they didn't really know Dad's wife either.

Nottingham had a great cancer unit though, and it agreed to take him in, but he refused to give in to his illness and eventually they told him he was well enough to leave, but these things are all relative. He ended up living in a motel in Kirby Muxloe, paid for by Ron Smith, one of his closest friends. On one occasion I went to see him and he was drugged up with morphine and really wasn't with it. He tried to tell me how much he loved me, but found it very difficult to say. Eventually he hugged me and managed to blurt out the words. He told me that he was proud of what I'd achieved, even though I hadn't done much on the golf course at that stage, and nothing of note off it.

It was a very emotional time for me. I found it difficult to deal with and failed to really tell him how much he meant to me. It is one of those big regrets of my life because it turned out to be the last time I saw him. I am also sorry that we didn't have more of an opportunity just to hang out more and discuss the things that fathers and sons should talk about. He was a naturally funny man and I did get on well with him, but circumstances dictated that our time together was limited. I suppose that is why my memories of him are still so precious.

Once, when I was about sixteen years of age, Mum and I drove through France with him to the Swiss Open at Crans-sur-Sierre, which was memorable because of its most stunning location in the Alps. Mum caddied for him and I supported from the sidelines. It will give you some idea of how useless I was as a supporter when I tell you that I cannot remember how well he did, but we then travelled together to Germany, where he was playing in his next event. We stayed in a hotel and Dad decided to pass the time by teaching me to play brag, but I beat him hands down every game and he got really upset, so the cards went everywhere, which was extremely funny. It was beginner's luck, which was something I fortunately always seemed to have.

That same year we were in Holland for the Dutch Open and the resort where we stayed had a flight of stairs that led to a veranda from the promenade. I knew that the gate at the top of the stairs was locked and that there was nowhere to go as I watched my father climb all the way to the top, scratch his head and then begin the long climb back down again. He wasn't too chuffed when he saw me splitting my sides with laughter, and he chased me back to the hotel.

I had been a big kid all my life and had never had to face any real responsibility or adversity, so when he passed away on October 9, 1984, it was by far the worst thing that had ever happened to me. He was only fifty-three years old.

Dad was a genuinely lovely person and many other people thought so, too. He hadn't wanted me to follow him into golf because he did not want me to stumble into the same pitfalls he had experienced throughout his career, but the thing he never realised was that if he had taken the time to coach me and teach me everything he knew about golf, then I could have avoided those particular setbacks. He also knew all the right people within the game and could have pointed me in their direction. I don't want this to sound conceited, but I always felt that I possessed the 'X-factor', that something that defines a winner from an also-ran. Yet because I didn't have the coaching earlier in life I never really became a great player in my own eyes. What I will say is that throughout my career to date I made the most of what I had, far more so than many other more talented golfers that I played with and against, individuals who should have gone on to achieve amazing things in the game, but who, for whatever reason, failed to reach their full potential.

CHAPTER SIX
THE INSURANCE
SALESMAN

In 1985, I decided that I'd had enough of Black's Camping and Leisure and quit. I was then out of work for the best part of two years, having made up my mind that I was going to give amateur golf my best shot and see where it took me. It was golf, all day, every day. I knew I had to do something else too, so also I signed up for a twelve-month college course in Leicester, which effectively allowed me to complete my business studies qualification. I enjoyed the studying immensely and, don't ask me how, but I somehow finished up with O-levels in sociology and business and management studies too, so it wasn't a complete waste of time.

Now I always emphasise to youngsters who want to become golf professionals how important education is, and that they should have something to fall back on in case their golf doesn't work out. I wish I had taken my own advice back then because after leaving college I found myself out of work for another twelve months and had to sign on the dole again. I recognise the risks now, but I don't suppose I did back then. I have seen far too many youngsters ignore their education, fail to make the grade in the sport they love, and then find they have nothing in reserve to use for gaining employment apart from their personality. If you've got the right sort of personality it can take you a long way, but often it isn't enough on its own, unless you are very lucky and get a break.

Then, lo and behold, in 1987, and at the age of twenty-seven, I landed what most of you would regard as my first proper job. It was with an insurance company called Manufacturers' Life, whose office was in the centre of Leicester.

Prior to getting that insurance job I applied for hundreds of posts. One vacancy was with a company that sold books. I went along to the interview and the first question I was asked was: 'So Gary, tell us, what was the last book that you read?'

'*The Hobbit*,' I replied. I immediately knew that my answer had gained me a black mark because *The Hobbit* is a work of fiction, and this company only wanted employees who read fact-based books, such as biographies, because they'd been told by some psychologist that people who read such literature would be more reliable employees. Naturally, I didn't get the job, but I was pretty upset because, in effect, what they were saying was that if you were somebody who read fiction then you were not worth employing.

On another occasion I went for an interview for a job selling office equipment and was told that I would have to attend a training course, which involved a ninety-mile round trip. It was on-the-job training held once a week, every week for about six months, and it wasn't going to be cheap.

'How am I going to do that?' I asked. 'I don't have a car.'

'You are going to have to get the train.'

'And will you be paying the train fares for me?'

'We will give you some money towards it.'

'But not the full amount?'

'No.'

That brief conversation told me everything I needed to know about that particular company.

So what can I tell you about my job with Manufacturers' Life? I think I may have described it as my first 'proper' job, but let's see what you think. There was no salary; instead, my fellow employees and I were lent a sum of money, which wasn't very much, to get us started. I was sent on a week's course, at the end of which I was entitled to sell just about every financial product known to man, apart from mortgages. The idea was that the money they gave me acted as a start-up salary to keep me going until the commission I was meant to earn from selling the company's various insurance products, investments and pensions, started to kick in.

If you wanted to sell mortgages, you had to attend a separate course. After a week-long set of lectures and instruction, what qualified me to advise people on how to invest their hard-earned savings, other than my blind faith in my new employer? I hadn't a clue what I was doing really, other than repeating facts from a manual, and I definitely didn't truly understand the product portfolio I was selling to my customers. My bosses told me what to say, and what to sell each client after making the appointment. So I went out, sat down in front of people, and repeated my script, parrot-fashion. In those days, it seemed the business was totally unregulated and that anybody could do it. Manufacturers' Life no longer exists, but it must have had some kind of credibility because the big prestigious company, Canada Life, bought it.

So how were we supposed to find our customers? What happens is that you have a team back at company HQ who phone likely prospects and set up appointments. Back then, however, it was down to me to find my own potential clients. I used to dread Tuesday nights with a passion, because that was the time I had to put aside for 'cold calling'. There isn't one person reading this book who hasn't put the phone down, or shut the door in the face of, somebody trying to sell them something they neither want nor need, yet here I was trying to convince complete strangers to give me the time of day. I hated it.

'No, I'm not interested. Why are you phoning me up? Where did you get my number from?' was my usual kind of response.

Remember that most of these people had been out all day at work, had come home, eaten their dinner and were now settling down to watch their favourite TV programmes, and here on the other end of the phone was some complete stranger doing his utmost to persuade them to arrange an appointment for him to come to their home to talk about a financial product that they supposedly needed. To be fair, personal pensions, savings plans, life insurance and the like are important, and people do need to be thinking about them, but perhaps advice dispensed by someone who'd only had a week's intensive product training was hardly worth having.

One of the clever things they do is to get you to sell to all your friends and relatives, because they know that these are the very people who will feel sorry for you when they learn that you won't earn a penny unless you shift a few policies, sell the odd pension or sign somebody up for an investment package. It was a clever tactic, but it was morally indefensible.

The theory was that by the time you had sold to everybody you knew, after about six months you would realise that you either liked the business and would stick with it, or that you didn't and would drop out. Some of the salesmen in our team were good, but I didn't believe completely in the product I was selling, and really wanted to do something else, although I still didn't know what. But it wasn't all bad. Most of my appointments were in the evening, and that meant I could spend most of the day playing golf and still make a living. It was also possible to sell some of the products to my fellow players if I was lucky.

I have done all sorts of things to earn money, but this was pretty tough. The irony was that I discovered that I was quite good at selling, so when I did get my foot through the front door I usually managed to persuade the person to sign on the dotted line. However, I knew I couldn't stick it for long – few could – and after almost a year I'd had enough, and left to take up an offer of something far better.

Obviously somebody up on high looked down upon me and decided that I had suffered enough. I played for the Midlands against the South-West in 1988 and faced a guy called David Powell, a solicitor who was a senior partner for a firm called Alsters, based then on College Green in Bristol. I immediately struck up a good rapport with him and when we met up again in 1989 it was obvious there was a possibility that we could perhaps find a way to work together, even though I didn't ever expect anything to come of it.

In 1988, David had been captain of the Gloucestershire

county team and he decided he wanted to strengthen the squad, having lost the services of Welsh international, Keith Jones, that year to the professional ranks. So he told the powers-that-be about me and informed them that he was going to try to persuade me to move south as a replacement. He duly contacted me and informed me that Alsters, and Gloucestershire, could do with a top golfer on their books – would I be interested in coming to work for him while playing for Gloucestershire? He was offering me a job in their debt recovery department, which was a new arm of the business, but I would effectively be promoting his law firm, earning far more money than I had ever done before (which was not difficult) and I would be driving around in a VW Golf GTi, which was the real clincher. Decisions, decisions... It took me all of ten seconds to agree. I had been saved.

That was it. I was off to Bristol. It was a definite step up for me, but don't run away with the impression that I was swanning around doing nothing, because that wasn't the case at all. I worked hard while in that town. David and the other partners insisted on it and there were no holidays either – it was just work and golf. However, things were a million times better than they had been.

Some people will point to the time I spent on the dole or the hours playing golf and say that was a holiday, but the reality is that, even now, I haven't had a proper holiday since I was a teenager. People will say that you can have a holiday for £250, but I did not have £250 to spare back then and, in truth, I still don't. The other thing is that, for me, it was work and/or golf. If you have to ask an employer for days off to go and play competitive golf, you can't also go to him and ask for time off to go on holiday. Officially, I had about eight weeks' annual leave, which was incredibly generous, but nowhere near enough if you really want to play in all the major amateur tournaments England offered back then, so I always seemed to be asking for more holiday time. There was one year when my golf commitments took me away from the office for twenty weeks, but David never once complained. He was a plus-handicap player himself, so I am sure that helped. He also knew, as well, that I was a valuable addition to the company.

When you go to foreign climes to play for England or for Great Britain and Ireland, it is never a holiday either, as some would claim. Not for me at least. It was always about winning. I was only interested in getting to know the course we were playing and in doing the very best that I possibly could for my country, and that meant early nights, so much of the time I never really got the opportunity to gain a proper experience of the places where golf took me, unless I was very lucky.

My social life wasn't much better either. Girls were interested in guys with money and a car and, until I moved to Bristol, I had neither. If I had been a footballer, cricketer or rugby player it might have made a difference, but your average pretty girl's eyes simply glazed over when the subject of golf was brought up, which meant I was always 'five down at the turn'. I was pretty much right up there with stamp collectors and train spotters. Yet it never really bothered me too much as I was focused on what the game could do for me. I was hooked on the glory.

Although moving to Bristol was the best thing I ever did, it still didn't improve my social life much – mainly as I didn't have a group of friends who were of similar inclinations. I was getting time off to play golf, and every spare moment was spent trying to improve my game, going to tournaments, testing new equipment and that sort of thing. Remember, too, that if I won a tournament I would end up going home with a trophy and, if I was very lucky, getting a voucher for £200/£300 to be spent in a golf shop. I was fortunate inasmuch as the better I got, the more likely it was that a golf manufacturer would give me something for free, but there was always something I needed though, whether it be a trolley, a new set of waterproofs, clothing or whatever. As an amateur there was no prize money, but at least I always looked a million dollars.

I entertained myself in those days, chilling out by going to the cinema or by watching videos. I just loved the movies – even now, I must still have at least 250 VHS films! I also enjoyed reading and bought a lot of books – you may have worked out by now that my money did not go on wine, women and song. I always like the story about George Best when he was asked how he had squandered his fortune. 'Basically,' he said, 'I spent most of my money on wine, women, fast cars and cigarettes and the rest I just wasted.'

I had a girlfriend called Michelle while I lived in Bristol, and we went out together for three years pretty much, but, as usual, golf got in the way and that relationship eventually fizzled out like all the rest. There was a Croatian hairdresser too who was absolutely stunning, but, again, I was away playing golf for long periods, so that also ended, this time after six months. In the end I reached the point where I didn't want or need the hassle a relationship would inevitably eventually bring me, and I couldn't be bothered with the confrontation that came with having to make choices between a girlfriend and golf.

A typical scenario might run like this:

'Golf is very important to me,' I would say. 'It helps to define who I am and I will be spending large parts of my life away from home playing in competitions.'

'So is it golf or me?' she would ask.

'Sorry, but I think you can guess the answer to that question.'

It may seem like a selfish attitude, but perhaps it helps to explain how I managed to achieve as much as I did on the golf course, despite lacking the talent that others had. The word I would use is 'dedication'.

There was another girl whom I felt might have been my soul mate. Her name was Clarissa and she was perfect, although she was forever telling me to stop staring at her, but she was pretty, so what else was I supposed to do? I just enjoyed looking at her, and she made me laugh. She even played golf, for goodness' sake, and it was my intention to ask if she might consider marrying me, but the day I was going to propose she told me that she had found somebody else. At that point I probably knew that I was destined never to have a meaningful relationship and that's the way it has turned out. Well, so far anyway. My sentiments are: 'The glass is still half full.'

I joined Bristol and Clifton Golf Club in 1990. Funnily enough, on the day of my interview when I first joined the club, I played eighteen holes with David Powell and had a hole in one at the seventeenth, so when we went in for the interview he turned round to the committee and said: 'You are now looking at the newest member of the hole-in-one club!' Not a bad introduction, wouldn't you agree?

As I started to win more and more important amateur tournaments around the country and began to attract press interest, the company realised that there was potential to be had from putting me into the marketing side of the business – basically going out and pressing-the-flesh and meeting people. I actually brought in quite a lot of new business for them. I was expected to play golf with clients and suchlike and I've got to say that it was hard work, because I had to make sure that the focus was on them, not me, and it goes without saying that, at times, some of the men and women I was expected to play eighteen holes with barely knew one end of a golf club from the other. Throughout the summer David would often also suggest we go to Bristol & Clifton GC at 6am to practise for an hour-and-a-half before getting into work by 8.20am. It made for a long day.

I suppose it didn't help that there were other people at the law firm who felt that it wasn't fair that I was allowed to play golf in company time, but they didn't realise that, for me, it was not a nine-to-five job. I would often start at 8am and frequently didn't finish until around midnight. David Powell would take clients to Bristol or England International rugby union matches – former England international Kyran Bracken worked for us for a while. By the way, I can exclusively reveal that Kyran has the longest tongue of any person I have ever seen in my life, and could easily touch the end of his nose with it, which was quite a party trick. When David took clients to these matches, I would often be expected to tag along as well, and no matter which way you looked at it, it was work.

CHAPTER SEVEN
COOL HAND GARY AND THE £50 FRUIT SALAD

One of the big plusses about my life in Bristol was playing county golf for Gloucestershire. The team spirit was excellent during my time and there were some real characters in the side.

I remember we were playing at Westward Ho! in 1992 and we had a guy in the team called Doug Young, who owned an old people's home near Bath. He was the joker of the team and he always seemed to have a bit of ready cash on him. He enjoyed being the centre of attention, a larger-than-life character who was forever instigating ridiculous bets or winding people up.

The team had played a practise round and had sat down for dinner and eaten the initial two courses on the first night when Doug, who knew that I was always up for a bet, turned round to me and said: 'Right then Gary, £25 if you can eat that gateau.' On the sweet trolley was a huge chocolate-and-cream gateau. As much as I could have done with the money, I knew that there was no way I could eat the cake, so I declined, but Doug kept raising the bet until eventually it reached £45. Still I refused. But he wasn't going to take no for an answer.

'Well if you are not going to eat the cake, how about that bowl of fruit salad?'

This was a bowl that would have been used to feed the entire restaurant for the evening, but he then upped the bet to £50 and I found myself thinking: 'Well, it's fruit. It will slide down. It can't be too difficult.' So I agreed, and managed to polish it off in just forty-five minutes. Towards the end though, it was a bit like the scene in the movie *Cool Hand Luke* where Paul Newman plays a convict who has to eat forty-five hard-boiled eggs. My stomach was swollen and I had to undo my trousers. Once I'd finished the fruit Doug pointed to the bowl and told me that I had to swallow all the pips and drink all the juice, too. I should tell you that after the bet had been struck, he offered to pay the hotel for the bowl of fruit but they said: 'If he is going to eat the entire bowl then you can have it for nothing.' Not only that, but the staff all stopped what they were doing so that they could watch. I had been told that I wasn't allowed to make myself sick and that if I did throw up I would lose the bet. I somehow got myself to bed and lay awake all night in agony. I thought I was going to die! When I came down the following morning I had already made up my mind that I wasn't going to eat anything, but there on the breakfast table was an industrial-sized tin of prunes, with another £40 bet waiting for me. No way! All credit to Doug – when he realised I had survived the night he duly paid up my £50.

On another occasion we were in Devon in early May for a county match and had played our practise round, had dinner and were out for the night walking by the harbour when Doug turned to Danny Thomas, one of the youngest members of the Gloucestershire team, and said: 'I bet you £25 that you won't jump into the harbour and swim over to that boat and back.' Without a second's hesitation, Danny took his shoes off, dived into the water and swam out to the boat and back. Now there are a few things you should consider – he had no idea how deep the water was, or whether there were any rocks beneath the surface, it was pitch black, and the water was ice cold. We helped him out of the water and he was absolutely freezing, but Doug had to hand over yet another £25 there and then.

Once year the Gloucestershire team was invited to take part in the Finnish Amateur Championship and off we went to Helsinki. On the eve of the championship was a big Am/Am tournament, after which there was a crayfish dinner, washed down with schnapps and various other alcoholic drinks. The idea was that throughout the evening we were given glasses of drink and had to stand up, sing a song, and down the schnapps in one. James Webber, a member of the team, quickly acquired a taste for schnapps, knocked back about ten glasses, and could hardly stand up. As the night progressed, James's condition deteriorated still further and eventually he disappeared. A group of Norwegians found him passed out in the lift and somehow discovered which room he was in, carried him back and put him on his bed.

The following morning, James was supposed to be one of the first players on the tee and, of course, he was nowhere to be seen, so we sent somebody off to find him and somehow got him to the course just ahead of his tee-time, still absolutely hammered from the night before. The entire team turned up at the first tee because we were fascinated to see what state he would be in – most of us were betting that he would miss the ball completely. Instead, he bombed his opening drive and, incredibly, by the turn he was one-under par. But then inevitably the wheels came off and he finished up eleven over.

It may not sound like it, but we did actually take our golf pretty seriously though and, as a team, we were very hard to beat. This was due in the main to the 'team spirit' we had because of the memorable experiences we'd enjoyed as a group, of which the above are probably the only printable ones I can remember!

CHAPTER EIGHT
ENGLAND EXPECTS

I was Leicestershire matchplay champion in 1984, 1985, 1986, and 1988. I won the Midland Open, and 'Closed' championship in 1986, the West of England strokeplay in 1987, West Midland Amateur 1987 and the Leicestershire Silver Fox strokeplay in 1984, and 1985. I also reached the Quarter Finals of the Amateur Championship at Royal Lytham, and the English Amateur at Hillside in 1986. However, despite these successes and quite a few other decent results in national events, I was only second reserve for the Home Internationals in 1986, and then first reserve in 1987 for the eleven-man Home Internationals team. In April 1988, however, I finally received the letter telling me that I had been chosen to play for England in the nine man team against France at the Berkshire Golf Club.

My early experiences within the England squads prior to this had been quite difficult because of what, to all intents and purposes, could be classified as bullying. There are different kinds of bullying of course. There is the blatant stuff, such as I had experienced when I was at school in

Australia, and I would never for one minute suggest it reached that level within the England squad back in those early days, but myself and people like Roger Roper, from Yorkshire, were made to feel uncomfortable because we were a bit 'different'. I was a short hitter who used 'solid' balls to help me hit it a bit further and my team-mates thought that was funny because they were all using Titleist balata golf balls.

I guess you would describe Roger as being like a boffin. He was far more intelligent than anybody else in the squad, and that set him apart from the rest. Peter McEvoy tells a great story about Roger. He was playing in the European Strokeplay championship in Austria, and arrived at the tee on a very tight par five; because it was such a difficult hole there were lots of ball spotters on duty down by the fairway and Roger asked his team-mates that evening: 'What are all those people doing here?' The guys said: 'It's for a long-drive contest that is part of the event, Roger.'

Roger was a very long hitter, so the next day, instead of taking an iron out and playing for position, he pulled out the driver and smashed the ball as hard as he could.

'I really got that one out there today,' said Roger. 'How do you think I am doing?'

McEvoy, who was one of the greatest amateur golfers these islands have ever produced, had a wicked sense of humour and told Roger: 'Yes it was pretty good Roger, but you are still only running third at the moment. There's a Norwegian and Swede in front of you.'

The next day Roger got to the hole and absolutely slaughtered it once more. He hit it so hard that he was off his feet at impact. Remember that this was a really tight hole with out of bounds, trees and thick rough everywhere and was probably the most difficult on the course, where it was really important to keep the ball in play, and here was Roger Roper, having been told it was a long-drive hole, smashing it as hard as he possibly could.

'I've got to be leading now,' he said that evening.

'No, sorry Roger, but the Swede is still ahead of you,' was the reply.

Not believing this, Roger asked an official on the course same question the next day, and, of course, the cat was out of the bag.

On another occasion, one of his team-mates phoned him up ahead of a county match and told him that the *Yorkshire Post* wanted to interview him. Roger was a proud Yorkshireman and so of course he agreed. Another man on the team, a guy called Duncan Muscroft, turned up wearing glasses and a wig and conducted this phoney interview and Roger didn't recognise him. He admitted afterwards that it took fifteen minutes before he began to wonder if it was a genuine interview.

I have always taken a pride in my appearance and believe that if you dress the part you play the part, so I would always make sure that my golf shirts and suchlike were neatly pressed and folded. On one occasion the team got into my room and then came into the dining room, one at a time, wearing my shirts.

'That looks like one of my shirts, but it can't be.' I thought.

Then somebody else would come in, then another, and by then the penny had dropped. To an outsider it may seem that I was over-reacting in getting so upset about something so trivial, but there was the sheer frustration of knowing that now I didn't have a 'clean' top to wear for the rest of the week, and they knew of my suffering. I guess they were just trying to wear me down.

I was expected to take it on the chin and accept that it was just boys having fun. I didn't think it was that funny – remember that we were all supposed to be on the same team. They wanted to bait me and a couple of others who were on the squad at that time. I know you will be wondering why they would want to do that. I don't know for sure, but I believe a lot of it was down to the fact that I was achieving things on the golf course, and had begun beating these guys regularly, when they felt I should not be able to do so. So I guess we are talking about petty jealousy, and when you add into the mix the fact that most of these young guys hit the golf ball a mile and I didn't, then it just made me seem like even more of an oddball. In their eyes at least.

They looked at me and saw a plodder, a guy with apparently no talent, and yet I was beating them. I guess it must have been pretty hard to take, and some of them must have hated it. I was also an easy target because, although I have always been fairly hot-headed on the golf course, in everyday life I was a completely different kettle of fish. It has always taken a hell of a lot to wind me up and they knew it.

Another example of the type of 'fun' they liked to have at my expense came in February 1986 when we went to Almeria in Spain with the England squad. There had been some problems on the first trip some months earlier, with Geoff Marks, the chairman, reading the riot act to the players at the airport before we left, telling everybody they had to be on their best behaviour.

I had managed to get my hands on some special new golf

balls – Casco 432s. These were three-piece, solid golf balls and were very advanced for the time. It was a great ball for me because it travelled further than most other conventional ones, and I needed all the help I could get in the distance department. They were considered to be 'rocks' by the bigger hitters when compared to the Titleist balata balls everybody else was using, and I knew that, although I would not be able to get much backspin with them, they would travel further. Just as long as I could chip and putt with them, I was happy.

We had played eighteen holes the first afternoon and were then supposed to finish for some final practice before dinner but, unbeknown to me, my so-called team-mates had decided to play an extra few holes and had opened up my golf bag, removed all bar one of my new golf balls, and gone out and played with them, coming into dinner at the clubhouse later and telling me: 'Those golf balls of yours are good, but they don't float that well.' They had knocked almost every ball into the various lakes round the back nine and I had just one golf ball to last me for the rest of the week – a week that was meant to be a bonding session. Some chance of me bonding with that bunch.

I had to buy balls to see me through the week which upset me a great deal, and I still went out and played reasonably well and beat most of them. And remember at that time I wasn't in the team. They'd taken my golf balls, tried to smash my resolve and still they couldn't break me. I had a head-to-head match with a chap called Freddie George, who was a fabulous athlete (capable of doing backflips etc.) on the final day; he had won the Berkhamsted Trophy and was one of the better players in the team, but I beat him 3&2 that afternoon.

Failing to respond to their infantile behaviour definitely won me some respect, but the bottom line was that I just didn't fit in with their view of the norm. They thought I was different and I wasn't the only one who was picked on either. I later discovered that Peter McEvoy had sat the squad down and given them something of a lecture, telling them that he was pretty certain it would be me who would have the last laugh. Peter had obviously seen something in me and became a friend and an ally throughout many difficult times. He was also my first England foursomes partner in that match against France in 1988 on the Red Course at The Berkshire; the pair of us lost, and even Peter admitted that it was his fault because, on the day, he had a stinker.

I was a loner and that was something else that set me apart from the rest. Maybe they respected me for what I achieved, but that didn't stop them hating losing to me, because they all felt they were better golfers than I was. I'd admit they were undoubtedly better strikers, but not better golfers – there is a subtle difference between the two. It just made me more determined than ever, however. The behaviour to which I was subjected could have ended up with me giving up on England, but it simply made me more determined than ever to play at my best. I suppose it was a case of: 'I'll show you.' It spurred me on.

In my first Home International series at the venerable Muirfield club I scored five points out of a possible six, so nobody could argue with my right to be on the team, but it had been a huge struggle for me to get the recognition I thought my golf deserved.

I may not have impressed the selectors with my play when they came along to watch me, but my results alone should have been more than enough to earn a place in the side. I didn't impress anybody through long driving and wonderful shot-making, and always gave the impression that I was scrambling to make my score, but was that really such a bad thing? It meant that no matter how poorly I struck the ball, I would almost always find a way to achieve the best result.

I have won getting on towards a hundred tournaments all over the world. I wish I'd had better funding and better opportunities earlier in life, because I believe that I could have been even more of a world-beater. My mother did a huge amount for me, including giving me her car for six months so that I could continue to play. She gave me money when I had none, but she was never really in a position to do any more. It made me completely focused on not letting her down and to make the most of the opportunities that she had given me. All my disposable income went on the game, whether that be the cost of lessons, equipment, getting to tournaments, entry fees, or paying for food and board.

Because nothing came easy it made me more determined to be the best, to get my name in the papers and, in the end, I am convinced it helped me cope with some of the tougher experiences I had too. Sometimes I lost through making stupid decisions, but I always tried to learn from them, and although I had to watch the pennies at all times, I was lucky to get some help and support from the likes of Maxfli, Titleist and Ping through my career – it was, of course, in their interests to have their logos on the golf bag of the country's leading amateur golfers, but I was always extremely grateful to get their help and never abused their generosity, as some apparently did.

Another story that comes to mind from those early years with England was when we were playing in the Home Internationals at Conway in Wales and I invited my girlfriend of the time to come along. I had my own hotel room and the plan was to ask her to join us for dinner after the final day's play and then sneak her into my room.

But my team-mates had other ideas. Bobby Eggo and Mark Wiggett, two fellow England internationals, somehow got hold of my room key, went upstairs and completely trashed my quarters. They threw my clothes all over the place, pulled the wardrobe over, turned the bed upside down and pulled all the drawers out. It was a mess.

Now at the time the Lord Chief High Justice for Northern Ireland was also staying in the hotel as he was also the President of the Irish Golf Union that year, and he had his security team with him, since these were the days of the troubles in Northern Ireland. They were watching the hotel from across the road and saw my two team-mates trashing my room through the window; as Eggo and Wiggett were coming down the stairs, laughing and joking at their handiwork, they were grabbed and questioned about what the hell they had been doing. I am certain the security guys were armed, and you can take it from me that Eggo and Wiggett were wetting themselves. I was sent for and was asked if I wanted to press charges against my team-mates, but I figured that they had suffered enough. Naturally, I had to forget about any thoughts of sneaking my girlfriend into the room; apart from anything else, it took an hour to put everything back together, DIY not being my forte.

I shared a room with Eggo in Denmark for the European Amateur Strokeplay. One night after dinner he disappeared for the evening and when he got back to the hotel he was so drunk that he could hardly stand up! It was about 3am when he fell into the room and slumped on the bed, and I lay there pretending to be asleep. Within seconds, he was snoring like a trooper, but then he seemed to stop breathing for fully two minutes. I lay there thinking: 'He'll be fine, he'll be fine. He will start breathing again ... in a minute.' But he didn't. So I jumped out of bed, switched on the light, and, as I did so, he gasped a huge gulp of air and started breathing again. It happened twice more that night, and I was worried he was going to die! Needless to say, I wasn't worth much the next day after a fretful night making sure that my roommate didn't expire.

Bobby was a legendary drinker in those days. Reputedly, when he reached the final of the English Amateur Championship in 1987 against Kevin Weeks, he'd made a pact with Kevin that if they both reached the final they would go out for a bender the night before. Now Kev was a man-mountain of a guy who could probably drink anyone under the table, so eventually Bobby came off second best in both contests – losing on the 37th in an epic match round Frilford Heath.

CHAPTER NINE

PLAYING WITH A LEGEND

In 1991 the Amateur Championship was played at Ganton Golf Club. I'd had a great run of form leading up to it, going close in the English Amateur Championship at Formby, *Golf Illustrated* Gold Vase at Sunningdale and the European Strokeplay at Hillside. The weather had been great too that summer, which suited me because it meant the fairways had more roll than normal and the greens were quick.

Ganton was one of my absolute favourite courses because it required tactical play rather than pure length, so I arrived with my confidence high. There were two qualifying rounds in those days, one at Scarborough Northcliffe, the other at Ganton, and I broke 70 in my first round at Scarborough, followed by a 72 at Ganton and finished as one of the leading qualifiers. I had met up at the tournament with a friend, Charlie Banks, who was a Nottinghamshire county player, and we both completed our second rounds early in the day. I knew that I was going to get into the championship proper, but Charlie was on the borderline so rather than let him hang around all day watching the scoreboards, I suggested that we went into Scarborough and spend the afternoon playing the slot machines, walking on the beach and eating candyfloss and ice cream. We had a blast and he won a bulldog soft toy, which became his mascot for the week. As it turned out, he qualified, too.

The draw meant that we could have met in the quarter-finals, but, in the end, Charlie lost to a decent Italian called Floriolli in the last sixteen, who I ended up beating in the quarter-finals in a low-scoring match. I vividly remember standing on the sixth green needing to two-putt from no great distance to win the hole, but the surface was so fast that I very nearly putted my ball off the green. Fortunately, I holed the one coming back and eventually got through to the semi-finals, where I met a Scotsman, Wilson Bryson, against whom I played what turned out to be an epic game.

On the third hole of the semi-final against Wilson, I pulled my drive short and left. As I strode down the fairway, Keith Wright, the then secretary of the English Golf Union, who had come up to support me, told me that he had found my ball but predicted that I wouldn't like his discovery. He was right. It was in a small gorse bush, resting about six inches above the ground. I studied my options carefully and pulled out my driver, with everybody thinking that I was preparing to take a drop under a penalty of one shot, but I gripped down the shaft of the club and swung nice and easy. It soared into the sky, exactly as I had envisioned, and flew into the stiff breeze the 190 yards towards the green. It was perfect, other than the fact that it leaked slightly right and finished in a greenside bunker just past pin high, no more than fifteen feet from the hole. Bryson, meanwhile, had put his second shot on the green, twenty-five feet from its target. He hit his first putt almost five feet beyond the hole and I splashed out the bunker and left my ball stone dead, so he now he had to hole his putt to half a hole that minutes earlier he was certain he was going to win. To his credit, he holed out, but shook his head all the way to the tee, in disbelief that I had got a half.

I won the next to go one up and we got to the seventh hole, which is a great par four. However, I pulled my second shot into another bunker where I found an absolutely horrendous lie. I could only play it with one leg out of the sand leaning on the bank and the other in the bunker. I had to get the ball up very quickly and carry it fully twenty yards to a flag that was located in a tricky rise on the green. Bryson was again on in two, once more ticking off the hole as a certain victory, but I somehow got the ball out of the bunker to about fifteen feet and holed the putt for a miraculous par. Unsurprisingly, he missed his birdie putt and from that moment on he was a beaten man.

Afterwards he told me that he had never seen two golf shots such as the ones I had played. 'I couldn't believe what you did from the gorse bush, and I certainly couldn't believe the bunker shot you played at the seventh,' he said. The best thing of all was that Wilson returned to the course the next day to watch me play in the final, which I thought was very sporting of him.

The Walker Cup had been played the week before, so the entire American team was at Ganton with the exception of Phil Mickelson who had to get home due to other commitments, as he was soon to turn professional. This incidentally was the last time that our Amateur was graced by the US Walker Cup team, due to the Amateur date being moved back to June every year, apparently for selection purposes. This, in my opinion, is sad, as we now no longer ever see the cream of American amateur golf in this country. I had missed out on selection for the Great Britain and Ireland team because by the time I ran into form, the side had already been picked. The likes of David Duval, Jay Sigel and Bob May were all in the field at Ganton though, but I avoided the American players in the earlier rounds until I got to the final of course, where I faced May. You may remember that later, in 2000, Bob ran Tiger Woods very close in the US PGA championship at Valhalla, only losing in a playoff.

Andrew Maw, a fellow Leicestershire county player and a good friend, had parents who lived in Scarborough and they put me up while I was playing in the championship. His father Peter also caddied for me, which made all the difference, because he was a member of Ganton too.

There was a crowd of more than 2,500 people for the final and May was the red-hot favourite, having beaten Duval in the other semi-final. I was two down after four holes and, as I was walking off the next tee behind a couple of R&A officials, I heard one of them say to the other: 'Well, that's that then.' Even though it was a thirty-six-hole final they were already writing me off. They couldn't have known it, but it was exactly the thing I needed to hear because it caused my hackles to rise and made me determined to show everybody that this was no foregone conclusion. I battled back and ended the first eighteen holes by holing a fifteen-foot birdie on the eighteenth green, to go into lunch two up.

One of my most vivid memories of that final day was sitting in my car listening to music between the morning and afternoon rounds and getting so fired up that by the time I returned to the course, I could have beaten poor Bob to death, I was so 'up' for the coming confrontation. When I am able to get myself in a bubble like that, I feel that nobody can beat me. I guess every champion you meet will constantly talk about 'Getting in the zone', but everyone has a different way of getting there. For me it has always been music.

In the afternoon I played the best golf I could have done, apart from the ninth hole, where I ran up a double-bogey but still won the hole. From the tenth hole in the morning to the tenth hole in the afternoon I was six-under par with a double-bogey on my card. May didn't stand a chance and I finished up beating him 8&6.

We shook hands and got a buggy ride back to the clubhouse, but it really didn't sink in that I was the Amateur Champion until I started to have my photograph taken with the trophy. Ganton was always good to me, but this was extra special, particularly when I realised what came with my victory.

Winning the Amateur Championship meant that I gained entry into The Open at Muirfield in 1992 and, most amazingly of all for me, was the trip to The Masters at Augusta National. If I was told that I had one more round of golf to play before I died, Augusta in The Masters is where I would choose to play it. Everything about the place is special, and the attention to detail is just amazing. The greens are so fast that you reach a point where it becomes incredibly difficult to release your putter, especially if you are putting downhill, because sometimes it's almost impossible to keep the ball on the green and you could find yourself putting off the surface into lakes, bunkers or back down the fairway.

When most youngsters stand over a putt they imagine that they need to hole it to win The Open, but for me it was always The Masters that held a special place in my heart, and I cannot adequately find the words to tell you how much it meant to me to realise my ambition of playing there. The first thing that happened was that I received a letter in early December inviting me to play and then I had to pluck up the courage to ask David Powell if I could have the time off work. He agreed, but there was, of course, a condition. 'Yes, you can have the time off, but only if I am coming with you and, oh, and I will be caddying for you, too.'

I couldn't very well refuse, could I?

Augusta National, and everything about it, took my breath away from the moment I arrived. Heading down Magnolia Lane to the clubhouse is everything I thought it would be and more. I was treated like a movie star right from the start. They gave every competitor a Cadillac to drive for the week. I couldn't believe my luck. What a fantastic car this was. Mind you I was stopped for speeding within forty-five minutes of picking up the keys and received a ticking-off from a police officer who looked like he had walked straight from the set of *Chips*.

Before one of the practise rounds, David went to pick up my golf bag and said: 'What on earth have you got in here, Gary? Your bag weighs a ton.' Most top golfers go out onto the course with no more than, say, ten golf balls in their bag, but I had put in about forty old balls because I wanted to have something to hand out to any of the children or other spectators who were looking for souvenirs. Needless to say, David did not appreciate my generosity, and told me that if I wanted to do that then I could carry the bag myself.

On the Wednesday I was informed that I had been paired with Arnold Palmer in the first round. Initially I was a bit disappointed as I really wanted to play with Nick Faldo, Fred Couples or Tom Watson, but then it began to sink in: Arnold Palmer – The King.

There is always a special dinner to honour the Amateur Champions from the US and Britain on the Tuesday night and I sat next to Alistair Cooke, of *Letter from America* fame, and he was one of the most fascinating men I have ever met. There was a whole host of other great amateurs there – men such as Michael Bonallack, Bill Campbell, Fred Ridley and Jay Sigel. It was a fantastic experience and it made me feel very special. These guys were there to honour me, and I felt humbled.

I had made a small presentation of some old replica golf clubs on a plinth on behalf of Bristol and Clifton Golf Club to Augusta National in thanks for the invitation to compete. I gave the gift to Jack Stephens, chairman of The Masters, and he was genuinely touched. He even came down to the first tee to have his photograph taken with Palmer and me before the first round, which was against the usual protocol, but Stephens was the chairman of Augusta, so I guess he could do anything he liked.

On the morning of the first round I was on the practise ground hitting balls and I became aware of a presence behind me. I turned round and there was Sevcriano Ballesteros, one of my all-time heroes, standing there quietly watching me hit golf balls. Let me repeat that – Seve Ballesteros, one of the greatest golfers ever to draw breath, was standing watching me hit golf balls. 'I have been watching you Gary,' he said. 'You are swinging the club great. Don't worry, you are going to do well today, have fun.' It was a wonderful gesture and it made me feel ten feet tall. Out of all the top pros, he was one of the few who made the effort to speak to me. The top British players hadn't said a word to me all week. I would like to think that if I had been at Augusta as a British professional and my national amateur champion was making his debut that I would ask him if he wanted to play a practise round with me, or simply say hello. At the very least, I would offer some tips as to how best to play this most difficult of golf courses, but there was nothing from any of them, and that is what made Seve's gesture so special in my mind.

I'd also had a note from Peter Alliss, telling me just to play my own game, that Augusta was just a course like any other with eighteen greens. 'Nothing changes, you still have to plot your way round as you would with any course,' he wrote.

On the day of the first round I had received a new set of woods by courier. I tried them out on the range that morning and told David Powell that I was going to put them in the bag and use them. Even now, I still can't believe I did that. David certainly couldn't believe that I was serious when I told him what I was going to do.

I then spent an hour on the putting green hitting putt after putt, just trying to get a feel for the pace of the greens in particular. I was a very good putter and I knew that if I could get a feel for the speed then I would have half a chance of doing well.

When I had completed my preparation in good time, it was still at least twenty minutes before my 10.30am tee-time, so I wandered down to the first tee to try and get a feel for what it was going to be like teeing off. I introduced myself to the starter and asked him if it would be all right for me to stand at the back of the tee and take in the atmosphere. He told me that would be fine and I duly watched the group in front of me tee off. Don't ask me who it was because I haven't clue. I suppose I was still in a daze. After they had hit off, there were still about 2,000 people beside the tee and there was polite applause, but now I was aware that more and more people were starting to flock towards the tee.

I could hear some noise in the background and it gradually got louder and louder until suddenly there was Arnold Palmer bursting through the crowd. It was a spine-tangling experience that left the hairs on the back of my neck standing on end. I knew that the Americans loved Palmer, but I had no idea how much.

Even youngsters were approaching him and asking him for his autograph.

I was standing on the back of the tee watching all this going on. Players are actively discouraged from signing autographs before they start a round at Augusta, but who was ever going to tell Arnold Palmer, The King, that he was 'breaking the rules'? I was also struck by the fact that he seemed to know everybody's name, and I am talking about officials and spectators alike. If you know anything about golf, you will realise that the fans at The Masters are known as 'patrons' and they return year after year, so I am guessing that many of these people have introduced themselves to Palmer over the years and he has shown sufficient interest to remember their names. What a truly remarkable man.

He was sixty-two years old at the time. The starter introduced him to me and I will never forget his words to me: 'Gary, this is an honour for me. I am really looking forward to playing with you today. I knew your father and he was a lovely man. I'm sure we'll have a great day.' He then shook me warmly by the hand and moved away. Then came the moment.

'On the tee, Arnold Palmer...' Once again, there was a huge round of applause, which Palmer duly acknowledged. He then propelled the ball 290 yards, straight down the middle. Further wild applause.

'Now on the tee, from England, Gary Wolstenholme...' Polite applause. I moved over to my bag and pulled out the driver, which was followed by these immortal words of wisdom from David Powell, my boss and trusted caddy: 'For God's sake Gary, don't miss the ball.' Of all the things you would want a caddy or friend to say to you at a moment such as this, that is probably the last thing you would expect to hear. Until that moment, it had never entered my head that I might miss the ball, but now, as I stood over my ball, that was all that I could think about.

I told myself to keep my backswing as slow as possible and less than a second later the blur slowed back to normal time and somehow I had managed to hit a beauty, 265 yards straight down the fairway. I had just been out-driven by almost thirty yards by a sixty-two-year-old man, but to be honest I couldn't care less. I was living the dream. I almost ran off the tee, with the applause for us both still ringing in my ears. I had to stop myself from racing all the way down to the first fairway, because I was so excited by it all. The atmosphere was electric.

The first hole was a drive and a seven iron to twenty feet below the hole for me, which was ideal. I swear to you that in my humble opinion the green staff at Augusta cut the first one just that bit faster than any other on the course in those days to try to catch out the players.

Remember that I had been on the practise putting green for an hour before the start, and I had worked really hard on the greens all week, so I knew what to expect. However, I hit my uphill putt on the first one fully six feet past the hole and thought: 'That's not possible.' Needless to say, I missed the next one and walked off the hole having dropped a shot, as did Palmer. I was thinking that I was going to shoot 90 as we walked off the green. Nothing was said between Dave Powell and I, but I am sure that he thought the same.

The second hole is a par five and we had to wait for the guys in front, who were going for the green. It gave me a chance to take a few deep breaths and get my thoughts in order. Eventually we got the all clear to play. Palmer launched another huge drive, while I hit a decent one just short of the bunker on the right. I then hit a five wood, leaving myself just over eighty yards to the flag. I hit my approach and I can still see in my mind's eye a chap sitting on his little Augusta stool behind that position and as my ball landed and bounced forward to the very lip of the hole he put his hands to his head in disbelief that it hadn't gone in. In the event it screwed back six feet but, thankfully, I holed the putt and I was off and running.

At the third I hit a driver and a nine iron and holed a fifteen-foot putt for another birdie. One-under par. The fourth is a tough par three, at which I hit the green with a five wood and two-putted, so I was still doing okay. The fifth is a long tough par four and I also played that in regulation. By now, I was feeling more relaxed and was beginning to enjoy the experience. I lipped out for another birdie at the sixth, but was happy to settle for a par. The seventh hole has changed a great deal since 1992, but back then I got home with a drive and a nine iron to eight feet. Guess what? I holed the putt. Now I was two under.

At the eighth I put an eight-iron approach four feet from the hole and made that putt, too. Three under. I hit a poor drive at the ninth, which left me blocked out with a four iron for my second and I hit a great shot that just carried the bunker but ran through the back of the green and left me with a very slippery chip, the sort of shot that anybody playing Augusta has nightmares about. It was straight downhill and I was at least forty-five feet from the flag and with about five feet of fringe to chip it over. I pulled out my sand wedge and David asked: 'Gary, are you sure you want to do this? Wouldn't you be better off putting it?' But I was adamant, even though I knew that the shot I faced was incredibly difficult. I produced the best chip I could possibly have played. It checked up and trickled down to the hole, leaving me no more than twenty inches from that spot. As I walked down to my ball, Palmer said: 'That was a great shot Gary, a brilliant touch well done.' Which made me feel great.

As I was walking to the tenth tee, three-under par, some wag in the crowd shouted out: 'Don't look at the leaderboard.' I obviously ignored the advice, as you do when someone says don't do something, and looked up and there it was: Gary Wolstenholme leading The Masters, tied with David Frost and Brad Faxon. In my first competitive round of golf at Augusta, I had reached the turn in thirty-three strokes, with a bogie. I've a picture at home where there was a guy leaning out of the scoreboard looking at my name and the bubble caption could quite easily have read: 'Who the hell is Gary Wolstenholme?'

I hit a reasonable tee shot at the tenth, but it left me with a three iron for my second shot. I was on a down slope and the golden rule under such circumstances is always to aim slightly left and allow for the ball to drift right. However, I forgot this basic principle and ended up in the right bunker, splashed out to six or seven feet and lipped out. I dropped another shot on the eleventh but made my par three at the twelfth, a short hole over water where Tom Weiskopf once took thirteen.

The thirteenth is a dogleg par five and because of my lack of distance from the tee I laid up with my second and produced a good approach to the green, but just missed my birdie. Another shot went at the fourteenth, which brought me back to level par. I made a par at the fifteenth and then we got to the par-three sixteenth, with water on the left. Palmer hit his tee shot long and left of the pin, which was on the top right-hand side of the green, while I put my tee shot on the right level, about twelve feet from the cup. This is the hole where you'll remember a few years back Tiger Woods produced that miracle chip, when the ball hung onto the lip of the hole just long enough for everybody to see the Nike swoosh on his ball before toppling into the hole.

One of the traditions of Augusta National is that people sit in the same spot all day long. They put their little seats down and walk away knowing that nobody will ever move that makeshift chair, or sit in it. They get to know every nuance of the hole they are watching, they know every slope, so the second that Palmer hit his putt the murmuring began. On and on it rolled, and as I watched it I thought: 'That's a pretty good putt. It's a good pace too, and on a good line.'

As it tracked in on the hole the volume of noise from the gallery began to grow and then the ball hit the hole and disappeared. If I thought that the roar that greeted his arrival on the first tee was loud, it was as nothing when compared to this. They went nuts. I have never heard a crescendo of noise like it. I could even feel it through the soles of my feet. It gives me goosebumps even now just to think about it all these years later. I have never experienced anything quite like it before or since. And Palmer loved it. The years fell away as he stormed up the green, putter raised high above his head.

Eventually the noise died down and I somehow had to try and focus on my putt. The perfect ending to this part of the story would be for me to tell you that I holed it, but sadly I lipped out. It didn't matter though. I was still smiling when I walked off the green, enjoying the reaction to a legend.

Palmer strode off to the seventeenth tee and as I followed him I heard somebody shout: 'Arnie, you're the man!' It is commonplace on American golf courses now, but that was the first time I had heard it, and I thought it was really funny. And then as I walked past the guy he said: 'And you're the man, too!' He hadn't the foggiest idea who I was, I am sure, but it was a lovely moment and made me laugh out loud. I was in heaven.

I stood on the seventeenth hole, still on level par, and got a decent drive away and put my second shot, with a four iron, just through the back of the green. Palmer was in a greenside bunker and played a wonderful recovery and I congratulated him. He thanked me and, once again, I had to wait for the noise to die down and concentrate on my pitch shot, which was another slippery chip, but in it went for the most unlikely of birdies. As we walked off the green, Palmer said: 'And that was pretty good, yourself.'

So I arrived on the final hole one-under par. It was

beyond my wildest dreams. I struck a good drive and was then stuck between clubs for my second shot, either a three or a four iron. I decided to go with a three and swung easy, too easy. The ball leaked right into the bunker. After everything that had gone before, I was absolutely gutted, but I had been playing really well and, apart from the three-putt on the very first green, my short game had been sharp, so there was no reason to think that I couldn't get up and down from the sand. I splashed out to about four feet, just above the hole. Unfortunately, I pulled the putt and dropped a shot.

I had played my first competitive round of golf at Augusta, in the company of the one and only Arnold Palmer, in level par 72, three shots better than Palmer himself. My finish disappointed me, but what an experience it had been. Arnie was an absolute gentleman and I now knew why so many people loved him.

We walked off the final green, signed our cards and handed them in. I asked whether it would be possible to keep mine, but they told me that they kept every card, but they did agree to sort out a photocopy for me. It was a great souvenir, especially as I wasn't playing with Palmer the following day. Now, you play with the same partners for the first two rounds in three balls, but not back then.

I thanked Palmer for his company and told him how much I'd enjoyed playing with him.

'Arnie, that has been just the most amazing day of my life. I have really enjoyed it,' I said.

'And so have I Gary. It's been great fun. Good luck tomorrow,' were his words.

During the second round – which I played with Bob Gilder, an extremely quiet American – there was one incident that really made me smile. I had just hit my drive at the seventeenth and was walking off the tee when I heard one of the gallery say: 'Gee Hank, even my wife hits it further than this guy.' And she probably did – but she never played in The Masters with The King.

Still, I finished my second round with a birdie at the final hole by holing a great putt across the green, which meant I had scored a 79. So I had the privilege of breaking 80 twice, which is no mean feat at Augusta in your first Masters. I missed the cut by five shots, but I could have played all four rounds – I put my tee shot in the water at the par-three twelfth and walked off with a five, and there were a couple of other holes where I dropped stupid shots, so I played well enough to make the cut. I sometimes wonder, even now, what might have happened had I played that second round with Palmer once again? But it wasn't meant to be.

However, the first round played in the company of The King was the most memorable of my life. After that round at Augusta I was interviewed for an hour or more, sitting on a bench outside the clubhouse. At one point there must have been twenty or so journalists recording the story of my round.

I would play in The Masters again, in 2004. As it turned out, I shot rounds of 76 and 77, so I can say that I have played this course four times in the event proper and broken 80 every time. There are many professionals who would love to be able to say they had broken 80 every time they played Augusta. It is an achievement of which I am especially proud.

When the professionals miss the cut they catch the first plane out of town, usually one that they own, but I was determined to soak up every single moment and watched

Fred Couples win the Green Jacket and David Berganio win the prize for leading amateur after making the cut and playing all four rounds. I savoured the whole thing.

I considered it a privilege to be able to use the clubhouse throughout the week, even after I'd missed the cut. It's an amazing place, full of tradition. Everywhere you look there are great pictures, and in the dining room there is a club in a display case from every winner of The Masters, which means that if you close your eyes you can go back in time and recall previous great tournaments. There is nowhere else quite like it apart from St Andrews, I guess.

Of course, everywhere there are reminders of the great Bobby Jones, who founded both Augusta and The Masters. Jones is a great hero of mine. Like me, he had a bit of temper on the golf course, and was a gentle soul off it, and I don't think it is possible to top his achievement of winning the US Open and US Amateur, and Open Championship and Amateur Championship in the same year. To win the US Amateur and complete the set, he had to beat eight opponents in matchplay. Anything could have gone wrong. Can you imagine the pressure he must have been under? I often wonder what he would think if he could see what they have done to the game he loved so much.

True golf fans don't like to see the best players in the world struggling in major championships, so why do the USGA, R&A and many other tournament organisers feel it is necessary to set up golf courses that are almost impossible to play? We all want to see great shots, lots of birdies and the occasional eagle. Making courses ever longer and speeding up the greens is not the way to get great champions in my opinion.

I was fortunate enough that week at Augusta in 1992 to

play with Jack Nicklaus in a practise round on the Wednesday before the traditional Par Three tournament. It was a brilliant experience. We were walking down the tenth when he told me that he had his own tournament, The Memorial, coming up at the fabulous Muirfield Village in Ohio later in the year. Would I like to play in it?

'Jack I would love to play, but unfortunately it's not up to me. David Powell, who is my caddy, is also my boss at the law practice where I work, and it is up to him.'

Jack nodded and winked at me. 'Leave it to me,' he said.

We got to the thirteenth hole and we had to wait on the tee for the group in front to get out of the way. Nicklaus, who is David's idol, put his arm around my boss's shoulder and said: 'David, I have a favour to ask you.'

I was looking in the opposite direction, barely able to keep my face straight, as I heard David reply: 'Oh Jack, anything, whatever you want.'

'I would really like Gary to come and play in The Memorial this year if that is okay with you. Would that be all right?'

'Oh yes Jack, of course. That would be fine.'

He had been ambushed, and he knew it. As we walked down the thirteenth fairway, David said: 'You little bugger, you knew he was going to ask that and there was no way I could turn him down.'

What can I say about The Memorial? It is a truly great tournament, played at a fabulous venue, hosted by the greatest golfer who has ever picked up a club. And it suited me down to the ground because I got free food and accommodation, as well as a Lincoln Continental car to drive for the week. The practise facilities were the best I had ever seen and the turf was superb. I hit twenty-four shots off the same spot, which you could never do at any course in this country. The fairways were immaculate and the greens were fast and true. Basically it's Augusta with rough.

I arrived at the venue on the Saturday and Nicklaus asked if it would be all right for him to have a practise round with me on the Sunday. I thought about it for all of a fraction of a second before saying yes. We were joined by Tom Weiskopf and before we knew it we were being followed by a crowd of about 400 people who were treated to an exhibition featuring the greatest golfer of all time, a former Open champion and some quaint English amateur golfer who played the game for fun. It was great, and I played really well too, which made for a perfect day.

Nicklaus and Weiskopf got into a conversation about course design, with Jack talking about the changes he'd made at Muirfield Village. After nine holes we stopped at the halfway house for a drink and a bite to eat and I had to pinch myself to make sure that I wasn't dreaming. Weiskopf had a call to make so he left us, and Jack and I sat there for at least half an hour talking about all sorts of things, with Nicklaus chatting to me as though I was a lifelong friend. A great memory.

By the time we reached the tenth tee, some members of Nicklaus's family had arrived, including his four-year-old grandson, who had got hold of Weiskopf's driver and was trying to hit the ball off the tee with it. As he hit the shot, I bent down to tee it up for him again and somebody took my picture, which Nicklaus later had printed and signed before sending it to me.

Unfortunately, the weather during the tournament was awful and the course was playing really long, far too long for me. There are some houses bordering the course and on the

Friday when the heavens opened, there was a rain delay and we were invited into somebody's home. While we waited for the rain to stop, the lady of the house put on a great spread for us. This was somebody we had never set eyes on before, and here she was feeding us in her own home. To be honest, I was quite sorry that we eventually had to resume play because I knew I was going to miss the cut.

I eventually finished off my second round on the Saturday morning. I'd played awfully and even managed to four-putt the 17th green, but was able to laugh about it and, because I was able to raise a smile, people patted me on the back and told me how good it was to see somebody play the game and able to shrug off such a disaster.

Jack asked me back to Muirfield Village after I won the Amateur Championship again in 2003, but I wasn't able to go because it clashed with the defence of my title at St Andrews. No prizes for guessing where I would rather have been though, but everybody had said that I couldn't beat the Old Course at St Andrews, and I wanted to prove them wrong. To be quite candid I don't particularly enjoy the course as it's just made for big hitters and you can get away with hitting fairways on adjacent holes and still have a shot. Bobby Jones said that you can't be considered a true champion until you have won at St Andrews, but I believe that's rubbish.

It does, however, have a unique atmosphere, and when you walk down the first, seventeenth and eighteenth fairways it is impossible not to stop for a moment and consider all the greats of the game who have gone before you. In what other sport is it possible for a novice to be able to share the same stage as the best players in the world?

It still doesn't change my mind about the Old Course,

which, in my opinion, isn't even the best course in St Andrews. The New and the Jubilee courses are fairer tests. After saying no to Jack, I comfortably qualified for the matchplay stages of the Amateur Championship, but lost in the last sixty-four, which was very annoying.

Winning the Amateur Championship in 1991 and 2003 got me into The Masters. But it did not get me into the US Open. It only allowed me to take part in final qualifying if I so wished, but did not give me direct entry. The US Amateur champion is allowed to play in The British Open though, and that is something that has always irked me. I wrote to both the R&A and USGA in an attempt to get them to address it, but it was a waste of paper and ink.

Peter Dawson, of the R&A, told me that the USGA would not give any ground, so I suggested that we should tell their amateur champion that his victory would only entitle him to take part in our final qualifying, only to be told that we couldn't do that. The Americans, however, were basically implying that: 'Our amateur champion is better than yours.' It blows my mind that the R&A is prepared to put up with such things.

The first Open I played was at Muirfield in 1992 , when Nick Faldo scrambled to a 72 in the final round and beat John Cook by a shot. The course was very tough that year and the weather wasn't good either. After the first round a national newspaper did a comparison, looking at how John Daly, the US PGA champion, played the course in comparison to how I did – we had little in common as you can imagine, but I did beat John's score.

I was drawn with Gary Player and Tom Weiskopf in the first two rounds, two former champions who were past their best. Weiskopf remained largely silent, although Player more than made up for it, and was good company. He is a lovely man to play with. I had a practise round with him at The Masters in 2004 as well. He is very opinionated, but so am I, which is perhaps why we got on so well. I did nothing spectacular, shooting a 77 and a 76, and I missed the cut by a mile. Mum stayed with some friends during that tournament and had a bad asthma attack, while I had problems finding somewhere to stay before eventually ending up in a small hotel. The whole thing wasn't a great experience, although I loved that moment when my name was announced on the first tee.

I always got friends to caddy for me so that they could enjoy the experience too, even though I might have been better off employing the services of a local caddy, but that's not my way. The thing is that professional caddies cost so much money, and it was all that I could do to scrape together enough to find accommodation. At The Masters, if I'd had a local man on the bag it would have cost me about $1,500 and I didn't have it, although I am pretty sure he wouldn't have said to me on the first tee: 'For God's sake, make sure you don't miss the ball!'

I also got into the 1992 Scottish Open, played at Gleneagles in those days. I was on the putting green and again felt that presence looming behind me. It was Seve again. 'Hello Gary, is it all right if I play a practise round with you?' he asked.

So myself, Peter Mitchell, Marc Farry and Seve set off, and poor old Seve was struggling with his game from the very first hole and was out of sorts with himself. Mitchell ended up giving him a playing lesson on the way round and by the time we came to the ninth hole the Spaniard was absolutely nailing it. He then produced the greatest burst of golf I have ever witnessed – on six straight holes he nearly knocked the flag out with his approach shots. By this time his mood had improved, so much so that he ended up giving me a personal bunker lesson by the 16th green .

As we were walking down the seventeenth hole the subject of back pain came up. I knew that Seve had suffered, as had I, and he started to tell me about an exercise he had been taught. Before I knew what was happening he was down on all fours in front of me, demonstrating this exercise, whereby he stretched one arm out in front of himself while stretching the opposite leg as far as it would go – a bit like a Superman pose. It was a great exercise and he was deadly serious about it all, but as I looked down at him I was struggling not to laugh out loud. There were spectators on the course and they had all stopped and were doing a double take. It was surreal. He looked up and said: 'You think this is funny? What's so funny?' He was clearly miffed.

'Seve, here you are,' I explained, 'my absolute golfing hero, in the middle of the seventeenth fairway on all fours doing this Superman impression, with all these people looking on wondering what on earth you are doing.' He looked around and then he, too, saw the funny side of it all.

We played the last hole for a sandwich in the clubhouse and wouldn't you just know it – Seve hit a monstrous drive, a five iron into the heart of the green and then holed the putt for an eagle. I was in awe of the golf I had seen him play that day, and I was certain that if he continued to perform like that, he would win the Scottish Open by fifteen shots. Unfortunately, the magic disappeared and he didn't win.

Golf fans know all about Seve's magical short game, but he was a prodigious striker of the golf ball too. My father

related a story to me from his tour days when he and Greg
Norman were playing a practise round at the Dutch Open
and they looked back to the tee and saw Seve on his own.
Dad had already played with Seve and suggested to Greg
that they let him join them. Greg, who was a long hitter,
had hit a decent drive and was waiting by his ball to play
his second. Dad waved Seve up and the Spaniard unleashed
his drive, which was still in the air as it passed over
Norman's head.

CHAPTER TEN

TOP OF THE TREE

After winning the Amateur Championship in 1991 I found myself playing number one for England. We went to County Sligo for the Home Internationals and I did pretty well there. I was now in a pretty unfamiliar position because suddenly when I turned up for tournaments I was the favourite, and everybody wanted to beat me.

There was regular press interest and there were also the fans who wanted to have a look at the son of Guy Wolstenholme, Amateur Champion. Most of them had read the stories about me being a late developer whose raison d'être was keeping the ball on the short grass and I guess they wanted to compare themselves with me.

At first it was hard work, but I had already experienced something similar when I broke through at county level. Everybody was watching me back then too, and I found that difficult early on, but I got used to it, although I could never handle the criticism too well. Selectors would have a go at me for not winning more often, but you can't win every time you tee up the ball, especially at amateur level if you are also trying to hold down a job.

Nothing was ever said directly to my face, but they would make comments to other people, knowing that the remarks would get back to me, things such as: 'He should never have missed that cut.' I didn't miss many cuts, and when I did it was usually because the weather was lousy, and I hated playing in the cold, wind and rain. In those days, I found that when conditions were inclement, physically my game wasn't strong enough to compete on some of the courses on which we were expected to play.

In 1992, I was selected to play for Great Britain and Ireland in the St Andrews Trophy against the Continent of Europe at Royal Cinque Ports and I found myself coming face to face with David Berganio, who had maintained he was American when winning the US Public Links championship, but who had suddenly reverted to being Italian.

At the time there was an Irish golfer in our team called Garth McGimpsey who broke all sorts of appearance records during his amateur career and he suffered a couple of very heavy defeats in that match that, in some people's opinion, effectively ended his international playing career. It was sad because he was a fantastic player, who won 207 caps for Ireland, which it's believed happened to be a world record, until I beat it in 2007. I am particularly proud of the fact that I played for England 218 times. Unsurprisingly, I was also England's record points scorer with 142.5. I won 130 matches, halved twenty-five and lost sixty-three. Remember that I was a late starter, and was representing a country for whom it is pretty damn difficult to get national recognition. I will be very surprised if anybody ever tops my figure because any amateur golfer who is that good nowadays will inevitably turn pro.

If I had perhaps been Welsh or Scottish, I might well have been capped a couple of years earlier and would probably still be playing international representative golf today. That is to take nothing away from those two countries, because of course they have less players to choose from; on the contrary, I am certain though that they would have realised I had something to offer their up-and-coming players and would have actively encouraged me to keep going. Funnily enough my paternal grandfather was Scottish, so I could actually have opted to play for the Scots, but it never once entered my head, as Dad had played for England too.

Quite apart from my performance in the St Andrews Trophy, I had played well throughout 1992 and into the following year, so it came as a bit of a shocker when I was told that I hadn't been selected for the 1993 Walker Cup team. They picked the youngest team ever, choosing to ignore the claims of three English golfers who should all have been shoo-ins – Warren Bennett, David Fisher and yours truly. I should also mention that the Great Britain and Ireland team that I played for in the St Andrews Trophy was a nine-man side, so I was good enough to get into that team, but just a year later I hadn't been considered good enough to get into a ten-man line-up. All a bit of a mystery to many.

Padraig Harrington was in the team that was annihilated by the Americans in 1993, but I still maintain that had myself, Warren and David been picked then the outcome would have been very different indeed. There were no experienced players in the side, and that I suppose will now be the norm as the match progresses because there will be no more career amateurs available for selection.

So how do you find a leader on the course without there being some perennial career amateurs available? You need somebody who will show the younger guys how to behave, what to do, how to cope with the pressure, what to say, what not to say, how to get the most out of your practice. The theory is that the captain is there to handle all that sort of stuff, but if you are struggling with your game, the last person you'd choose to go and talk to is the captain, because all you want to do is go out and play, and if he realises you are not at your best he will not take the time and trouble to find out why – he will just leave you on the sidelines, making up the numbers.

CHAPTER ELEVEN

TAMING THE TIGER

At heart, I am a showman and I love playing in front of big crowds, and I guess that could be why I loved the Walker Cup so much. The bigger the crowd the better I play. In America they always seemed to limit the size of the galleries, but not in Britain, and it was such a buzz.

If I had 10,000 people watching my singles match it would suit me down to the ground. It reduced some guys to quivering wrecks, but I fed off it. I have always struggled to lift my game if there is no atmosphere.

When I turned up for a thirty-six-hole competition in early spring and it was cold, wet and windy, the course was in poor condition and I had spent my last few quid to pay for travel and accommodation, the thing that would drive me on to play well was the incentive of qualifying for those big team matches, whether it be for Great Britain and Ireland in the Walker Cup, the Eisenhower Trophy, or to make the England team for the Home Internationals. It pushed me on.

Some guys just cannot perform under those pressurised

circumstances, but I could. And I often became that leader on the course, which I alluded to earlier. If, for instance, one of the guys was struggling with their putting, they knew that they could always come to me and ask me to take a look at their stroke, and because putting was the strength of my game it usually didn't take me very long to identify what was wrong. I practised less than I wanted to, often because I was helping other players.

The Walker Cup consists of two ten-man teams and the selectors decided in 1995 to pick eight players and leave the last two places up for grabs until the last minute. Fortunately, I won the inaugural British Mid-Amateur at Sunningdale, playing possibly the best golf of my life. The course was made for me, the fairways were running and the greens were fast and true. I played a young guy called Simon Vale in the final and I had two twos, a hole-in-one with a four iron and a three on the four par threes. I was unstoppable and would have beaten just about anybody on the planet that day. Clive Brown, the Great Britain and Ireland captain, came up to me afterwards and said: 'Gary, that performance has just secured your place in the Walker Cup team.'

The decision to leave two places open led to a young golfer called Gary Harris, who came from the same Broome Manor Golf Club that produced David Howell, phoning the English Golf Union to tell them that since he wasn't one of the eight selected players, which had been widely expected, he was going to turn professional. Paul Baxter, chief executive of the EGU, used all his powers of persuasion to try and talk Harris into delaying his decision, assuring him he would get one of the final two places, but Harris was adamant and turned pro anyway. So Jody Fanagan and I were named as the final two players in the team.

My breakthrough victory in what could be regarded as a major amateur tournament had come at the Midland Open in 1986 at Little Aston GC, and I had been a consistent performer in important national and county tournaments ever since. This led to my victory in the 1991 Amateur Championship, of course, and that was actually the start of a run of some very good years for me which included wins in 1993 – the Chinese Open Amateur Strokeplay championship, in 1994 – the Duncan Putter Strokeplay, the English County Champion of Champions and I finished leading amateur in the European Tour's Benson & Hedges International at St. Mellion.

Just prior to the 1995 match I'd had a great season, culminating in my victory in the British Mid-Amateur, which I also won again in 1996 and 1998. I also got the opportunity to travel to the UAE, where I became United Arab Emirates Open Amateur champion too.

The Walker Cup match was played at Royal Porthcawl and our captain was, appropriately, Welshman Clive Brown, while the Americans' non-playing captain was Downing Gray. We were still smarting from the 19–5 thrashing we had suffered at the hands of the USA at Interlachen in 1993 and to make matters worse everybody was talking about this phenomenal young golfer called Tiger Woods. It was generally agreed that he had half a chance of turning out to be a pretty decent golfer.

I suppose that most outsiders looked at Fanagan and I and regarded us as afterthoughts who were unlikely to have much of a part to play in proceedings, but the two of us felt we were at least as good as anybody else. Clive Brown is a lovely man, and, notwithstanding this Woods kid, we had a decent side of our own.

There was Gordon Sherry, the giant Scot from which so much was expected. He had already finished as leading amateur in the Scottish Open and would play all four rounds in The Open at St Andrews, too. We also had Padraig Harrington, playing in his third and final Walker Cup before joining the professional ranks. David Howell was somebody I had played with and against – he represented Wiltshire and I faced him while playing for Gloucestershire. David was a fine golfer and a very funny young man, ideally equipped, I was certain, to cope with the pressure of a Walker Cup match. Lee James, a temperamental player, also came from my neck of the woods and was another who was capable of producing fantastic golf when called upon. Graham Rankin was a big, burly Scot who seemed, to me at least, to be lacking the self-belief that his play deserved.

And then there was Barclay Howard, another Scot, and somebody who had lived life to the full... and then some. Barclay had been an alcoholic and had fallen foul of the authorities on more than one occasion, but it is to his eternal credit that he eventually straightened up and became a great, great player. He and I were the old men of the team and we enjoyed each other's company and became good friends.

The other members of the team were Stephen Gallacher, the nephew of Bernard, and Mark Foster, who was a contemporary of Lee Westwood at Worksop Golf Club in Nottinghamshire.

Apart from Tiger, the American team included John Harris, Notah Begay, Chris Riley, Buddy Marucci, Jerry Courville and Trip Kuehne, who remains one of the great US career amateurs. Trip has a brother Hank, who plays on the PGA Tour and a sister, Kelly, who was one of the better players on the LPGA Tour. So, as good as our ten players were, we knew that we were going to have our work cut out for us if we were going to beat the Americans.

The one thing we knew that we had in our favour was that Royal Porthcawl, in the nicest possible way, was a baptism-of-fire sort of a place to play golf, particularly when the weather was not good and especially when the greens were less than perfect, because they were affected by a fungus at that time. The green keepers had battled for five weeks to get conditions correct, but the surfaces were fast and bumpy – not at all what the Americans were used to.

The course wasn't in a good enough condition to host the event really, but there was nowhere for them to turn because there wasn't time to find another venue. In any case, the R&A hadn't truly realised the problems with the greens until about two weeks before the match was due to be played, so we had to make the best of a bad job.

We were all staying in the Copthorne hotel just outside Cardiff, so we had a forty-minute bus journey to and from the course each day, which was a long time, especially when we had early starts. There were lots of official dinners and other functions to attend, including one on the Wednesday evening, where we went to a seafood restaurant a little way down the coast. The idea was to get both teams together so that we could all get to know one another better. From our point of view it was a great idea because it helped us realise that they were all, well, just regular guys. Meant in the nicest possible way. We needed to meet these Americans and we needed to convince ourselves that we could beat them, because Great Britain and Ireland's record in the competition was dreadful, so much so that it had been nicknamed 'The Walkover Cup' by some of the media.

As we were sitting on the bus waiting to leave for the dinner somebody asked where Chris Riley was. One of the American players was sent to look for him and, needless to say, Chris had fallen asleep. When he finally got on the bus everybody was having a laugh, taking the mickey out of him, but he took it all in good part and it helped to break the ice.

I was sitting opposite Downing Gray, the American captain, and he turned to me and said: 'You know, if that had been Tiger, none of my team would have said a word.' Even then, within the US team it was a case of 'him' and 'us'. The year before, a sports journalist called Alan Fraser had gone to Paris to interview Tiger after he'd won back-to-back US Amateur Championships as a teenager and had been selected for the US Eisenhower Trophy team, which America duly won. It was obvious even at that stage that Woods was destined for greatness, so Alan went to see him, only to be told that Tiger wasn't interested. Have you ever heard of an amateur golfer turning down an interview with a national newspaper journalist? Woods did just that. The same journalist tried again at Porthcawl, and again Woods said no, so you can imagine the sort of press coverage he got in Britain. Let's just say that it wasn't very favourable.

Downing though become a good friend of mine. Everything that this man did during the week was perfectly polished and he simply outclassed poor Clive. When he gave a speech he had us all laughing and crying with him. Peter McEvoy – who would replace Clive in 1997 – was also a very good captain, but even he would have struggled to hold his own with Gray. The man was simply born to do the job, and happened to be a marvellous entertainer.

The day after the meal at the seafood restaurant we went

out for a practise round and discovered the Americans were already on the course, playing as a nine-ball. There was no sign of Tiger. The official line was that he had food poisoning and didn't feel well enough to play. My view is that he just really didn't want to be there. He was probably hoping that Royal Porthcawl was going to be another Sunningdale, that the weather was going to be glorious, that he could reduce it to a pitch-and-putt course and tick off the Walker Cup from his 'to do' list.

Eventually he joined his team-mates on the course on the Friday, for the final practise day. Later on was the opening ceremony and for everybody representing Great Britain and Ireland this was a big deal, something we wouldn't have missed for the world. There were hundreds of Welsh people there, all singing their hearts out. It was a horrible evening, but the supporters were undaunted by it all.

The teams were then introduced to the public and that was followed by the announcement of the pairings for the following day's foursomes. I was left out. Clive decided not to play me, even though I considered this to be my forte. It could be argued that he made an error of judgment, but I am man enough to admit that the captain has a difficult and delicate job to do in picking his players for the first day, trying to make sure that everybody gets a game. Foursomes golf was what I was born for.

Anyway, after the foursomes pairings had been announced, it was time to announce the singles match-ups. Clive had told me beforehand that I was due to play in the anchor match. I was standing next to Gordon Sherry, and after a couple of the games had been read out there had still been no mention of Tiger, and Gordon turned to me and said: 'You've got him.'

'Um, I know,' I replied, and I turned and looked at Gordon and we shook hands – the photographers took a picture of us and I am sure that almost everybody who was at the ceremony was wondering what on earth we were up to.

I had played the anchor role for England on a regular basis and I was used to it, but we believed it was odds-on that the USA would put Woods out first. Downing Gray had other ideas, and it turned out that Gordon and I were spot on. 'For the United States, Tiger Woods. And for Great Britain and Ireland, Gary Wolstenholme.'

There was an audible 'Oooh!' from the gathered throng of about 4,000 people, and Woods must have wondered what on earth all the fuss was about, but it was because they all knew that here was this young American kid who hit the ball into the middle of next week taking on the Englishman who could barely hit it 200 yards. Peter McEvoy came up to me afterwards and said: 'Gary, you were the only man in our team that I would have wanted to play Tiger.' Needless to say, that made me feel pretty good. Everybody had said they wanted to play him, I guess because there was no risk – if you were playing the best amateur in the world you were expected to lose, but if you managed to win you would be hailed the hero. I didn't particularly think that way. I just wanted to win every match, regardless of who my opponent was.

I was sharing a room with Lee James that week and he asked me how I was feeling about it and I told him, quite honestly, that I was looking forward to it. Being out-driven by 150 yards did not trouble me at all. The difficulty for me was in not playing the foursomes, because I didn't feel that I was going to be into the match and I didn't really have a feel for how the course was playing.

THE LONG AND THE SHORT OF IT

We got on the bus on the Saturday morning when it was still almost dark and when we got to the course we all headed off to the practise ground, which was at the far end of the golf course. I hit a few shots and then I went down to the first tee to support and watch everybody tee off before going out onto the course myself and playing a few holes on the front nine, just to keep me nice and loose. Then I went back to the clubhouse and had an early lunch before heading back out to watch the conclusion of the foursomes.

Sherry and Gallacher lost to Woods and John Harris: the Americans' top pair, Foster and Howell managed to get a half, and Rankin and Howard, the all-Scottish combination, also lost, but Harrington and Fanagan kept us in it by winning, so we were one point behind.

I still had lots of time to kill because Tiger and I were last off, so I went back to the range and hit more balls. Normally, I like to get to the course, spend ninety minutes warming up, and then go out and play, so my normal preparation was pretty messed up. Eventually we were called to the tee.

The first is a short par four, which Tiger almost reached with an iron. Fortunately, he failed to make his birdie so we started off with a half. I missed the second green short right and to my surprise, he missed it too, long and left, out of bounds. I was one up. Then I won the next. Two up. We halved the fourth, but then we reached the fifth, a par five, and he was hitting an eight iron for his second shot while I needed a driver and a five wood to get to the front of the green. Woods hit his shot and it seemed to stay in the air forever, but in a surreal moment I noticed a guy sitting on a wall behind the green – I remember that he was bald – and the next thing we knew was that Tiger's ball hit him flush on the top of the head and ricocheted out of bounds. At the same time, the chap who had been sitting on the wall suddenly disappeared, having been knocked out by the impact. As I said, it was a surreal moment, and it meant that after five holes I was three up.

He nearly drove the next, another par four, and got up and down to win it with a birdie. He then pitched too far at the next hole, or so I thought, but screwed the ball back miles to finish fifteen feet away. I was twelve feet away, but he holed and I missed.

The match continued in this fashion, with Woods hitting the ball 100 yards past me on every long hole, but I was just about managing to keep my nose in front. I had never seen anybody hit a golf ball like that and it was fantastic to watch. Also, even at that age, he had a glorious short game. He could putt and he could chip. It was a good job really because he was so wayward at times.

After thirteen holes we were all square. The fourteenth was a par three and he put his tee shot through the back – it was an elevated green, so it wasn't the place to be, especially when I dropped my shot fifteen feet from the hole. He chipped the ball way past the hole, but then holed the putt back and gave it the full 'Tiger Woods' punch in the air. I figured that if I could hole my putt for a two and win the hole that it might knock the wind out of his sails, and that's exactly what I did. After the match, a US journalist who had followed Woods from his days as a top junior said: 'For the first time in all the tournaments I have watched him play, I could see that when you drained that putt it put the seed of doubt in his mind as to whether he was going to win that match. He knew you weren't going to roll over and that you were not intimidated by him.'

That may or may not be true, but it didn't stop him winning the next hole, hitting a drive and an eight iron into a strong headwind, while I hit a drive and a five wood and still didn't reach the green. We were all square again.

At the sixteenth hole there are bunkers and a big mound at about 280 yards and you have to make the decision as to whether you are going to lay up short or go for the big bomb. Tiger, who had the honour, went for it, and failed to connect properly. He stared at the ball, looking anxious, but, amazingly, it easily carried all the trouble and he was left with just a nine iron for his second shot. I hit a poor five wood off the tee, the same club again just short of the green and chipped up to six feet. Thankfully, he cleared the green yet again, chipped back to eight feet and, to his credit, holed for a par. I followed him in so we were still all square with two holes to play.

The seventeenth was a downwind par five, reachable in two shots, and he would have been standing on the tee thinking that he was a certainty to be putting for an eagle three. I wasn't so sure I would though, but I hit a driver and a five wood, which just went through the back of the green, and he went in with a seven iron for his second, also through the back. I chipped up to seven feet and lipped out for a birdie, while Tiger chipped to five feet, and then lipped out for his birdie; those of you who have watched Woods will know that he almost always gives the hole a chance and this was no different because he rimmed it out at least six feet past but, again, he made his par putt under enormous pressure. So we stood on the eighteenth tee all square.

He hit a one iron and I chose my driver and was left with a five wood for my second shot – have you noticed a pattern emerging, by any chance? There were about 8,000 people

GARY WOLSTENHOLME

around the eighteenth green stretching up the fairway to create a magnificent amphitheatre. It was organised chaos; the crowd was about ten deep, with everybody jostling for position. The only place you could not afford to miss the eighteenth green was on the right-hand side, where the rough was really thick and you would have no shot. We both knew that. My five wood just trickled off the right edge of the green, but it was fine and left me with an easy chip from less than thirty feet. Tiger's caddy was a guy called Mark Benka, a fine golfer in his own right, and he later revealed that for the first and only time, Woods asked him for a second opinion and they agreed that he should hit a seven iron. The ball was lying below his feet, just off the fairway in a tufty lie with the wind blowing off the left and he hoiked the ball way left.

Colin Edwards, my caddy, said: 'I think he has just knocked it out of bounds.'

'I don't care what he's done,' I replied. 'All I am interested in is getting down to my ball and making sure that I do no worse than take a four. He could still make a five.'

All credit to the nineteen-year-old. He stayed where he was until he got word that his ball had gone out of bounds – it was found in the small ditch just left of the green. Most players would have walked down the fairway, joined the hunt for the ball and then headed back to play another shot, but not him. He dropped another ball and put it to fifteen feet, which meant that if he holed it he would make the five I had predicted.

As we had walked down that final fairway the sun came out, probably for the only time that day, and there was this golden carpet of sunlight reflected off the water in the

128

Bristol Channel. It was spectacular, one of those great-to-be-alive moments. If ever I had wondered why I played golf, at that moment I got my answer.

The rest of the boys had done really well and we were one point ahead. I knew the situation as I stood over my chip, which certainly got the adrenalin going. I hit the ball and left it about thirty inches past the cup. Tiger missed his putt and conceded the hole. I had beaten him on the final green. Yes, he had knocked the ball out of bounds three times, but I had played pretty darn well too. Mum was there, and my team-mates all rushed up with their congratulations and to slap me on the back. At the end of the first day I had beaten the world's number one amateur and we were two points in front of the USA – not bad, I am sure you will agree. The atmosphere on the bus on the way back to the hotel was fantastic. Gordon had put a Billy Connolly tape on the bus's tape player and everybody was laughing and joking, a mood that continued throughout dinner.

Graham Rankin, who lost both his matches on that first day, that told Clive that he'd hurt his wrist, that meant that I was then picked for the final-day foursomes, to play with Lee James. He was my roommate and the two of us got on pretty well together, so I was looking forward to our match against Jerry Courville and Buddy Marucci. But, only two holes into the match, everything changed. He was – and is – a very good player but, after he had hit two bad shots, his spirits just dropped. I tried to encourage him, but it didn't seem to help. It was so frustrating, and I just hate not being competitive in any match never mind in a Walker Cup, that's it lucky there wasn;t anything sharp to hand! We were beaten 6&5 my worst ever loss at international level. I hated every second of it, and didn't set me up well for my re match with Tiger.

Fortunately, Mark Foster and David Howell won their match, and Padraig Harrington and Jody Fanagan brilliantly beat Woods and John Harris, so we went into the final series of single matches with our two-point lead intact.

Harris and Woods were the USA's best players and all logic dictated that they should have been sent out in the first two singles to try to make up the deficit, but Downing Gray put them out again in the last two matches instead, which was great news for us. We got off to a fantastic start, with Gordon Sherry, David Howell, Stephen Gallacher and Jody Fanagan winning the first four matches. Barclay Howard and Mark Foster both halved their games, so it didn't matter that Padraig Harrington was beaten by Harris or that Tiger got his revenge on me with a 4&3 victory, because we had won the Walker Cup by the time Woods and I had reached the twelfth tee.

The weather was dreadful too, with plenty of wind and rain, so I asked the referee if I could concede the match, but he told me that I couldn't. I was one down at the time, but I just wanted to go in and celebrate with my team-mates. We'd won the trophy and I'd already beaten Tiger Woods once, which was enough for me. I just wanted to get back to the clubhouse and join in the celebrations, and who could possibly blame me? When all the putts had been holed and the scores were added up, we had overcome this awesome USA side 14–10. What a feeling.

For me personally it hadn't been a particularly satisfactory day from a playing point of view, but I wasn't concerned. I'd got the crucial point yesterday and had been the hero of the day, and that was good enough for me.

When I got to the clubhouse somebody gave me a bottle of champagne and I drenched Rankin in the stuff. I said that Barclay Howard had pretty much solved his problems with booze and eventually he did, but every now and again he was still up for a tipple or two, mainly after the tournaments, and had to be taken to bed at 3am on the Monday morning, with Graham, his roommate, guarding the door. I was actually one of four last men standing because I didn't want the day to end. It was fantastic to be part of a winning Walker Cup team.

We returned to our hotel to get ready for the big gala dinner that would bring the curtain down on our victory. There were hundreds of people in the dining room with us, but there was one notable absentee – Tiger Woods did not join his team-mates for the dinner. On top of that, he had hardly signed any of the souvenir programmes either, which is a last-evening tradition for the teams.

I look back now and admit that he was head and shoulders above me and everybody else when it came to playing ability – it was only eighteen months later that he would go to Augusta and break every record in the book, winning by twelve shots during his first Masters as a professional. I knew that I had played with somebody special, but as a human being and as a team player he fell some way short. In saying all of that, he is one of the very few golfers in the world that I would go out of my way to watch. I love the fist pumping and I love the seemingly impossible shots he is capable of producing too.

Back in his early days as an amateur, however, he made some serious errors of judgment, and failing to join his team-mates for that final dinner was one such mistake. The following day he had the opportunity to add his signature to those of his team-mates on the souvenir programmes, but he refused to do so. I guess you could say that he has become the Michael Jackson of golf, and I just hope that, ultimately, he does not suffer the same fate.

Apparently when he was aged just four, he was put in an empty room and there was a golf club and tennis racket on the floor. If he'd picked up a tennis racket then we might have been watching him win Wimbledon ten times, but he picked up the golf club and the rest is history. I understand that he had a sports psychologist from the age of eleven for goodness' sake, and a father who instilled the competitive spirit in him – that feeling of never knowing when you're beaten. As he grew up, perhaps more people should have been around to tell him about the other stuff he needed to do – the sort of things that were the appropriate actions to do as befits a truly great champion, and a sporting icon.

CHAPTER TWELVE
CAPTAIN'S ORDERS

Malcolm Lewis was my England captain from 1998 until 2001 and he was not only a good man but also a great friend and former Gloucestershire county colleague. He had played for England and in the 1983 Walker Cup, and was top of the tree for about three years. However, essentially he gave it up when career and family came along, and Malcolm went on to become an accountant. I first met him at the Amateur Championship at Lytham in 1986, which was his last major tournament.

It was Malcolm who first approached me about going to play in Finland in 1987 and who also opened the doors that got me into tournaments in Hong Kong and China too. When I moved to Bristol to work for David Powell, I used to see Malcolm on a fairly regular basis, and I remember a discussion with him that went something like this:

'Right Gary, we need to get your career on track, so you need to set yourself some goals,' he said.

Malcolm was talking about goals in connection with my

job, but the only goals I was really interested in at that point were with my golf.

'I want to play in the Walker Cup, Malcolm,' I said. 'After that, we will see.'

'What about a house and family?'

'After the Walker Cup, Malcolm.' I replied.

After I had played and beaten Tiger Woods, there was no way I was ever going to give up my amateur career – I was well and truly hooked on the glory. Malcolm told me it was time to get on with the rest of my life, but I had long since decided that I wanted another Walker Cup under my belt. And then another.

As a captain, Malcolm would always put me out first or second, or last. It used to make me feel appreciated, because I knew that if he was putting me out in the first matches it was because he expected me to get an early point on the board for England, and if he put me out last it was because he had done his sums and worked out that the last singles match would be crucial. Whenever we played Ireland, he would always try to find a way of getting me drawn against Garth McGimpsey, who was their best player at the time. I had a great record against Garth, who always inspired me to play well.

If it wasn't me at number one, it would be Simon Dyson. Malcolm used to call him his 'red meat' player because he didn't care who he played, he would just go out and try and eat them for breakfast. Malcolm knew that Dyson was a banker, too. The same thing applied to Phil Rowe, who could be hacking the ball all over the place, but always found a way of raising his game for England when it mattered most.

Malcolm was a great one for making sure that everybody

was comfortable when they played for England, and one of the ways he did that for me was by ensuring that I had my own room when we were away on international duty. You have to remember that I was a good deal older than most of my team-mates, so it made sense. Plus the teams were usually made up of odd numbers, nine- or eleven-man teams usually. We were playing in the European Amateur Strokeplay in Sweden and Malcolm came into my room and stopped dead in his tracks and looked in astonishment at the spare bed.

All of my clothes were laid out for each of the days, together with socks and underwear, my daily intake of vitamin tablets and the packet of cereal I would be eating each day. For me, it was absolutely normal, but he shook his head and said: 'Gary, I knew you were organised, but this is ridiculous.' Preparation has always been everything for me, and that was part of it, down to the finest detail.

Malcolm had a better understanding of my game, and how I managed to score well, than almost anybody else. He will tell you that I try to take risk out of the equation, and he is correct. He will also tell you that I hit the ball much further than people give me credit for, even though, despite his words, I know how far I trail behind most decent players.

I don't like taking risks off-course either. Malcolm was instrumental in helping me to land a job looking after a driving range because he felt I needed to make a change in my life at that time. I had been told that the owner was happy for me to take time off to go and play in amateur tournaments, the money was good and that I would be allowed to hit golf balls to my heart's content. We shook hands on the deal one evening, but I started to worry about it and at 3am I phoned Malcolm and left a message: 'Malcolm, I can't sleep. Can you get me out of the deal please?' Thankfully, he did. I can't really explain why I felt so uncomfortable about it, but I just knew that it wasn't right for me, so I stayed with David Powell at Alsters.

Malcolm used to spend a great deal of time working on the mental side of things, and took great pride in putting the right players together in the foursomes. However, he did get it wrong on the odd occasion. During the Home Internationals at Royal County Down in 1999, he partnered me with a great Yorkshire golfer called Aaron Wainwright and for a while we were unbeatable. Aaron was a big strong hitter and we got on great for the first couple of days.

On the final day we faced Ireland and Aaron and I were four up after six holes and all was still well with the world, but then inexplicably the wheels started to come off. As Malcolm approached us to find out how we were doing, Aaron was walking about fifty yards behind me. I look back on it now and realise that the moment I started mis-striking the ball I started to retreat inside myself and had essentially stopped talking to Aaron. I was self analysing what was wrong in my game, but failed to realise that it was ruining Aaron's performance in the process, as he needed my reassuring confidence to satisfy himself that all was okay.

Malcolm asked me what was happening and I said: 'I'm struggling with my game a bit because of the strong wind mate, and Aaron's lost his driving.'

Aaron told him: 'I don't know what I'm doing wrong, and Gary isn't talking to me either?'

It was just a case of crossed wires I guess, but, needless to say, we ended up losing our match and my chance of winning six out of six of that Home Internationals. Malcolm realised that he couldn't play us together again which was a shame. Confidence is a big thing I guess.

CHAPTER THIRTEEN
HEARTBREAK RIDGE

The 1995 Walker Cup match was a watershed moment for me, but afterwards I knew that it was time to make some changes in my life. I had been in Bristol for seven years and I would count them as being among the happiest of my life, but I ended up heading back to Leicestershire when I was offered the post of Director of Golf at Kilworth Springs Golf Club, near Lutterworth. They had been looking for a Tour player, somebody to promote the club, but they couldn't find anybody for the money they were prepared to pay, so Jennifer Prentice, a journalist and a mutual friend of myself and Roger Vicary, the owner of Kilworth Springs, persuaded Roger that he should employ me instead, as I'd probably get them as much, if not more, publicity than any Tour pro.

It made sense, because no Tour player would have taken the job for £20,000 a year. I, on the other hand, was very happy to do so. Every time I won an event I was described as Gary Wolstenholme of Kilworth Springs, so I helped raise their profile from that point of view alone, and because of all the publicity that I got them, the club never spent much on advertising. There were pictures of me on all the walls (and still are), as well as regular articles in some publication or other, mainly thanks to the efforts of Jennifer Prentice and her husband, David, who got articles about me published whenever I did something of note.

It was difficult to get my feet back on the ground after the events at Porthcawl, but I had no choice and soon returned to normal life. I continued to play some great golf, and in 1996 I won the Mid-Amateur again, as well as the Berkshire Trophy, Finnish Open Amateur Strokeplay and the Duncan Putter (again). On top of that I was English County Champion of Champions again and became Gloucestershire County Champion for the fourth time. The following season was another Walker Cup year, during which I won the Berkshire Trophy for a second time and the Welsh Open Amateur, as well as the Leicestershire and Rutland County Open Amateur Salver and the Failand Cup.

Clive was again Great Britain and Ireland captain for the 1997 match, to be played on American soil at Quaker Ridge in New Jersey. We had a fantastic team once more that included the likes of Justin Rose, Barclay Howard, David Park, Craig Watson (he beat Trevor Immelman in the final of The Amateur Championship the previous year), Keith Nolan and Steven Young, a wonderful young Scottish player who was, like Nolan, based at an American college. Leading up to the event we were all playing really well and were confident that we were going to retain the cup. Yet again, we were staying miles away from the course, which wasn't ideal, and the greens, which were incredibly undulating, were unbelievably quick. Certainly faster than anything we were used to back at home.

I don't think Clive knew quite how we had won the Walker Cup in 1995 and if he did, he had forgotten by the time we arrived at Quaker Ridge. We'd probably made the mistake of allowing the warm-up sessions to be too intensive and on top of that, Clive kept us at the course all day during the practise days, from 8am until 5pm. All we did was hit golf balls all day long – everybody, that is, apart from Steve Young and Craig Watson, who refused and instead spent most of the afternoon in the clubhouse, eating doughnuts and watching TV. They knew exactly what they were doing.

My problem is that I love hitting golf balls and I didn't realise that we were simply practising too much. Justin was a schoolboy prodigy, and he couldn't get enough of it either, and the rest of the team were the same – they just wanted to soak up the atmosphere and play as much golf as possible on this fabulous course. Michael Brooks, another member of the Great Britain and Ireland team, was worried about his short game and seemed to spend entire days chipping and putting with his father, Andrew, a long-time professional, at his side giving him advice.

Michael and I became great friends through these matches in particular, and I can tell you that he is one of the world's great shoppers. He would spend £200 on a tie because it was a limited edition, and would then have to buy a jacket to go with it – one that I would have been frightened to wear in case I ruined it. Years later, I travelled to Hong Kong with him before we played in the Eisenhower Trophy in Manila in the Philippines, and we ended up in the seediest part of Hong Kong in a market that sold fake watches, one of which Michael ended up buying. It looked great, but, typically, it broke within months. The reason he bought it was that he realised just how rough the area was and he felt that if he didn't buy something there was every chance we would get mugged or worse.

On the Wednesday before the matches at Quaker Ridge were due to begin it was decided that we were going to watch a New York Mets baseball game, which meant that we had to leave the course at 2pm and then head back to the hotel to get changed. It was a sweltering hot day, but we had to put on our team uniforms – as a result, we all fried.

Before the game started we were upstairs enjoying the hospitality of Nelson Doubleday Jr, the co-owner of the Mets, when there was an announcement, welcoming the British Walker Cup team and saying that Clive Brown was going to deliver the opening pitch. That was the signal for Clive to get in the lift along with his wife, son and Doubleday Jr, with me as official photographer. On his way down to throw the pitch everyone wanted to watch as there were bets going round that Clive wouldn't reach the catcher with his pitch; we all knew it was a pretty safe bet as we had watched Clive practising back at Quaker Ridge with a golf ball. Before the lifts doors closed at least another sixteen people squeezed in. This was a lift that was designed to hold twelve people, and there were twenty in it, some of whom were big guys. Guess what? It broke down. Inside it were the owner of the Mets, both Walker Cup captains, and what seemed like both teams, plus some wives.

After thirty-five minutes stuck in the lift the temperature soared to 120°F. We had Downing Gray, the American captain, pressing the intercom button and announcing: 'We have a situation here.' It was just like something out of a bad American disaster movie. Craig Watson sat on the floor, while I, in my position as official photographer, was taking pictures. We were laughing because it was such a ludicrous situation to be in. The women, meanwhile, were beginning to panic, and the co-owner wasn't feeling so good. We were stuck in that lift for fully forty-five minutes before it was eventually cranked down to the ground floor and the doors were forced open.

I could not believe the sight that greeted us. Remember that we were only stuck in a lift, but there were doctors and nurses, security teams, stretchers and ambulances with flashing lights. The only thing missing was Paul Newman and Steve McQueen and we could have done a re-make of the *Towering Inferno*. Somebody tried to give me oxygen, but that was ridiculous and I refused. It did at least mean that Clive did not have to throw the opening pitch, much to his relief I guess.

Having practised nonstop, Clive then announced that on the Thursday and Friday we were going to get to the course at 6am because this was the time we would leave for the actual matches and he felt we should 'acclimatise'. It was August, and we were getting up at 5am when it was still dark. The result of all this preparation was basically that we were all shattered by the time the event got under way.

The opening ceremony was held on the Friday evening in glorious weather and was attended by thousands of people. I suppose it was a bit like when the Americans lost the Ryder Cup to Europe for the first time – they had come to regard the trophy almost as their property and had lost interest in it, but that interest was renewed when the cup was taken away from them. The Americans weren't used to losing the Walker Cup, so turned up in huge numbers to cheer on their boys and to have a look at the team that had dared to beat them two years earlier.

One of the features of the ceremony is the raising of the flags, but guess whose flag only went to half-mast? It was Clive's job to raise it, but he couldn't get the knot undone properly. I was standing there thinking: 'That's a bad omen. If we don't get beaten it will be a miracle.'

The weather had been so hot and sticky that we had all struggled, despite the fact that Graham Rankin (who was in the team again) and various other players, came to breakfast every morning and piled their plates with doughnuts and other sugary delights. They couldn't believe their luck. However, filling your body with sugar in the early morning is probably the worst thing you can do. After all our exertions, when the first day arrived, we all felt as flat as pancakes.

Before the match got under way we were summoned to Clive's suite for a final team meeting. Clive, bless him, was giving us a pep talk about the Walker Cup and what it would mean to beat the Americans on their own soil. He said: 'I want you to realise how important this week is...'

He was in full flow when Graham stood up and decided that it was his duty to take over the entire meeting. He delivered a diatribe about how we were the greatest team, that nobody could beat us – I doubt that even the legendary Scottish hero, William Wallace, could have matched his passion. Graham went on for about fifteen minutes, almost without stopping to draw breath, and told us that we had to be prepared to go out there and die for our country. It was quite extraordinary. 'I'm gonna go out there and I'm gonna play great and beat these guys,' he said. That's just the way he always was, but this had come like a bolt from the blue. For some unfathomable reason, he had decided that it was his job to lead us into battle. Eventually he paused for breath, realised he had nothing more to say and sat down. As you can imagine, there was a stunned silence in the room, and Clive was standing there, open-mouthed, before he eventually said: 'Right, thanks for that Graham. That's great.'

The rest of us sat staring at each other in disbelief. Rankin was red faced, but not with embarrassment – he was burning with passion. I don't think I have ever seen anybody so fired up for a game of golf. Next, he decided that he was going to sign the glass table top around which we were all gathered, and before we knew what was happening, the rest of the team were signing it too. Why? I haven't a clue really, but I guess it was a good team-bonding session.

It was a weird moment among many that week and we did, of course, get slaughtered. The final score was 18–6 to the Americans. How did that happen? We had a great team. We should have beaten them but we didn't.

Clive was nonplussed. He partnered Justin Rose with Michael Brooks in the opening foursomes series. Justin was a seventeen-year-old boy who needed to be paired with an experienced player, somebody like me, for instance. And what did Michael do at the very first hole? He let Justin hit the opening tee shot. Justin would have been incredibly nervous anyway, without being handed this responsibility. The first hole at Quaker Ridge is a long tough left-to-right dogleg that requires a confident, solid drive to find the fairway. Michael should have taken responsibility and shown Justin the way, but he failed to do so. It came as no great surprise when Justin blasted his drive right, way into the trees, and the ball was never seen again. Michael then snap-hooked his drive into the woods on the other side: they were already one down, without having put any pressure on their opponents.

I played John Harris in the singles on that first day. We had an epic match that culminated in me three putting the last from thirty feet to lose my match by one hole. I had played so well, on the back nine in particular, and shouldn't have lost.

On the second day, Clive finally decided to partner me with Justin and we played extremely well together, summed up by the sixteenth hole, at which he hit his drive into the right hand fairway bunker, and, undaunted, I played a recovery to about five feet, which he duly holed. It was a horrible snaking downhill putt to win the hole. We went on to win 2&1, and the result announced Justin as a force to the world.

I remember that Walker Cup and its aftermath for the saddest of reasons. We had played in the US Amateur Championship in Chicago after Quaker Ridge – which was won by Matt Kuchar – and by this time Barclay Howard had got himself together, remarried, had a little girl, and it was her first day at school on the first round of the matchplay. He played through the first two qualifying rounds and comfortably qualified for the matchplay stages of the tournament. Then he said to me: 'Gary, I don't want to be here. I just want to go home, I'm feeling dog tired, and it's my girl's first day at school in a couple of days.' With that he walked into the recorders' tent and said: 'I am awfully sorry, but I am going to have to disqualify myself.'

The officials were mortified. He was a British Walker Cup player and they wanted him in their championship. He said: 'I was playing with a black Titleist and I changed my ball to play the eighteenth and I used a red Titleist for the hole. I have only just realised.' I should explain that in America they have something called the 'one-ball rule' where you must start and finish with an identical make of golf balls. The president of the USGA at the time was a lovely lady called Judy Bell, who said: 'Are you sure Barclay. There must be a way that we can find to let you play.' But dear old Barclay was adamant: 'No, no, I've broken the rules.' It was nonsense, of course, but he didn't feel one hundred per cent and he was now desperate to get home.

It slightly backfired on him because suddenly he was being hailed as a hero and interviewed by all the press, whose general feelings were: 'Barclay, what an amazing thing you have done. You epitomise everything that is great about amateur golf and have set a fantastic example to your fellow golfers.' The newspapers also singled him out and wrote amazing tributes. I don't know how he managed to keep a straight face, but at least he got home to see his daughter's first day at school.

Tragically, not long after he returned home, he went to see his doctor because he wasn't feeling well. The doctor told him to take a couple of aspirin and said he would be fine. A friend urged him to seek a second opinion and he went back to see another doctor who immediately sent him for tests. He was rushed into hospital that same day. His body was riddled with leukaemia, a form of cancer. Barclay was told afterwards that if he hadn't sought the second opinion he would have been dead within three weeks. Although he did not enjoy a great quality of life afterwards and lost a great deal of weight, he survived for a further eight years and at least he managed to see his daughter through primary school. He was a great friend and I miss him still.

I called him my Little Tank Engine because he was short, squat and as tough as old boots. Yes, he always struggled with his demons and yes, he could be a trifle belligerent on occasion when he'd had a few drinks, but he was a great guy and a loyal friend who was good to be around. He was a genuine character and there just aren't enough of those in the game these days.

CHAPTER FOURTEEN

PETER PERFECT

Peter McEvoy was named as Walker Cup captain for the 1999 and 2001 matches. I was delighted with the appointment, because I had a great deal of respect for him. Prior to the 1995 Walker Cup match I was told by the selectors that I probably wasn't going to be chosen for the England team to play in the Home Internationals at Hoylake, and neither was Colin Edwards. It was bizarre, because many people felt that Colin and I were two of the best players in the country at the time, and Peter McEvoy, who was then the England captain, told the selectors: 'Gary and Colin are not only going to play, but they are also going to be the first two players on my list. I want them in the team.' The other selectors had wanted Mike Welch and Lee Westwood because they were young bombers, but they were duly named as first and second reserve, although before the match, two members of the original eleven turned pro so, as it turned out, myself, Colin, Lee and Mike happily all made the England team.

Colin and I played really well at Hoylake that year. Lee

struggled and suffered a couple of bad defeats, which could have destroyed his confidence, but even back then it was clear that he was made of stern stuff and he went on to turn professional just a few weeks later, and made an almost immediate impact. Amazingly, the young and hugely talented Mike Welch almost completely disappeared from the scene after those Home Internationals after he, too, had played poorly. Mike and Lee, who played foursomes together, scored only one point between them, which further enhanced Peter's reputation as a good judge of character.

One of the things that sticks in my mind about the Home Internationals is that when they were played in Walker Cup years, a lot of the guys who had represented Great Britain and Ireland didn't really want to play, claiming that they were too tired and deflated after the high of the Walker Cup. I could never understand that attitude, because I just couldn't get enough of playing for my country and I have always believed that the more competitive sport you play the better you will become. It is sad that the Home Internationals seem to have lost some of their kudos these days. I lived, breathed, ate and drank representative golf, but now the emphasis is on individual performance and I believe that golf will suffer for that. It is a selfish enough sport without taking away all these wonderful opportunities to play in national colours. I loved it. What could be better than hearing: 'On the tee, representing England, Gary Wolstenholme'?

My problem was that even though I wanted to play, it seemed some of the selectors, for reasons best known to themselves, didn't want to pick me for certain matches. They were wrong of course. Bearing that in mind, it was a big deal for me to have somebody like Peter McEvoy on my side; someone who was prepared to go in and bat on my behalf.

Once again, my form leading up to the 1999 match was pretty good. In 1998, I won the Mid-Amateur for the third time, as well as the St Mellion International Amateur and I also became the English County Champion of Champions winner for the third time. In 1999, I was the Duncan Putter champion for the third time and also won the Berkhamsted Open Scratch Trophy.

The 1999 match was played at the magnificent Nairn Golf Club in northeast Scotland and I just knew that we were going to win. McEvoy is a master tactician and man manager, and we all knew that he would leave nothing to chance.

When Peter was named captain he introduced lots of changes. For instance, he made sure we all had umbrellas with wooden handles; it may sound trivial, but it was that kind of attention to detail that made us feel special. We were given top-of-the-range golf bags, the very best shirts, cashmere sweaters and he also got Saatchi and Saatchi to produce a video, a copy of which was given to each player. It began with stirringly powerful music and then there was a golfer hitting balls, with the music building up. Then the commentary began: 'This is a team that has won six of the past eight European team championships, this is a team whose players have won the Amateur Championship three times in the past five years, this is a team that has won more major amateur championships than any other, this is the team … that the Americans have got to play.' Then the music died down and the golfer strode off, apparently walking across water. 'That's who the Americans have to play – YOU. The greatest team in the world.' It was a fantastic thing to have, even though it only lasted for about five minutes. I played it at least fifty times and nearly wore it out.

McEvoy knew that Prince Andrew was both a golf fanatic and a member of the R&A, so he managed to arrange for us to go to Buckingham Palace to meet the Prince and have tea with him. This was a man you wanted to do well for.

An example of his ability as a man manager was in the way that he moulded Graham Rankin, who was again selected, despite never having won a single Walker Cup point. Some people asked: 'Why has he been selected again? He is not going to make a contribution.' To be fair to Graham, his Walker Cup record might well have been dire, but he kept winning domestic tournaments, did well for Scotland, and left the selectors with no option but to pick him, no matter how reluctant they might have been to do so. He had pretty much won everything there was to win in Scotland. He was a big hitter with a delicate touch round the greens and he was a good team man.

Peter sat Rankin down and told him that he wanted the Scot to be his vice-captain, his eyes and ears on the course and in the team-room. It was a stroke of genius. Nobody would have thought to pick Graham Rankin as a vice-captain, but Peter did. 'If the players want anything Graham, they have to come through you,' Peter said. 'You will be my link to the players, and vice versa.' Outwardly, Graham had never been short on confidence, but this one gesture made him feel that he wasn't only needed, but that he was an important part of the team to boot. If Peter McEvoy had singled him out, it meant he was the best player in the team, too.

It gave him a sense of purpose, and it was very clever. McEvoy wanted Rankin to be successful both for himself and for the team, and that's the way Peter was. He knew which buttons to push with each and every player, thus ensuring that he always got the best out of us. He recognised the strengths and weaknesses in each golfer. He had been England captain for four years with a great record of success, so he knew me inside out and there was nothing new for him to say to me, but that didn't matter.

Whenever he would see me on the course, he would wander over and ask how I was doing, and the conversation would go something like this:

'How are you doing, Gary?'

'I am two down.'

'That's not very good. I am just going to see a few of the others, and by the time I come back I want you to be no worse than one down, but I would rather you were all square.'

Four holes later he would come back.

'How are you doing now?'

Feeling quite pleased with myself, I would reply: 'I'm all square, Peter.'

'All square? I am sure that I asked you to be one up by now. Right, I am off again, because there are other players in this team that I need to talk to. I don't need to talk to you. When I see you again though, I want you to have won the match. You are on a roll. He's not as good as you. Look at him – he's frightened to death of you.'

With that, he would point at my opponent, who would be wondering what on earth was being said about him.

It always had the effect of relaxing me and making me laugh and, before I knew where I was, I would be shaking hands with my opponent, having beaten him as requested to do so by my illustrious captain.

With me, he knew that the right thing to do was to find a way to make me laugh. It almost always worked.

When I was playing in foursomes and we would see Peter striding across the fairway towards us, I would say to my partner: 'Right, here he comes. We will get the funny comment in ten, nine, eight...'

And, right on cue, he would deliver the funny line, and then ask: 'Gary, what were you counting for?'

'No reason, Peter. No reason. Don't worry about it.'

'How are you doing? You are winning aren't you? Don't tell me that you are not winning, because I put you in against these two because I knew you would win.'

Once again, we had a great team for Nairn. For a start, we had some Scottish players in David Patrick, Lorne Kelly and Graham Rankin, so we knew we were going to attract plenty of local support. Then there was the hyperactive Yorkshire terrier Simon Dyson, one of the grittiest and gutsiest men you could ever wish to meet, Graeme Storm, Luke Donald, Paul Casey, Phil Rowe, Paddy Cribben and myself. Luke and Paul were unbeatable that week. When they played in the foursomes they were in such good form that Luke would ask Paul which side of the fairway he wanted to play his approach from, and if Paul said the left, that is precisely where Luke would put his drive.

The Americans knew all about Luke and Paul because they were at college in America and were both breaking records right, left and centre, so it must have been pretty demoralising to get to the first tee and find them waiting. They won both their foursomes and both their singles matches, which meant that we were six points to the good before anybody else had struck a ball. This was yet another decent American team by the way, featuring Matt Kuchar, Bryce Molder, Jonathan Byrd and the US Champion David Gossett.

I'd hurt my back through hitting too many golf balls as per usual, so on the eve of the match I was sent to the physiotherapist for treatment. I still felt a bit stiff on the Saturday morning, but told Peter I would be fine to play. However, Peter wasn't totally convinced and put me in the foursomes, but not in the afternoon singles. So out I went with my little buddy Phil Rowe and together we beat Molder and Kuchar, the Americans' star pairing, after Phil holed a fabulous twenty-five footer across the final green to win the match one up. The pair of us virtually ended up doing the Highland Fling on the green. Despite that, and the efforts of Luke and Paul, we trailed 7–5 at the end of day one. I had to sit out the singles chomping at the bit, which the USA won 5–3. And Graham Rankin still hadn't scored a Walker Cup point.

On the second day Phil and I beat Kuchar and Molder again, 4&3 this time, and we were absolutely flying. Luke and Paul came up trumps again, as did Graeme Storm and Graham Rankin, who had finally secured his first point, so we had won the foursomes 3–1 and everything was level going into the final series of singles matches. It couldn't have been more perfectly poised, and we were confident of winning in front of a huge home gallery.

I had to play David Gossett, the US Amateur champion, in the last match. It was a beautiful day and almost 20,000 spectators turned up to cheer us home. It was a fabulous sight. First out was Graham Rankin and, buoyed by his win in the morning foursomes, he beat Steve Scott one up. Peter had said to him: 'You are my vice-captain and I want you to go out there and lead from the front.' Privately, Peter told me: 'If he had gone out and lost, it wouldn't have hurt the cause that much because it would be out of the way quickly and not be so crucial.' But he won, against a strong opponent. There was some controversy, however, because Peter chose to leave out the other two Scots, Lorne Kelly and David Patrick all day, which hardly endeared him to the Scottish fans. Better players than those two have been left sitting twiddling their thumbs, though – Michael Bonallack didn't hit a single shot in anger in his first Walker Cup match. The rules have now changed though, so that there are ten singles matches, meaning that everybody gets at least one game during these.

Surprisingly, Simon Dyson lost the second match, so there was still everything to play for. But then the unthinkable happened, and Paul Casey, Graeme Storm, Luke Donald, Phil Rowe, Paddy Gribben and myself all won our matches. We had won the singles 7–1 and the Walker Cup 15–9 – a record victory for Great Britain and Ireland.

To give you some idea of just how much the record victory meant to Peter, he came out onto the course and told both myself and Phil Rowe that he didn't want us to muck about, that we had to keep our focus and win our matches because not only did he want to beat the USA, but he also wanted to do so by a record margin and to achieve that he needed victories from the two of us.

The celebration afterwards was one to remember. I ended up with the Union Flag and Paddy Gribben bagged the Tricolour. We had the biggest crowds in Walker Cup history and the right result to boot. What more could any of us have asked for? Just after the last putt was holed we all headed for the press centre and drenched the media in champagne. Why? Let's just say that it was our way of making a good-natured point to the journalists who had doubted us.

It was great for Peter's kudos and I have to say that as good a man manager as he was, he was also interested in his own reputation. It went through the roof after that. He won virtually everything with England and everything with Great Britain and Ireland, apart from a St Andrews Trophy defeat Villa D'Este in Italy, and to this day I still don't know how we lost. It was the only blemish on his otherwise immaculate record.

We even managed to win the Eisenhower Trophy under Peter's leadership, and that was pretty special too, but not much tops beating the Americans, other than beating them on their own turf, and that was the next thing on his agenda.

The 2001 Walker Cup was played at the Ocean Forest Golf Club in Sea Island, Georgia, and I was picked for the team again. It was my fourth appearance and I had earned it. I won the Sherry Cup International Strokeplay at Sotogrande in both 2000 and 2001, and in 2001 I won my fourth English County Champion of Champions title, the Leicestershire and Rutland County Strokeplay and the Selbourne Salver. My stroke average in 2000 was exactly 70 for the year, which, let me tell you, is pretty impressive. Coming up to the age of forty I was playing the best golf of my life.

We were desperate to win and headed across the Atlantic with another strong team. Apart from myself, there was Marc Warren, Nick Dougherty, Luke Donald, Graeme McDowell, Michael Hoey, Nigel Edwards and Steven O'Hara. Before the team was finalised, Peter had told me that the choice for the final place was between Warren and

Barry Hume, and asked me who I thought would be best for the team. I didn't really know either player that well, but I knew Warren by reputation and was well aware that he was an excellent golfer and some of the other England players of the time had suggested that he would be their pick so I told Peter what the others had said: that he should pick Marc. I often wonder what might have happened had I gone the other way. Would Marc Warren still have gone on to become the excellent tournament professional that he now is? Probably. But maybe not. It's funny how chance conversations such as that can seal somebody's fate.

As for the Americans, they were no slouches either and fielded a team that included Lucas Glover, who would go on to win the 2009 US Open, D J Trahan, Bryce Molder and Jeff Quinney. They also won the humanitarian vote too when they named Erik Compton in their team. He was a great player, but he attracted a huge amount of publicity when the press got wind of the fact that he'd had a heart transplant when he was twelve.

We practised at various courses and Marc was playing like an eighteen-handicapper, shooting 90-odd every time we went out and leaving me to wonder what the hell I had done in recommending to Peter that he pick him for the team. Worse than his scores was the fact that, similar to my experience of playing with Lee James some years earlier, if he played one hole badly it could really affect his concentration. It was painful to watch. Peter had to put his arm round him on the eve of the matches and tell him he wanted to speak to him in his office. Peter didn't have an office, of course, but it was just another of his ways of getting it over to players that he was prepared to give them his undivided attention to resolve any problems or issues that were troubling them.

'You are one of our best players and I need you at the top of your game. You have to pull your weight,' Peter said. 'I know what it's like when things aren't going right because I have experienced it myself. I wanted you in the team Marc and picked you specifically before anybody else.'

In the matches, I teamed up with Steven O'Hara in the opening day foursomes. We were the first match off and the honour of hitting the opening drive fell to me. The first hole at Ocean Forest was a shortish par four with water all the way down the left side of the fairway, and mounded rough and trees down the right. It was a daunting tee shot. I was as nervous as I had been standing on the first tee with Arnold Palmer at Augusta, but I hit a corker, straight down the middle, and we went on to win our match 5&3, as did the all-Irish pairing of Michael Hoey and Graeme McDowell.

Jamie Elson and Richard McEvoy halved their game, so we had our noses in front heading into the singles. I played Compton and I am here to tell you that, heart transplant or not, he seemed a pretty fit specimen to me and beat me 3&2. America won five of the eight singles, so led by a point going into the final day. And Marc Warren? He played pretty well against John Harris, who had been previously unbeaten in singles, and won 5&4. It was a significant feather in Marc's cap and, once again, McEvoy had worked his magic.

I didn't play in the foursomes on the Sunday because Peter wanted me rested for the singles. We won them 3–1, although Steven O'Hara ended up in a right old state after he and Marc Warren lost their match 7&6. Peter made a mistake not putting me out with Steven again and his confidence was in tatters after that defeat, so much so that I ended up spending forty minutes on the practise ground with him afterwards, helping to sort him out. Nick Dougherty had also been struggling with his swing, so I gave him some of my time, too. We were all on the same side and all trying to achieve the same objective, so why wouldn't I help out two young team-mates?

We then thrashed them again in the singles, winning six-and-a-half points to their one-and-a-half. For the record, I beat Nick Cassini 5&3 and Luke Donald completed his stellar Walker Cup career with a 3&2 victory against Lucas Glover. Whatever I told Steven obviously worked because he, too, won, and comfortably, beating Harris 4&3. This time, Warren beat James Driscoll 2&1 and holed the putt that won the trophy. Or so the record book says. The truth is that I am pretty certain that I got the winning point on the fifteenth green a few minutes earlier, but in the grand scheme of things it didn't matter. It suited the TV cameras for Marc to be credited with holing the winning putt because Peter McEvoy and most of the team were behind that green with its spectacular backdrop of the Atlantic Ocean. The important thing is that it was just brilliant to be enjoying that winning feeling again. We had equalled our 1999 score, winning 15–9 again in what I believe is the greatest performance by a British golf team. The victory also meant that I had become the first man to play on three winning Great Britain and Ireland teams too, a record that I am certain will never be broken. It was also the first time in the event's seventy-nine-year history that Great Britain and Ireland had retained the trophy and only the second-ever time we had won on American soil (the other victory coming in 1989).

CHAPTER FIFTEEN
BLOWING HOT
IN CHILE

Right up there with the Walker Cup, for me at least, is the Eisenhower Trophy. Back in my early days, it was the ultimate amateur event, because it was the hardest team to get into. You had to be at the very peak of your powers to get into Great Britain and Ireland's four-man team, although it has changed now, as England, Wales, Scotland and Ireland now enter separate teams. Even getting into a four-man England team takes something special, though. I played in the Eisenhower four times – twice for Great Britain and Ireland and twice for England.

The other major difference from the Walker Cup is that you are facing the best amateur golfers from all over the globe, and the event is often staged on the best golf courses the world has to offer, too.

The first one I played in was staged in Manila, in the Philippines, in 1996. It is impossible to describe the heat and humidity. In the first round I drank eight litres of water and didn't have a pee once, so obviously didn't drink enough. It was ninety per cent humidity and 105°F. The sweat just ran off us, to the extent where it was almost impossible to hold your club because your hands were so wet. I have never experienced anything quite like it, and I love hot weather. However, I played pretty well, even though we were never really in contention as a team. My team-mates were Keith Nolan, Michael Brooks and Barclay Howard. We travelled to Hong Kong first to compete in the Hong Kong Open – Barclay was first, Keith was second and I finished third, with Michael in seventh or eighth place, but I guess that we all peaked just a bit too soon.

Michael nearly left Manila with a wife, too. We were given local women as caddies and the girl who carried Michael's clubs fell in love with him. It was the funniest thing because she barely stretched to 4ft 10in, while he was at least 6ft 3in tall. I had seen the way she looked at him and realised there was something going on in her head. Michael, however, was oblivious to it, so I took her to one side and asked her if she liked him. When she told me that she did, very much, I decided to have a bit of fun and informed her that he wasn't married. The next day she arrived at the course with her entire family, who had obviously come to size up this potential husband. He wondered what on earth was going on, and nearly wet himself when I told him what his caddy had planned for him. Fortunately, he eventually saw the funny side of it, but the poor caddy and her family had to be let down gently.

We had decided not to stay in the city of Manila, partly because if we had it would have left us with a long bus journey to and from the course each day, as we would inevitably have got stuck in the daily traffic jams, but the main reason was because of the crime that goes hand in hand with the grinding poverty, and we did not want to put ourselves at risk. Manila is a very poor city and we were fortunate to be able to stay in the hotel on the golf course – a guest residence that had opened that very week. The R&A footed the bill for everything, which meant that for once in my life I wasn't watching the pennies. What a difference that makes, I can tell you.

We always used to fly business class, which made us feel special, and there was never any penny pinching. Whatever we needed, we got – matching shirts, shorts, trousers, hats, socks and bags. So we looked fantastic, and that always made me feel better. In truth, it was also a great incentive to ensure that you tried with all your heart and soul to get on to these teams and to do your best. I still have much of the team kit they provided. What an incredible contrast from my early days in amateur golf. Peter McEvoy used to say I was pecunious, but that was unfair. I admit that I liked to get nice things, but I always appreciated everything I got. If there was a spare tie I would have one whether I needed one or not, though – I admit that. On one occasion in the 2001 Walker Cup at Ganton, Peter's Walker Cup waterproof jacket ended up in my golf bag – I think my caddy at the time found it and thought it was mine and put it there. It didn't enter my head to keep it and he seemed genuinely surprised when I gave it back to him a month or two later when we next met up. He hadn't a clue where it had gone, but why would I want to keep Peter McEvoy's waterproof jacket?

Two years after Manila, in 1998, we were in Santiago, the capital of Chile, which was one of the most enjoyable places I have ever been to, and we also had a good team that year – myself, Luke Donald, Lorne Kelly and Paddy Gribben, with Peter McEvoy as captain. In those days, when we were still representing GB&I, there always seemed to be more of an emphasis on getting the right mix of nationalities on the team rather than necessarily selecting the strongest possible line-up, hence we finished up with an Irishman, a Scotsman and two Englishmen.

It went against the grain for Peter, who always wanted to travel to every event with the best possible team. When he was appointed captain and attended his first selection meeting, he'd said: 'Right, do we want to pick a winning team, or do we just want to pick a team?' He almost always got his way. He argued so logically and if he sensed that he had a struggle on his hands he would target the men he regarded as being the most amenable among the other selectors and would work away at them until he got them on his side. He was a winner and he wanted to surround himself with winners. He once said of me in a magazine article: 'If there is one man I would want to be tied to on a mountain side, in a blizzard, and needing to get home, it would be Gary Wolstenholme.' Which from Peter was a compliment indeed.

He didn't always get his own way, of course, and he didn't quite manage to pull it off in 1998. If national prejudices had been put to one side it might have been possible to pick an even stronger team than the one we took to Chile, but the four of us clicked really well.

There were two courses, a long modern layout and an old-fashioned tree-lined one in the city, and we had to perform two rounds on each, with the first two rounds dictating the order of play for the final thirty-six holes. In total, there were would be about forty-four teams, but only a handful of them were capable of winning.

The golf courses were in superb condition, and Santiago

was clean and modern. It took many of us by surprise. If there were any slums, we didn't see them. Interestingly, General Pinochet, the dictator who had run Chile with a rod of iron, had been arrested in Great Britain and the British women's team decided to withdraw from their event the week before. Indeed, it was touch and go as to whether or not we would take part, but eventually we got the green light. I had always been convinced that there wouldn't be a problem and there was no way I wanted to stay at home. The climate was perfect – every day we would wake up to blue skies and temperatures of 80°F.

The best three of four scores counted from each round – although that has also since been changed, so that now the teams consist of three players and the best two count each day. Again, this was an area in which Peter McEvoy excelled as he would walk round the course and make a point of knowing exactly how everybody else was getting on. He even kept us in the picture about the 'minnows' of the event, so we would be told exactly who was vying for last place – Estonia had shot an 90, while their rivals from Slovenia had fired an 86 to move them up to forty-second position. It was a bit of fun really, but it had a purpose, as it helped Peter take some of the pressure off our shoulders, particularly as we were in contention. Laughter is a great stress buster.

Every day he would tell us that he had a feeling in his water that we were going to win. He said it so often that, after a while, we all just took it as read that we were going to pick up the Eisenhower Trophy come the final day.

We would sit down for dinner and it was the same. 'Yes, I've got it in my mind. You guys can win this,' he would say. It helped enormously that Luke and I were playing well, so it meant that we only needed one other score each day from Lorne or Paddy, both of whom had been spraying the ball about the place that week. We didn't have a coach with us, so Peter started off by building them up mentally, telling them they were the greatest thing since sliced bread, and he then started to give them the occasional tip. Lorne was struggling with a hook, and Paddy had one of his best friends with him, acting as a minder/supporter, but the important thing was that we had lots of fun throughout the week.

Both courses suited Luke and I and we both opened with rounds of 70, Paddy chipping in with a 71, so we were off to a decent start. In the second round Luke had a 70 and I scored 71, with Lorne's score counting, despite shooting a 77. The pattern continued in round three, with Luke recording a 69, myself a 74 and Lorne a 72. When it came down to the wire, we were in the penultimate group on the final day, trailing Australia and the USA, which meant we would be setting the target for the others to shoot at. Peter was darting about, staying abreast of the scores and keeping us informed.

The course finished with a par five and a par four and as we played them we realised we were in the lead. I was genuinely nervous, more than I had ever been while playing golf previously. I missed my chance of a birdie at the seventeenth, and then had to make the greatest up and down of my life to save par at the last. By this stage we knew precisely where we stood.

I had played what was probably the best round of golf of my competitive life, shooting a 67 on the tight city course, which was the best score of the day. I pretty much did everything right that day. Luke then kept his composure to finish with a couple of pars and a round of 71 and we realised that unless the Australians, who were by now in second place, all finished with birdies we had won the Eisenhower Trophy. They failed to do so and we had won. The feeling of elation to land the greatest prize in world team amateur golf was special and I will never forget it. For the record, Lorne's final round was a 70 and Paddy shot a 72, to leave us four shots ahead of second-placed Australia.

We met the president of the USGA, Buzz Taylor, and were treated to a private champagne reception before coming out to receive the trophy in front of all the other competing nations. I don't mind telling you that there was a lump in my throat as the Union Jack was raised and I stood alongside my team-mates, each of us wearing our gold medals, as we listened to our national anthem being played. It was as close to the feeling an Olympic athlete must experience as I will ever know.

Everything about that week had been wonderful – the courses, the city, the hotel and the food. The quarters in the hotel were among the best I have ever stayed in, and we each had a room to ourselves. We also discovered a pool table and each night Luke and I took on Lorne and Paddy; they may have been struggling on the golf course, but they more than made it for it when it came to shooting pool. These guys were really good and every evening we would go into the last frame trailing by $50, and each night Luke and I would somehow win the last frame and wipe out the debt.

It was a very tall hotel, and Paddy's room was on one of the highest floors. Each night would end with the two of us in the lift and just before I would get out I'd press every single button, so he had to stop at every floor before reaching his own. He never cottoned on to what I was doing until the last evening.

On the second or third night of our stay in Santiago we were in the main hotel restaurant with Peter and his wife, Helen, and the other selectors; I guess there were about ten of us sitting down to dinner when I noticed a woman whom I assumed was another guest, waiting to be shown to her seat. It turned out she was anything but a guest and she lifted Helen's handbag while we weren't looking and cleared off with it. When Helen realised it was gone and raised the alarm Peter flew up and dashed out of the restaurant in a vain attempt to find the woman. I have never seen him move so fast.

Everybody else followed him and I was left trying to get hold of a hotel official. The thief was obviously part of an organised gang and there was no way we thought that Helen McEvoy was ever going to see her handbag again. She was in tears, because her bag had contained some precious photographs and other personal belongings. Incredibly, though, at midnight, her bag was handed in at reception. Everything was still in it, except for the money of course. This had happened a couple of days before play got under way and it could have ruined the week for everybody, but we refused to let it do so.

Winning the Eisenhower Trophy in Chile is my crowning achievement, my ultimate moment in golf. I was thirty-eight years of age and was at my peak. I loved every single moment of my round with Arnold Palmer at The Masters, Walker Cups, Amateur Championship wins and the like, but here I had been a key member of a four-man team from Great Britain and Ireland that had won the most prestigious trophy in amateur golf, and I was stoked. Sergio Garcia was a member of the Spanish team that year, Sweden had Peter Hanson and Henrik Stenson, Aaron Baddeley and Brett

Rumford were playing for Australia, Jean Hugo and Trevor Immelman for South Africa and Matt Kuchar and Hank Kuehne for the USA, so we had beaten some serious golfers.

The day after our victory we had to fly home, from Santiago to Buenos Aires and then on to London. As I have said, we were travelling business class, which was great, but when we got to the airport I was told that I had been upgraded to first class. A friend back home in England had pulled a few strings on my behalf after hearing that we had won. As I was walking to check-in Peter McEvoy wandered over. 'Don't say anything to anybody Gary, but Helen and I have been upgraded to first class and none of the others have, and there's been some words said,' he whispered. He had no idea that I'd been upgraded too, so I just said something like: 'Oh, really? Well that's interesting.' Even Sir Michael Bonallack hadn't been upgraded, and if anyone was a Platinum member of BA it had to be him and his wife Angela, who were as close to golfing royalty as it is possible to get. Angela had enjoyed almost as successful a career in the women's game as her husband had in the men's.

I knew why I had been upgraded, but I hadn't a clue why Peter and Helen had been. Just their lucky day, I guessed. We all got on the plane and Peter did a double take when he saw me in the seat opposite. 'What are you doing in here? Business class is back there,' he said.

'Well, you are not going to believe this Peter, but I got upgraded as well,' I explained.

I have never flown first class before or since, and this was something else. We were flying with British Airways, of whom I have always been a huge fan. We even got our own pyjamas on that flight, and I still have them tucked away somewhere. Blue trousers, white top, British Airways first-class logo on the chest. I checked out all the DVDs, got my own bottle of champagne, caviar, the lot. I thought: 'This is the life. This is what it's all about. I have arrived.' We had air hostesses fussing around and I jokingly mused: 'Well if I don't join the mile-high club on this trip, I am going to be disappointed.'

When we landed in Buenos Aires, one of the air hostesses told me that I would have to disembark. 'I am really sorry Gary, but it is procedure. You will be on the ground for about an hour-and-a-half, but don't worry – we will keep your champagne chilled for you and you can get it back just as soon as you get back on board.'

When we all reassembled in the departure lounge with the rest of the party, it was a case of: 'So where were you then? Are we not good enough for you?' I told them it was hell and that I didn't know how I was going to manage for the rest of the trip. Eventually, we all got back on the plane and set off on our journey again until, forty-five minutes into the flight, there was an announcement: 'Ladies and gentlemen. This is your captain speaking. I am afraid that we are going to have to return to Buenos Aires because we have had a slight problem with the undercarriage.' It turned out that they couldn't get the wheels up and they didn't know whether they were locked in place or not, so we flew around for a while, jettisoning fuel over the River Plate basin. Unknown to Peter and I, a woman who was sitting next to Paddy back in business class was saying: 'We're all going to die! We're all going to die!' Paddy then got himself into a bit of a state and started downing whisky after whisky. Before long, he seemed to be completely out of his tree. The flight crew had to move the woman who had caused the panic in the first place and then get Paddy's mate (the one who had come on the trip to keep an eye on him and keep him company) from economy to help keep him calm, because Paddy gave the impression of wanting to get off... at 35,000ft!

When we came in to land everybody was braced, prepared for the worst, and it didn't help to see dozens of fire engines, ambulances and police cars ready to deal with the potential full-scale emergency. As it turned out, the undercarriage was fine and the pilot landed the plane perfectly. By the time we got out of the airport and into a hotel arranged for us by British Airways, it was past midnight. We spent the night there and were told that the plane could not be repaired, so we were all starting to worry about how we were going to get back home. Peter was adamant that he had to return as soon as possible because he had business to attend to back in England. Our luggage, meanwhile, was still on the plane back at the airport, so we all had to go out and buy clothes and toiletries and I remember asking myself whether I should get an Armani shirt or a Versace one. Lorne and I ended up choosing Armani ones. Well, the R&A were footing the bill. Rhodri Price, our R&A 'minder' for the week, was having kittens, but after everyone else had done something similar, we thought: 'What the heck?'

We were then told that the choice was that we could go home that day, but that we would have to fly economy, or we could go business class the following day, but it would have meant going via Amsterdam. Like Peter, I had to get back to work, so we had no choice. Kilworth Springs gave me a lot of time off, but it wasn't unlimited, so I opted for the economy flight, along with Peter and Helen. Apart from anything else, Amsterdam has just about the worst reputation in the world when it comes to losing luggage, and I wasn't prepared to take that chance either.

I was not happy at having to sit with the 'riffraff', but the woman at check-in reiterated that the flight was full and that there was no chance of being upgraded. Peter, Helen and I were sitting in the same row, and I was aware that he was deep in conversation with the steward. Because I am so tall, I hate economy class because there is no legroom and it is incredibly uncomfortable, especially on such a long flight, and I made no attempt to disguise my discomfort. 'Don't you worry,' said Peter. 'I think that I may have fixed it for us.' It turned out that not only did Peter know the steward, but he knew him really well and a few minutes after we took off, he reappeared and told us to follow him, whereupon he guided us to three seats in business class. So much for the flight being full.

Thank God though, as we ended up getting home a full twenty-four hours before the rest of the party, and managed to do so without any of us being struck down by deep-vein thrombosis back in economy. The biggest disappointment of all was that if we'd been able to stay on our original flight, we would have been met at the airport back in London by the media for a full-scale press conference after our victory. Unfortunately, that had to be cancelled, so we never really got the publicity our achievement deserved. And do you know what? I never did get to join the mile-high club either. What a shame not to have been able to do the whole first-class thing from start to finish.

Bizarrely, I wasn't selected in 2000 for the next Eisenhower in Germany, even though I was playing fantastic golf that year. My stroke average of 70 for the year would apparently have put me in the top ten on the European Tour, but it wasn't good enough to secure my place in the Great Britain and Ireland team, which finished second, albeit a staggering sixteen shots behind the USA. Remember that we played some great courses, and very often not in great condition or in fine weather, certainly when compared to what the Tour professionals have to face, so I was pretty hot that season.

In 2000, the English Amateur Championship was played at Royal Lytham, which is one of my favourite courses, and I turned up for the tournament in good spirits, having won the Sherry Cup in Spain, tied for second in the European Amateur, and just missed out on qualifying for The Open at St Andrews. I also reached the last eight of the US Amateur Championship at Baltusrol, which was no mean feat – Luke Donald and I were in opposite parts of the draw and could have met in the final, but I went out in the last eight and he lost in the semi-finals. As a rule, British golfers have never done particularly well in the US Amateur, so going so far in the event did wonders for my confidence.

I played really well at Lytham, giving my opponents little or no chance, and before I knew where I was I had reached the final, where I faced Paul Casey, then, as now, one of the biggest hitters I have ever seen. He attended university in Arizona, and strangely had never actually represented England at International level. I played really nicely for the first thirteen or fourteen holes of the first round and then managed to lose three of the last five holes and found myself four down at lunch.

Everybody thought it was all over, but I knew how well I had been playing and I was determined that I wasn't going to lose without a fight. Casey had already won the English Amateur the previous year and I was determined that I wasn't going to be another one of his victims, so I gave myself a good talking to at lunch and came out for the afternoon round firing on all cylinders.

The first thirteen holes of the afternoon round were about as good as it gets, but Casey somehow, and I still don't quite know how, remained one up. I had clawed three holes back, but felt that it should have been six or seven. Paul played some spectacular recovery shots and holed a whole host of breathtaking putts to keep himself in it.

I then lost the fourteenth and fifteenth from nowhere and, suddenly, I was three down with three to play and really struggling again. At the sixteenth I went for a birdie putt, rolled it four feet by and missed the return and, with it, the match. Having played so brilliantly to get back into it, the conclusion was a real anticlimax and it remains my only defeat in a major final. I was disappointed to lose, of course I was, but sometimes you learn more in defeat than you do in victory and that was one of those occasions. And Paul wasn't a bad opponent to lose to either. The following year, 2001, I was in contention nearly every time I played and got my handicap down to plus 5.5, which was the best of my career.

Between 1997 and 2005 I would have backed myself to beat just about anybody. Apart from missing out on that Eisenhower Trophy side, I was being chosen to represent England for every team, I was being selected for GB&I and I was even being picked to play for Europe in the Bonallack Trophy against the Asia Pacific Confederation. I was travelling all over the world and had become one of the most instantly recognised amateur golfers on the planet.

I was back in the Eisenhower Trophy team in 2002 in Kuala Lumpur, Malaysia, and in 2004 in Rio Grande,

Puerto Rico, but by now the format had been changed and I was representing England in the tournament, not GB& I. How would I ever have had the opportunity to visit these amazing places had it not been for my ability to hit a little white ball into a hole? And had it not been for the EGU and the R&A, I wouldn't have had these incredible opportunities.

Jamie Elson, Richard Walker and myself formed the team in Kuala Lumpur, and I was comfortable there; apart from anything else, all the road signs in Malaysia are in English and almost everybody speaks the language, too. The great landmark is the Petronas Towers, which we visited, and we also ate in a revolving restaurant perched on top of another tower – it was hundreds of feet tall and featured a partly glassed floor. We dared each other to lie flat on the glass and look straight down, but there were no takers. I was prepared to kneel on it, but I couldn't bring myself to lie on it. How strange was that? Remember that this would have been reinforced glass. We loved walking round the city in between rounds and most of us bought something interesting from the market stalls.

The golf course was great, but was lush and very hilly. Richard Walker was a links-course specialist, having won the Brabazon Trophy at Birkdale, among other things, and it didn't suit his game really. Most top amateur events in Britain are played on links courses each year, and teams would then be picked for tournaments abroad that were almost always played on inland golfing venues, which I always thought was ludicrous. Richard, never the fittest of players, found that the humidity in Kuala Lumpur really did not suit him, and the course certainly didn't.

Due to Richard's difficulties it was left to me and Jamie

to try and produce the counting scores every day, hoping that he might just pull a miracle out of the bag; Jamie played well, and I did my best, but we never quite got going. Richard was a very talented golfer, who eventually turned pro and ended up returning to the amateur ranks, but at least he was able to say that he played in an Eisenhower Trophy, which was something to be proud of.

Jamie had a run-in with Peter McEvoy in Kuala Lumpur after Peter told us all that he wanted us to go out in our final practise session and treat it as though it was a proper round of golf, at the end of which he wanted to know our scores. Jamie lost a ball on our tenth hole and lost concentration after that. Peter blew his top, having tried everything to get Jamie 'on side'. He later told me that if he had been able to send Jamie home on the next flight he would have done. It was the first time I had ever seen Peter lose his temper.

In Puerto Rico it was James Heath, Matt Richardson and myself – a good team that could, and should, have done significantly better. Matt was a fine player and James had played brilliantly to win the Lytham Trophy earlier in the season – I completed on nine-under par in that tournament to finish third, but was a country mile behind James. He broke all records for the trophy, finishing with rounds of 66, and 65 and an 18-under par total on an Open Championship venue beating Ross Fisher into second place. It was quite phenomenal.

We travelled with high hopes and, once again, I loved the country, but wasn't too keen on the very grainy greens we had to play that week. We played decently, but were never in contention and struggled horribly on those surfaces. To make matters worse, the rain arrived and reduced the event to three rounds, which scuppered any chance we might have had.

Several years later, it is a surprise to me that neither James nor Matt has gone on to achieve genuine success in the game, as I always thought they both had the tools to compete at the very highest level. James, in particular, was capable of producing some amazing scores. I would have loved to have won the Eisenhower Trophy with England, but it wasn't to be. I believed that we had a great chance in 2008, when it was played in Adelaide, but I wasn't chosen, of course, and Scotland went on to win.

I also played in seven European team championships (1995, 1997, 1999, 2001, 2003, 2005 and 2007) and only won it once, on the final occasion at Hillside in 2007. In the strokeplay part of the championship we would win by twenty-odd shots as a matter of routine almost every year, but we consistently struggled in the two foursomes and five singles of matchplay, usually against Scotland in the semi-finals. There is no logic to it, but for the Scots I imagined it was always a case of 'Braveheart' all over again – the Mel Gibson film whose driving theme was fierce loyalty to Scotland and antipathy to England. We, on the other hand, were just playing golf.

CHAPTER SIXTEEN
THANK YOU FOR THE MUSIC

In 2003, the Amateur Championship was played at Royal Troon. By that time of the year I had been playing pretty well and felt particularly good about my game. Keith Williams, the lead national coach at the time, had said he thought I could win, as I was hitting the ball so well just prior to the championship. Maybe he should have been doing my lottery tickets that week, too.

I always feel as though I am going on holiday when I go to Scotland, and I am especially fond of the west coast. There is something special about looking out to sea and seeing all the islands, and I love the light you get up there during the summer – when it is not thumping down with rain and blowing a 'hoolie'. In truth, I have almost always had decent weather when I have played in Scotland, so all these comments about the inhospitable climate are a conundrum to me.

I was well organised that week. I got myself a room at a Travel Lodge just outside the town and I had remembered to bring my own pillow – I have never been a great sleeper, and if I don't have my own personal head-rest then I toss and turn all night. The Amateur Championship involves long days, so it is essential that you get sufficient sleep and that you feel fresh each day.

Two courses were used for the qualifying – Barassie and Royal Troon itself – and I liked both of them. I got myself into a nice comfy routine where I would head down to the practise ground every morning and hit balls, and every day as I walked into the club I was greeted by a local caddy called 'Fall down' Pete.

'Gary, can I caddy for you?' Pete would ask.

'No, I am all right thanks.' I'd reply.

This went on every day and, eventually, I felt sorry for him because he clearly didn't have a bag for the week. I told him that if I made the cut then he could caddy for me.

I had a decent first round, was playing well during the second round and with three holes to play I felt that I had done enough to qualify safely for the matchplay stage. I got to the sixteenth, which was a par five, and knew I had to avoid a ditch that ran across the fairway, 280 yards from the tee. I hit a beauty of a five wood and set off down the fairway thinking I would be in an ideal position to reach the green in two, but, to my amazement, the ball was nowhere to be seen. It had finished in the ditch. I was gutted.

I dropped out, but that meant incurring a penalty shot. I wasn't too worried because I knew that I could still make the green and if I did so I could make my par, or even a birdie four, and move on, but I put my third shot into a greenside bunker and failed to get up and down in two, so I walked off the hole with a six. Not ideal, but still no cause for panic.

I parred the seventeenth and then did the hard thing at the final hole, which was to get my drive into the middle of the fairway, leaving a five iron for my second. I hit what I thought was a decent shot, but it got a dreadful kick and shot forward. I knew that out of bounds lay behind the green and prayed that my ball was okay. When I got there I found that it had very nearly run into this forbidden area, before stopping a couple of feet short. As it turned out I made it into the matchplay stage by a couple of shots and now I was feeling more relaxed.

This, of course, meant that I had to employ the services of 'Fall Down' Pete, so named because of a story of when he'd had too much to drink he keeled over and fallen asleep where he landed. There was never any question of Pete being able to carry my clubs without living up to his nickname, so we sorted out a trolley for him to use. All I really needed was somebody to keep up and shut up, and that's exactly what he did. There was no advice on club selection or yardages, I did all that myself, so it was a bit like having a very expensive trolley, except that he was a very positive supporter too, bless his heart, and I knew that I had somebody on my side.

To win the Amateur Championship you have to get through six matches, the last of which is played over thirty-six holes, and I made steady progress. Unusually, each day I played somebody from a different country. I played a Finnish golfer in the last sixteen and beat him pretty comfortably, and by now the BBC were present and were taking pictures, which helped to get the juices flowing.

Next up was a guy called Craig Smith, whom I beat 3&2. We both played really well and he later joked that I 'stole' the match, but it's the result that counts. In the semi-final I was drawn against Francesco Molinari, a stocky little Italian who would go on to become one of the best players on the European Tour. He took me down the last, but I beat him two up, which gave me a great deal of confidence for the final and now the BBC and the media generally were sensing a good story. I faced a teenage Raphael De Sousa of Switzerland in the final, and I before I squared up to him I heard some great things about his game.

De Sousa was the up-and-coming star of European amateur golf and I was told before the start of the final that I would need to be at my very best if I was to have a chance of beating him. He was yet another of those young long hitters, but in my favour was the fact that he hardly used his driver because he didn't have sufficient confidence in it to keep the ball in the fairway. I got off to a pretty good start and then he fought back. It was nip and tuck all the way, but the fourteenth hole in the morning round was the big turning point. Raphael had got back into the match and I hooked my second shot into a greenside bunker on the long par four. My back was sore because I'd hit so many balls all week, both in practise and in play, and I got to the ball and found it in a very awkward lie. I wasn't looking forward to playing the shot because I knew it was going to hurt, but I actually played it pretty well and got the ball out to twenty feet. I then holed the putt for an improbable par to halve the hole, when only moments before my opponent was thinking he had the winning shot in the bag. A familiar story, I hear you thinking.

I was two up after eighteen holes. In a thirty-six-hole final, most players will go into the clubhouse after the first eighteen holes, but again I followed my own routine, which involved getting into the car and listening to some music – at various times I have been inspired by the likes of Queen and Jean Michel Jarre etc. While I was listening to my music I would eat a bowl of fruit and cereal. I did it because it meant I wasn't depending on anybody else. I didn't want to have to wait for somebody to serve me my food, so I always thought it best to take control of things like that myself. In the 1995 championship I remembered that Michael Reynard played Gordon Sherry in the final at Royal Liverpool and he was kept waiting for his lunch, missed his appointed time to restart the afternoon round and was penalised a hole.

So, suitably refreshed, I came out after lunch and birdied the first hole in the afternoon to go three up and when De Sousa made a mess of the second it was effectively all over. My golf bag fell over when I was leaving the tee on the par-three eighth hole, the world-famous Postage Stamp, but even that bad omen did not knock me out of my stride, and normally it would have done. I am hugely superstitious about stuff like that, but not on this day. He staged a brief fightback, but I won the ninth and the tenth, and was putting superbly and eventually closed out the match 6&5. I was walking on air. It may sound daft, but throughout that week I got into a routine that I was happy with – every day I had a pint of Guinness, a pint of water, ate the right food and kept the routine running exactly the same during the whole time. It's silly, but it obviously works for me.

Twelve years was a long time between titles, and winning the second meant far more to me than the first. Garth McGimpsey said: 'Gary, you can win the Amateur Championship once and have people tell you that you have been lucky, but do it twice and there is no way luck can have been involved. It's a great achievement. You have got to be a great champion to do it.' Hearing something like that from a player of Garth's ability meant a lot to me. Incidentally Peter McEvoy won it back-to-back, which is really impressive, and Sir Michael Bonallack won five Amateurs with three in a row, which is the mark of a true legend.

It was after winning at Troon that I began to regard myself as a good player, and the fact that I was forty-three made it all the more satisfying, because the Amateur Championship was supposed to be the domain of the young player, something he won before going on to make his mark in the pro game. It got me back into The Open, although unfortunately for me that year it was played at Royal St George's, which is not a course that ever suited me particularly well, and, of course, it gave me a way to return to my beloved Masters as well. I am privileged to have played in The Open on two occasions, but how I wish that they had been at Lytham or Birkdale, courses that suited my game. I am certain that I would have had a far better chance of making the cut at both those venues, as I had performed really well there in the past. But it wasn't to be.

I played all right at St George's and had Phil Rowe, my buddy from my England and Walker Cup days, on the bag, and we had a lot of fun together. I learnt after that tournament that I had quite a following, particularly on the internet, with a large number of gamblers backing me to beat my playing partners, Mark O'Meara and Mike Weir, in the first round – I shot a 74 with a double-bogey at the last to tie with both of them. I had hit a good drive and a decent second shot, but the ball found a horrible lie just off the left edge of the green and I was desperate to go to the toilet, so ended up playing the shot virtually with my legs crossed and, of course, I made a complete hash of it. The thing is that when you have thousands of people gathered around watching you, where do you go? You can't very well have a pee behind a bush, can you? And you can't very well turn round to two men who have each won major championships and ask them to hold on a minute while you go and find the gents.

The words of Jack Nicklaus when I played with him in practise at The Masters all those years before came back to haunt me: 'Gary,' he said. 'I have learnt an awful lot of tricks of the trade throughout my time as a professional golfer and one of the best tips that I can give you is that when you have the chance to go to the toilet you should always take it, even if you don't really need to, because you just never know when you will be able to go again.'

There should be a toilet on every tee at major tournaments for people like me who need to go regularly, as I drink lots of water during a round. But because there wasn't one to be found anywhere, I rushed off the green, signed my card, handed it in, and found a gents as quickly as I could. Soon afterwards I was told by a buddy of mine that all these people had lost money by betting on me. All for the sake of a missing portaloo.

On the twelfth hole of the second round I had put my ball in a bunker, taken three to get out and then holed my next shot from about 120 yards. Talk about 'if only'. I failed to break 80 in the second round and thus ended my second appearance in The Open. Phil kept me going right to the bitter end, despite my frustration with the way I was playing.

I really don't like the way the course has been changed over the years at St George's. They spoilt a brilliant par four at the fourth by extending it and turning it into a par five, and they ruined a perfectly good par three at the eleventh by once again deciding that it wasn't long enough. However, it seems as though this is the price we have to pay for the progress in equipment.

To play with O'Meara and Weir was a great experience, though. Weir had never played links golf before apparently, and O'Meara was great company, a man who chatted all the way round the course. He was charming and was also an old-style pro, a golfer who was capable of moving the ball from left to right or from right to left, at will. He could make the ball fly high or penetrate low through the wind – not many pros can do that any more. O'Meara only got a little tense towards the end of the second round when he realised that he was right on the cut line, and he did not want to come all the way to Kent and not play seventy-two holes. As it turned out both made it through to the weekend on the mark – excuse the pun.

I was better prepared for The Masters in 2004 and got together with a group of people so that we could hire a house. It was expensive, but everybody who stayed chipped in and it ended up costing me nothing at all. Lots of relations came over to watch me too and I was able to get them tickets, but I was shocked when I got to Augusta because by now they had tried to 'Tiger-proof' it, so it was longer, and they somehow managed to groom the fairway grass to grow towards the tees, which meant the amount of run on the ball was reduced significantly. For somebody who is as short a hitter as I am, that was a huge handicap.

But before I got to Augusta, there was a nice little bonus to look forward to. After I won the Amateur Championship for the first time I went to America and played at the Golf Club of Georgia with the professional, Archie Lemon. It was a glorious golf course and with its fast greens it provided ideal practise conditions for The Masters. Lemon had the idea that it might be a good plan to get the amateur champions of Britain and the USA together to play eighteen holes just ahead of The Masters.

I agreed that it was a fantastic idea. It wasn't until quite a few years later that it was instigated though, but it has now become a tradition. They called it the Georgia Cup, it began in 1998 and I played in it in 2004, by which time it had become established as a major charitable event, raising money for all sorts of good causes. I played Nick Flanagan, of Australia, who was the then-US Amateur champion, and we were treated like movie stars while we were there. They gave us each a leather holdall, a golf bag with our names on it, along with clothes. Not only that, but our match was televised. We started off with a crowd of more than 1,000 people and here I was facing yet another long hitter, but I won every one of the four par fives – I had an eagle and three birdies and finished up winning 3&2, and then did a question-and-answer session with the gallery. Although the eighteen-hole match was played on the Thursday prior to The Masters, we were looked after for almost an entire week – they took us to a basketball game and even put on a special dinner for us. It was amazing.

Beating Nick Flanagan to pick up the Georgia Cup also meant that I could say that I had won on all five continents, which is something that very few other golfers can boast – not even Sir Nick Faldo has managed it.

The golf club even set up a small museum, to which I donated a panama hat I had worn all week, together with my golf glove and ball. I also presented the club with a china lion, because my star sign is Leo, and that also went into the museum. And as well as the golf bag they presented me with, they kept one with my name emblazoned on the side to be placed in the men's locker room. As if all that were not good enough, I also received honorary life membership of the Golf Club of Georgia, so I can go and play there any time I want. I haven't a clue how much membership would be, but it was, and is, very expensive, so it's an incredible prize to receive.

I had to pay my fares to get there, but the club took care of everything else, and to think that it all came out of a chance conversation between myself and a club pro years before.

It got me into a great frame of mind before I headed to Augusta National. The course had been about 7,000 yards long when I had last played it, but it was now nearer to 7,400 yards. In saying that, I was a better player than had been the case in 1999 and had better equipment. Once again, I had a friend on the bag, Colin Edwards, who also caddied for me when I beat Tiger Woods in the Walker Cup. I should have bitten the bullet and accepted that it was going to cost me $2,000 to pay for a local caddy, but I always enjoyed giving a friend the experience of a lifetime by caddying for me in a major. That decision might have cost me my chance of making the cut, but sometimes it's not always about that and Colin enjoyed the week as much as I did.

I'd had a good practise round on the Tuesday afternoon

with Justin Rose, Ian Woosnam and Ian Poulter, with Rose and I taking on the other two and losing 3&2. Poulter was not a particularly impressive golfer in those days, so much so that I was amazed that he had said he fancied his chances of winning. Woosnam, even then, was a great player. He started off hitting the ball quite poorly, but I suggested a couple of tips later in the round and suddenly everything was coming out.

At the start of the round I got the feeling that Woosnam and Poulter didn't really want to play with me, but as it progressed they realised I wasn't a bad bloke after all – for an amateur. You have to remember that neither of them really served apprenticeships in the amateur game, while Justin did, and the two of us got on like a house on fire.

In the par-three competition I played with Sandy Lyle and Jose Maria Olazabal, behind Woods, O'Meara and Palmer. Arnie had a hole-in-one on the ninth and I stood and watched it from the eighth green, which was probably the best 'seat in the house' for that particular feat. Everybody went berserk.

In the tournament I was extremely privileged to play with Tom Watson and Briny Baird and shot a 77 in the first round without a solitary birdie, although I had at least six really decent chances. Watson was great to play with that day, all the more so when I later discovered that his caddy and great friend, Bruce Edwards, who had fought a long battle with Lou Gehrig's Disease, had died on the eve of the tournament. Watson had turned up five minutes late on the first tee with an official at his side, which I thought was a bit odd. We played the whole round together and although Tom chatted to us he didn't mention what had happened to Edwards – we didn't find out until later that day, after we had finished playing. Under the circumstances, he was an incredible gentleman to be with.

In the second round I started with a triple-bogey and I also had a double-bogey at the fourteenth, but still went round in 76 – if I hadn't dropped those shots I would have made the cut.

CHAPTER SEVENTEEN

BACK WHERE I BELONG

G arth McGimpsey was named captain for the Walker Cup matches in 2003 and 2005, the first of which was played at Ganton, which is my 'home from home'. It was where I won the Amateur Championship in 1991 and I had great memories of the place. Once again, I was playing well leading up to the 2003 match.

The previous season I had won the South African Open Amateur strokeplay, the Berkshire Trophy, the Lagonda Trophy and the Wiltshire Trophy, and in 2003 I had, of course, won the Amateur Championship for the second time. That was the icing on the cake, but I also picked up the Scottish Open Amateur strokeplay championship the following week and the Northamptonshire County Cup, as well as finishing the year as EGU National Order of Merit winner.

On paper, the Great Britain and Ireland team was good, but not great. We certainly didn't have a Luke Donald or a Paul Casey in our ranks. The team comprised Nigel Edwards, Noel Fox, Graham Gordon, David Inglis, Stuart

Manley, Colm Moriarty, Michael Skelton, Oliver Wilson, Stuart Wilson and myself. Yorkshire's Richard Finch, who has gone on to enjoy considerable success on the European Tour, should have been in the team in my opinion, but it was felt by the selectors that he had such a negative attitude when he was playing poorly and I believe that was why he was overlooked. Even then he was a fantastic player, as good as anyone, but there was just that something missing in his make-up, so Michael Skelton was the 'must have' Yorkshire representative playing before his home crowd. The only problem was that when he arrived for the match he was playing like a dog.

The American team was captained by the ebullient Bob Lewis and contained another host of potential superstars in Ryan Moore, Casey Wittenberg and Bill Haas, the son of PGA Tour star Jay. Trip Kuehne was also back in the team.

Once again, I wasn't used as part of one of the main foursomes pairings. Garth would make his selections and then it seemed to be a case of: 'Right, who is Gary going to play with? Who is left?' It was pretty frustrating.

For reasons I still cannot fathom, he put me out with Skelton against Haas and Kuehne in the Saturday foursomes, so I found myself paired with a golfer who was really struggling, but Michael actually played really well for ten holes, after which we were one up. But then the wheels fell off. Michael and I were the only ones to lose, which at least meant that we led 3–1, but with a little more planning, could it have been 4–0?

In the singles I was drawn against Bill Haas. He has taken his time to break through on the PGA Tour, but I knew from the first moment that I saw this young man swing a golf club that he had it in him to be something pretty special, and on that Saturday afternoon at Ganton Golf Club the two of us had the most amazing singles match. We threw birdies at each other, holed long putts and played great recovery shots when required to do so. I looked at the scores afterwards and I would have beaten every other American player, but not Haas, who beat me on the final green. By the end of the day I was sick of the sight of him!

Bob Lewis was a bit like Seve Ballesteros. When Seve captained the European Ryder Cup team he wanted to hit every shot, and Lewis was the same. When one of his team missed a putt or hit a poor shot, he would roll around in anguish. It wasn't an especially edifying sight, and most of the American players didn't want him around, but they did perform heroically for him in the first day's singles. Our only winner was Nigel Edwards, and Oliver and Stuart Wilson also managed to half their matches, as the Americans turned things around and finished the first day 7–5 ahead.

On the Sunday I was partnered with Oliver Wilson in the foursomes. I'd woken up that day with a really sore neck and the last thing I needed was to be playing Haas and Kuehne yet again, but that's what happened and, lo and behold, they almost drove the first green. I also realised pretty quickly that Oliver was struggling almost as badly as Michael had been the day before, so I was pretty certain that this was going to turn out to be a Walker Cup I would want to forget in a hurry.

We managed to get a half on the first and then I pulled my drive on the second and Oliver could only knock our ball back onto the fairway. The Americans were looking for theirs miles further down the left just off that area when I played our third shot to ten feet. The next moment they were claiming that I had played out of turn, but they had been searching for their ball way ahead of where I had played our third, so I just assumed that it was us still to play. In the end, they couldn't find their ball and had to go back to the tee, but they were still insisting I'd played out of turn and that I should have to play the shot again – you can be sure that if I had hoiked it into the rough they wouldn't have said a word. Fortunately, the referee disagreed with them.

Eventually, Haas and Kuehne holed out for a six, which meant that we had two putts from ten feet to win the hole and get our noses in front, but Oliver inexplicably knocked the ball five feet past. This was not how I wanted things to unfold, but somehow I managed to sink the putt and then the fog rolled in and we were taken off the course for almost two hours. It turned out to be heaven-sent because it gave me a chance to get some physio on my neck, which by that stage was killing me. Fortunately my osteopath from Leicester, a guy called John Lovett, eventually got my neck to click into place. Without that treatment I'm sure I would not have been able to play on. All Yorkshiremen describe their county as 'God's country' and I believe he may have been on our side that day.

We got back out onto the course an hour-and-three-quarters later and I played a series of wondrous shots from some horrendous places because poor Oliver couldn't hit the ball straight, but as we started to take control of the match he somehow managed to find his game as well and we won 5&4. We were the only winners, though, although the points were shared because we halved two games and lost the other, which meant we went into the final series of singles trailing 9–7. The USA needed three-and-a-half points to win, while we required five points to retain the trophy. Turning it around was going to be a huge task.

During the break between the foursomes and singles I was being interviewed by the BBC. It was a live interview, so when I became aware of team officials trying to tell me that Garth was holding a team meeting there was nothing I could do but carry on with the interview. 'We have been in this situation before where we have been trailing at this stage,' I said. 'We can definitely win this match. The course is to our favour, so yes, we can turn it around.' That was precisely what Garth had wanted to get across in the team meeting, so they all just listened to what I had to say instead. I don't suppose our captain was too happy with me, but what could I do?

Oliver was first out against Haas and I was in the match behind him, playing Casey Wittenberg, who was a precocious teenager who possessed tremendous self-belief and had talent in abundance. He thought that he was the best thing since the invention of the wheel. The American team were using the men's locker room while the British team availed itself of the women's facilities, which were actually the better of the two. There were pictures of me in the men's locker room and Wittenberg was apparently instrumental in turning them upside down. The reason I was so popular with the Americans was that prior to the Walker Cup I had been interviewed for a newspaper article in *The Sunday Telegraph*, during which I revealed what I considered to be the secrets of getting under your opponent's skin in matchplay, so every match I played at Ganton I was aware of the Americans looking me in the eye as we shook hands before teeing off, and marching quickly away from the tee and down the fairway. They were trying to play me at my own game, but I thought it was hilarious and just let them get on with it.

They were so concentrated on me, and in trying to find ways to beat me, that it took the focus off everybody else in the team. It didn't bother me – why should it? Years earlier I had gone head-to-head with Tiger Woods and beaten him, so I definitely wasn't going to be put out of my stride by Casey Wittenberg et al. He was going to beat me apparently, there was no doubt in his mind, and the US were certain they were going to bring home the trophy.

Things didn't quite go to the USA's plan, though. In the match ahead of us, Oliver Wilson managed to find a way to scramble out of trouble against Bill Haas and finished up beating him one up, which was miraculous given the way he had performed up to that point. That wasn't in the script either. It was a fantastic result, crowned by an unbelievable eight-iron shot onto the green from behind some trees at the final hole.

Meanwhile, I was also doing all right against Wittenberg. He was one up playing the eighth hole and I decided to engage him in conversation. He had no choice but to answer my questions and before he knew what had happened, the barrier he had tried to put up between us had come crashing down. Afterwards, one of the American journalists told me that he had never seen Wittenberg talk to anybody on a golf course before.

Coincidence or not, he blocked his second shot at the eighth and only stopped it going into the trees because it hit a marshall. By some miracle he had a decent lie, but failed to get up and down in two so I won the hole. All square. With the help of my pretty lady caddy Sara Garbutt, a local golfing hero in her own right, to keep my feet on the ground and temperament in check, I began to see a chink of light.

The next was a par five that he could reach in two all day long. I hit a driver and a five wood to ten feet though, while he put his second shot in the greenside bunker before nearly holing it, so he made a four. However, I holed my putt for an eagle three. One up. Suddenly, Casey Wittenberg started to lose the plot. I know that he was thinking: 'There's no way this guy is going to beat me. No way in a million years is he going to beat me.'

But I was beating him.

Then we came to the par three 10th. I hit the green, but he missed it, took a wild swing in anger and removed a huge chunk of turf from the tee. Now I knew he was a beaten man, even though he did manage to get up and down for a half. I won the next and went on to take the match 3&2.

Things were going the way of the GB&I team generally and when Stuart Manley beat Trip Kuehne it meant that we couldn't lose, but we didn't want to retain the Walker Cup by drawing the match, so it all came down to Nigel Edwards, who was playing against an affable American lad called Lee Williams. He did everything the right way, whereas Nigel was all over the place, but scrambled brilliantly. At the fourteenth, Williams hit a great approach shot to twelve feet, while Nigel went through the back of the green into the rubbish, but holed his chip. It was the Welsh Wizard at his best. Unsurprisingly, Williams missed his short putt and lost the hole. At the next hole, Nigel blocked his tee, shot into the bushes, and even he couldn't find a way to win that one. He got a decent par at the sixteenth then hit a shocker of a tee-shot at the par-three seventeenth, while Williams put his on the green. Incredibly,

Nigel holed out again from fully thirty yards with a putter, to a huge roar from the partisan crowd, so he had won that hole too, and found himself all square playing the last.

On the eighteenth, he was inches from the hole for the par that secured the half point that meant we had won the Walker Cup for the third time on the trot. The young American was left with an eight-foot putt for his par and we were all urging Nigel to concede it. 'Just give it to him. We've won the match and it doesn't matter.' Garth wasn't happy about that, though, and insisted that he wanted Williams to hole it. 'Come on Garth,' I said. 'This is a great opportunity to show what golf is all about. Give him the putt.' By now we were all shouting for Nigel to pick the ball up and, eventually, he did concede it. Yes, he could have won one up, but it wasn't a big deal and it had no effect on the outcome of the match. Victory was in the bag and it was a great gesture that went down well.

We beat them $12^1/_2$–$11^1/_2$ in front of a crowd of almost 22,000 people and a television audience of 4.5 million. A brass band played, the champagne flowed and again I counted my blessings. What a result, and what an honour to be part of it all once again. At the end of it we were given an official video of the match that had been produced by TransWorld Sport. Which was a tremendous memento. Needless to say, I have watched it many times since.

CHAPTER EIGHTEEN
MY KIND OF TOWN

I didn't know it at the time, but what would be my sixth and final Walker Cup appearance came in 2005 when we defended the trophy in Chicago. Once again, we had a sensational line-up – myself, Richie Ramsay, Rhys Davies, Robert Dinwiddie, Lloyd Saltman, Nigel Edwards, Gary Lockerbie, Brian McElhinney, Matthew Richardson and Oliver Fisher. There wasn't a weak link anywhere, and we initially thought that the Americans had played right into our hands by staging the match on a British-style golf course. The Americans however had an awesome line-up that included Anthony Kim, J B Holmes, Jeff Overton and, once again, Lee Williams.

I had played at the Chicago Golf Club before and loved the course because it was tight, with firm running fairways and fast undulating greens. However, when we got there we discovered that Bob Lewis had ordered the green keepers to soak the fairways – he had several very long hitters on his team so it made sense for him to find some way to give them an edge, and the way to do that was by drenching the fairways and eliminating all roll on the ball. So come the match I didn't find the course quite so perfect because it was playing significantly longer than usual. I don't blame the Americans – I would have done the same thing. You have got to find a way to give your team an advantage. Unfortunately, the R&A would never do such a thing, and I really don't understand why not.

Despite everything, I still believed we had a great chance of winning. Two years earlier, Peter McEvoy had been part of the team as Chairman of Selectors and had worked really well with Garth, but by the time we got to Chicago it was obvious that Garth was now in charge and that he had decided to do things his way.

Lloyd Saltman wanted to play with me in the foursomes, and I wanted to play with Lloyd, but Garth decided this wasn't going to happen. 'What about Matt Richardson?' he asked.

'I've absolutely nothing against Matt,' I replied, 'but you've asked me who I'd most like to play with and I would really rather play with Lloyd.'

Yes, Matt and I had played fifteen times together for England and had lost just once, and Garth had wanted me to partner him in Chicago but when he asked me who I wanted to play with I told him that Lloyd was my preference. He was a good friend and I believed our styles of play would combine well together.

Garth was determined that everybody would get a game on the opening day, and in the end he left me out of the foursomes and put Lloyd out with Richie Ramsay. To be fair, they turned out to be our only winning pair, although Nigel Edwards and Rhys Davies halved their match. The most baffling of Garth's combinations was pairing young

Oli Fisher with Matt Richardson – if I wasn't going to be paired with Lloyd or Matt, then I should have been the one to help the teenager through his first Walker Cup experience, or play with Matt. Oliver played well, but he was only a kid and he needed somebody to guide him, something I knew Matt would not do.

I would rather have played in the foursomes and been sidelined for the singles, of course, and if that had happened I am confident we would have been leading at the end of the Saturday morning. Instead, we were one point in arrears and I was drawn to play J B Holmes in the singles. I thought Tiger hit the ball a long way, but this guy was something else. On two of the par fours he asked for pin placements because he knew that he could drive the green. He actually went through the back of one of them. 'It's golf Jim, but not as we know it' were my sentiments.

To my credit, I managed to stay with him and even chipped in for an eagle at the sixteenth to square the match. On the seventeenth I hit a five wood for my second shot and as I struck it I thought that it didn't quite feel right. No wonder – the head fell off my club and flew into a bunker as I hit the ball. To compound things, he holed a monstrous putt from fully forty-five feet to win the hole with a birdie, and it was not the first time that day he had found his putting touch. I was sure that somebody had told me J B Holmes couldn't putt. One down.

I had a putt to square the match on the final green but missed and very disappointingly lost one down. So I hadn't played in the foursomes, which was my speciality, and I had been beaten in the afternoon by a guy who allegedly couldn't putt, but who had holed the biggest combined yardage of putts in the history of the game on the afternoon he played me. I was not a happy man, understandably, but at least we managed to come out of the singles 4–4 and only trailed overnight by a solitary point.

On the Sunday morning I was inexplicably left out of the foursomes again. I nearly asked Garth if he was deliberately trying to lose, but I bit my tongue. We shared the points, so went into the final series of singles still behind by a point.

I was in the first match out, and this time my opponent was Anthony Kim, yet another huge hitter, but this time I played out of my skin. Over the first ten holes I was four up, despite being out-driven by eighty-odd yards on each of them. I was producing some glorious golf, but Kim kept battling back and battling back and he made a couple of birdies late on that put me under a great deal of pressure. I may have been four up, but he clawed himself once more into contention and by the time we played the eighteenth I was just one up.

A decent drive was followed by a seven iron, which I pulled slightly long and left of the flag, while Kim pounded a drive away and put his second shot twenty-five feet from the hole. On the Friday evening before the first series I had been practising the exact shot that I had now left myself, so I knew pretty much how it would react. I played the most exquisite of golf shots, leaving it stone dead, or so I thought. I handed my club to my caddy and fully expected to be told that the putt was good and that it would have been conceded, but when I looked up I realised that the ball had rolled at least six feet past the hole.

Kim made his par, and I was left to hole the putt that would give me victory over yet another huge-hitting young American golfer and also to break Michael Bonallack's Walker Cup points record. Fortunately, I rattled it straight in. I had given us a real shot at winning again, and I then headed out to see how the rest of the team were getting on. I watched on the 18th Robert Dinwiddie chip in for a birdie, Lloyd Saltman hole from off the green and Oliver Fisher sink a huge putt for another birdie. Fisher and Dinwiddie both halved their matches, while Saltman won one up, and when Matt Richardson thrashed J B Holmes, now minus the golden touch on the greens, by 5&4, it seemed as though we were on course for yet another famous victory.

Lee Williams beat Gary Lockerbie, which meant that the outcome of the entire match hinged on the game between Nigel Edwards and Jeff Overton. There was some bad feeling at the seventeenth hole when Overton found himself in the right rough – he took lots of practise swings with his wedge, swishing away at the grass, and when he came to play the shot he suddenly handed the club back to his caddy and pulled out a six iron. I watched it afterwards on TV and I didn't think he had done anything wrong.

Eventually it all came down to Nigel having to hole a twenty-five-foot putt across the eighteenth green. If it had gone in the scores would have been level and we would have retained the trophy, but he narrowly missed it and the USA had pipped us by a point. We couldn't believe what had happened, and I guess that I still put it down to Garth McGimpsey deciding to leave me out of both sets of foursomes, but who knows?

Don't get me wrong. I was disappointed at the outcome, but I am not bitter about it because I had the experience of being on four previous winning teams. No British golfer has ever done that before and I don't believe anybody will ever come close to doing it in the future either. However, I was disappointed for the others, who never got to savour that special feeling of a GB&I win on American soil.

I wasn't selected for the match at Royal County Down in 2007. Did I deserve to be dropped? In 2006, I won the European Mid-Amateur championship, and I successfully defended it the following year. I won the South of England Open Strokeplay and St Mellion International Amateur Strokeplay and I won the 2007 Centenary New South Wales Amateur championship against one of Australia's top players, Tim Stewart. So you can draw your own conclusions.

There was one hole at County Down, the ninth, where if we were playing into a headwind I struggled to reach the fairway, and on that basis I got the distinct impression that I was left out. If that was the case I'm sorry, but I always thought that golf was played over eighteen holes, and there were other players in the team who couldn't make the carry either. If they had played me in my beloved foursomes I wouldn't even have had to hit a tee shot on the ninth. So it was ridiculous if that was the reason.

We played a strokeplay practise session for the event a few months before matches on the course, during which both Rory McIlroy and Lloyd Saltman failed to break 80, but I shot a 75. Where was the logic in their thinking? However, Lloyd and Rory were both shoo-ins at that stage.

It was felt by many that Colin Dalgleish, the captain, was not as good as the likes of Peter McEvoy when it came to man management. In the end we lost in Ireland, albeit only by one point. It was a shame because I felt that with the advantage of a huge home support, and a very British links, we should have cruised it. I had been told that Colin didn't want me to be a 'disruptive influence'. If that was so then that attitude annoys me, because I am not disruptive and nobody has ever been able to give me a reason as to why some people seem to hold that view of me. I just don't see it, not in a million years. All I want is the team to win.

If I saw something that I did not think was right then I would come up with constructive suggestions as to how I believed it might be improved. Why should we accept mediocrity? The powers-that-be in amateur golf should have been grateful that people such as myself were prepared to take the time and trouble to make a contribution rather wanting us to keep quiet and disappear from whence we came.

I have always been an ideas person. When we were in Chicago, Garth left it to me to work out the breakfast menu for everybody after I pointed out that we should not go back to doing things as we had in the past, with everybody eating food that was full of fat or sugar. There was nothing healthy on the menu, but I knew that we needed food that would give us energy and set us up for the day. There was no fruit, yoghurt or natural bars until I made sure that they were available. No matter how you look at that, it is not disruptive. It is a constructive approach, surely? The players certainly thought so, and nobody felt fatigued halfway through the morning that week, so I guess it worked. I also encouraged the players to take fruit out on the course with them. Garth left it to me to liaise with the chef and I'm sure everybody benefited as a result.

I often did my own thing, I admit that, but always for the good of the team. Always. If there was a problem, why did nobody ever sit down with me and say: 'Gary, we think it would be better if...'

So my Walker Cup career was over. It meant everything to me. For an amateur golfer who comes from these isles it is the ultimate golfing experience, and a great honour. People will say that the Eisenhower Trophy is the pinnacle and, while it is harder to get into what used to be a four-man team for the event, the history and the tradition didn't come close. It was also a rare opportunity to get involved in matchplay, and I still find it difficult to put into words what it meant to me to be part of a series of teams that turned the tables on the Americans, who had been thrashing GB&I for years.

I fear that the future of the Walker Cup could be in the hands of kids who are simply marking time before turning professional. There is nothing wrong with that as such, but the essence of the event is that it is an amateur team competition and with my departure into the professional ranks, and the fact that Nigel Edwards – a fellow 'old timer' – was dropped for Merion in 2008, the nature of the Walker Cup has probably changed forever.

There are also no guarantees in golf, of course. Just because you are picked to play in the ten-man Walker Cup team, it doesn't mean that you will be playing at the peak of your powers when the match comes along. I saw it at first hand with a number of excellent young, but inexperienced, players.

It always surprised me that the R&A did not appoint a coach to accompany the team, so much so that before the match at Royal County Down I eventually offered my services: if I couldn't play then perhaps I could contribute in another way. I told them that I would get to the venue under my own steam and that they could make whatever use of my talents as they saw fit. Peter Dawson, the secretary of the R&A, said he thought that it was a great idea and he would discuss it with Colin Dalgleish. In no time at all, Dawson was on the phone to me saying thanks but no thanks.

'Okay, that's fine,' I said. 'But even if you have decided that you don't want me, you really ought to have somebody there for the players.'

The most surprising thing is that everything else is taken care of, right down to the finest detail. The players are given the best possible kit, they stay in good hotels, transport is laid on for them and it all runs pretty smoothly, but the one thing you would think they would want to try and guarantee is the form of the players, and that can only happen if you have coaches on your side to give advice when things aren't going to plan.

CHAPTER NINETEEN

THE VOICE OF GOLF

I have been lucky enough to dabble in TV coverage of golfing events. My godfather is Peter Alliss, the doyen of golf commentary, and he put in a good word for me and got me the opportunity to do some work at the 1994 PGA Championship at Wentworth. Through the then producers, John Shrewsbury and Alistair Scott, I was sitting in the commentary box watching how things were done, having never spoken into a microphone in my life, when they told me that I was on air.

Talk about being thrown in at the deep end. If I'd been given some warning and the chance to think about it, I am sure that I would have been fine, but it all came as a bit of a shock to the system. I battled through it as best I could through the first day, and then they decided that it might be better to put me out in the open to do some on-course commentary and analysis, and I took to that like a duck to water, because I was talking about what I was seeing first hand. At that point, I was off and running.

They often used to give me Tiger to follow, and because

I was fitter than everybody else they had doing the on-course stuff, they used to make me jump through hoops.

'Gary, we need you on the twelfth,' someone would say.

'But I am on the sixth.'

'I understand that, but we need you on the twelfth right now. You will be on air in two minutes.'

I would be running around the golf course like a headless chicken and nearly had a heart attack on one occasion because I was out of breath when they put me on air and I had to try to talk without panting, so effectively I was talking without breathing. I do not recommend it to anybody. They never needed to ask me if I wanted to say something, because I always found something to say.

When Mark O'Meara won The Open in 1998, he finished tied with an American golfer called Brian Watts, but the most remarkable achievement of that year was that of seventeen-year-old Justin Rose, who finished two shots off the lead in fourth place while still an amateur. I was on the 18th fairway with him in the final round when he holed his approach to the final green for a round of 69. It meant that he finished with a total of 282, six-under par, and had bettered my father's best amateur finish of five under, achieved at St Andrews in 1960. When Rose broke the record, it was a real buzz to be there, working for BBC Television. He would go on to turn professional and initially miss a whole host of cuts, but I always knew that, one day, he would come good. He was just too talented a player not to succeed.

In 1999, The Open was played at Carnoustie and was famously (or should that be infamously) won by Paul Lawrie after Jean Van de Velde came to grief at the seventy-second hole. Much was said and written about the difficulty of that golf course, but I was commentating on that Championship and on the Tuesday I was allowed to play a round, teeing off at 6am, and I managed to complete it in 75, which included two bum steers as to the line to take off the tee given to me by Mike Hughesdon, a fellow on-course commentator.

I was amazed when the tournament began to see just how difficult the world's best golfers seemed to find it to hit a fairway, even with an iron in their hands. A couple of holes were too tough though – you could spit across the lay-up area in the sixth fairway, so that was an error of judgement by someone. And yes, the rough was a tad too thick, but if you are in the world's elite and you can't hit fairways, even with an iron, then you don't deserve to win.

Tiger Woods had left his driver in the bag for the entire tournament, until fatefully he felt he was falling too far behind Van de Velde, so on the sixth tee, out came the driver. He started blasting away with it, and really that's how he lost it. If he had stuck to his game plan, I believe he would have won The Open in 1999. Hindsight is a marvellous thing.

I have also worked in America for the Golf Channel, covering the Walker Cup with Billy Andrade and Steve Melnyk, who are two really lovely guys. I enjoyed every minute of it, but I don't know whether I will ever get the chance to do it again because the channels are always looking for what they would call celebrity commentators, ex-tournament pros such as Johnny Miller, Nick Faldo, Sam Torrance and the like.

Then there are people like Rob Lee, another former golfer who has turned out to be a star for Sky TV when it comes to presenting their golf coverage. If I was ever fortunate enough to be offered a contract I would have to think very seriously about accepting it because, for me, it's like falling off a log. Just imagine talking about golf and getting paid for it. It has got to be the best job on the planet.

I have listened to so many so-called golf commentators talking about amateur golf and cringed because they just don't know the game at that level. They don't even understand what exemptions the US Amateur champion is entitled to for instance, but I do. Not many in the media these days know more about the amateur game than me, so perhaps I may still get my chance, and with my possible success on the Seniors Tour other chances of working on the pro tournaments, where all my amateur contemporaries are now doing so successfully, might well arise.

And I have witnessed some fabulous moments as an on-course commentator, such as the head-to-head between Costantino Rocca and John Daly at The Open at St Andrews in 1995. I was standing yards away from Rocca when he faced his chip on the seventy-second hole (with the Italian needing to hole it to win) and I turned to Mike Hughesdon, with whom I was doing the on-course commentary, and said: 'He's going to duff this.' He was taking long practise swings and decelerating the club, which is a cardinal sin; on shots like that you always have to accelerate through the ball. Sure enough, he hit one of the worst shots I have seen in such circumstances, but then followed it up with that magnificent tramliner of a putt that got him into the playoff with Daly.

Sadly, there was to be no happy ending for Rocca, who lost the playoff. Although it wasn't my first close-up experience of Daly. After he won the 1991 US PGA Championship and I achieved my first Amateur

Championship, we were both invited to play in the Australian Masters and the Australian PGA Matchplay and I got the opportunity to get to know him. He was a genuine, down-to-earth guy, but even then he was eating fast food and knocking back six packs of lager for fun. I made the cut at the Australian Masters and ended up playing with Ian Baker-Finch in the third round, so the organisers had the current Open champion and Amateur champion playing together, which was pretty unique. Daly needed a guiding hand early in his career. If there had been somebody to guide him properly, who knows what he might have achieved? Certainly the saddest statistic about John's career is that he is still the only eligible two-time major winner never to compete in a Ryder Cup, which I personally think is a great shame.

In the matchplay I lost in the first round to the talented Kiwi Grant Waite, who went on to enjoy a successful career on the US Tour, but on that day he needed to hole a huge putt on the final green to beat me one up. It was a great experience on an amazing course at Kingston Heath in Melbourne, where the greens were so fast that they were just about unplayable, running at 14.5 on the stimp.

CHAPTER TWENTY
CARRYING THE LOAD

Why me? Why do I always seem to have problems with caddies? It has pretty much been a constant throughout my career, notwithstanding the occasions when I have had friends (or my boss) on the bag.

At on event in America, we were all provided with local bagmen and at one point were asked if any of us wanted to change them. They were all caddies from the local golf club and mine was no good. I'd had poor caddies at other American events too – maybe it was because I was last in the alphabet when it came to dishing out the caddies. Who knows? Anyway, I was able to replace the first one I was given, but the second one was equally poor. I wanted to change again but they wouldn't let me.

'You've got to have a local man carrying your bag,' they told me.

'That's fine,' I said. 'I don't have a problem with that, but if I've got to have a club caddy then I want a good one, somebody who knows the game and the course like the other guys seem to have. It's not too much to ask for, surely?'

But apparently it was. I should point out that the caddies get paid quite a good salary over there!

I don't believe that you need to be a genius to be a good caddy. You want somebody who knows how far you are from the flag. You want somebody who knows when to offer a supportive word and, most important of all, knows how to 'keep up and shut up'.

I always seemed to get on well with everybody else's caddy, just not my own, so I ended up being accused of being too picky. Throughout my amateur career I usually lugged my own clubs around the course, just to avoid any potential conflict. The thing is that I know I could well have won so much more if I'd had the right person at my side. I have blown tournaments through mental incompetence or because of making catastrophic decisions that a decent caddy would hopefully have stopped me from making.

On occasions when I lost my cool after hitting a bad shot, I needed somebody to help calm me down. I have always been too quick to come down hard on myself – I am my own worst enemy in some people's opinion, although sometimes it drives me on and makes me play better – a bit like John McEnroe used to be. It is difficult to get the right man (or woman), but it can make a huge difference to your game. Lee Westwood has finally found the perfect caddy in Billy Foster, a straight-talking, no-nonsense man who tells Lee what he thinks and who knows when to break the ice with a funny story. Fanny Sunesson and Nick Faldo were another great combination, but when Fanny left the Englishman and joined Sergio Garcia she had a less happy time. Maybe he was too young and too volatile and he was certainly very different from Faldo, who was like a machine on the golf course.

I can relate to the relationship Faldo established with Fanny because I have always preferred having a female caddy, especially if she happens to be good-looking too. I suppose the bottom line is that with a woman on the bag, I just wanted to show off, and her presence made me find it much easier to control my temper when things went wrong. It might well be that finding a glamorous woman to carry my clubs could be the secret to succeeding on the European Seniors Tour. If it stops me losing thousands of pounds it will be money well spent.

I have made some elementary mistakes on the course that I am almost embarrassed to talk about, such as getting on to a tee and forgetting that it has been moved forward, so I have hit a driver instead of an iron and found myself in a hazard. I have always played the game too quickly, when taking an extra moment or two might have possibly allowed me to register what I needed to do.

And that brings me on to my biggest bugbear of all – the five-hour round. Three-and-a-half hours is plenty long enough for any threeball to get round any eighteen-hole golf course. In my opinion if it takes you five hours to play, then maybe you need to be thinking about taking up another sport.

I spent years complaining to the English Golf Union about slow play in the likes of the Brabazon Trophy. The crazy thing is that even players who have no chance of making the cut and are playing badly still seem to take forever to play their shots. There is no excuse for it. Things are beginning to improve, but they still have tournaments where it takes five-and-a-half hours to get round. If you are having a nightmare and are hitting lots of shots I can just about understand why that would happen, but not if you are playing well. Slow play has also caused untold damage at some of the best tournaments in the world, including The Majors.

I watch golfers going through never-ending pre-shot routines and it nearly reduces me to tears of frustration. If you walk up to a golf ball, take a practise swing and then strike the ball with the minimum of fuss and without a multitude of swing thoughts going through your mind, the chances are that you will play better golf. If you take account of every potential hazard, have umpteen practise swings, step away from the ball and then stand over it for an eternity waiting for inspiration to strike, it is a pretty safe bet that you will score plenty.

I have played a lot of golf at Morecambe and Heysham GC's, where if you take more than three hours and fifteen minutes to play a medal in a threesome there will be questions asked. Perish the thought if you take longer than three-and-a-half hours. They say things like: 'Where have you been? We called out the RNLI but nobody could find you.' It tends to focus the mind.

It's been mooted that Amateur golf in England is, in many areas, rather quaintly organised. For instance, the English Golf Union have a fourteen-handicapper at Chairman of Championships responsible for setting up the courses at their major competitions. How does a fourteen-handicap golfer get into that position? Yes, he loves the game, but he has never played it to championship standard. We are talking about a lovely man, the sort you would enjoy spending some time with over a drink or two, and one who would do a highly professional job, but not necessarily a good enough player to be setting pin positions for some of the amateur game's biggest tournaments. And yet there is an ex-England international called James Crampton working for the EGU, so why not give him the courses to set up?

I put together a detailed letter and submitted it to the EGU. To my way of thinking, it contained lots of common-sense stuff. For instance, if you have a 465-yard par four hole in a championship and the wind is blowing a gale into the face of the players, you don't put the tee as far back as you can and the flag at the back of the green, otherwise it will slow play down.

I offered to help put together a group of former internationals, or, at the very least, top county golfers who would go to championships and set up courses for them. The EGU weren't interested. It would have been, I believe, the right thing to do. I sometimes wonder how I have managed to reach this stage of my life without being led away by men wearing white coats.

The EGU was originally transformed by Keith Wright. When he took over as secretary in the 1980s it had been run from a room in the back of Ian Erskin's house near Wokingham, but Wright turned it into a genuine professional operation based in Leicester. Keith's big problem however was that he was something of a Walter Mitty character. He claimed to have played for Leicester City, which he had, but then he claimed to have been a first-class cricketer – which he wasn't – a national-standard diver, a rugby player – name a sport and he'd played it at a high standard. It eventually became a bit of a joke.

Whenever he came away with the England team certain individuals would sit down before dinner and decide which sport we were going to catch him out on. The most memorable discussion involved diving, and it always seemed to be Peter McEvoy who got the ball rolling. Ricky Willison was a member of the team in those days, and his brother had dived at national level, so Ricky knew the subject pretty well.

'Have you ever dived, Keith?' asked Peter.

'Yes, yes. I was a very good diver.'

'What was your specialist dive then, Keith?' piped up Ricky.

'An inward.'

'An inward? An inward what?' demanded Ricky.

Now the thing about Keith was that he knew a little bit about lots of things, which is how he had picked up the word 'inward'.

'An inward inward, Ricky.'

There is, of course, no such dive. An inward pike, maybe, but an inward inward? No way.

'And what height did you dive from?' Ricky asked. 'Five metres? Ten metres? Thirty-five metres? Or was it the fifty-metre board?'

Quick as a flash, Keith replied: 'Yes, it was the fifty-metre board.' Which, again, was complete rubbish – you could kill yourself off a fifty-metre drop.

On another occasion we were at Valderrama on an England squad session, and while we were there the San Roque course was officially opened and we were invited to a cocktail party. At the time, the Football Association were looking for a new chief executive. The guys had been chatting to some girls and persuaded one of them to come in and say: 'Is there a Keith Wright here?'

'Yes, yes, I'm Keith Wright,' answered Keith.

'The Football Association are on the phone for you,' the woman said.

His chest puffed out and he said to the group: 'The Football Association, eh? They are probably going to ask me to advise them on who the next chief executive should be.'

Off he went and picked up the phone in the lobby, but, naturally, there was nobody on the other end of the line. When he came back in nobody said a word, but he tried to persuade us that the FA had been on the phone to ask for his advice about the appointment when asked about the call.

On another squad session we were in Almeria in southern Spain and we all had to take part in a series of fitness tests. Keith always thought that I was fat and lazy and I do admit that I was no Arnold Schwarzenegger, but I did keep pretty fit. Now Roger Roper, on the other hand, had to be physically stopped from doing any more sit-ups or press-ups because he was like a machine. There were twenty of us and we all made an effort, apart from a golfer called Alex Robertson, who might agree to do two press-ups and one sit-up on a good day. He couldn't see the point, so he always deliberately came last when the fitness test results were given out.

We were at dinner and it was Keith's job to give out the results. 'First, Roger Roper. Fantastic effort as always Roger. Second, Freddie George. Third, Gary Wolstenholme – no, that can't possibly be right.' He started going through his notes because he was convinced somebody had made a mistake. There was no way I could be the third-fittest man on the squad because I was a 'fat git' according to him, but actually I was reasonably fit and made an effort to do all the tests too.

Then there was a match in the south of France and as I

got up from the dining table, Keith yelled across the restaurant: 'Wolstenholme, you're fat!' Why would he do that? He was secretary of the English Golf Union and I was an England international. He was an oddball and yet the year I won the Amateur Championship for the first time he travelled all the way to Ganton from Leicester to watch me play in both the semi-final and final, which I greatly appreciated. I actually really liked Keith, and was very sorry when he eventually suffered a breakdown. Despite everything, English amateur golf owed him a great deal for the way in which he dragged it into the modern era.

CHAPTER TWENTY ONE

DROPPED FROM A GREAT HEIGHT

Golf has kicked me in the teeth many times. During the winter of 2004–05, I got a phone call from Peter Dawson of the R&A to inform me that the championship committee had met and had agreed that they wanted me to become a member of the R&A. What a fabulous honour, and a fitting tribute to everything I had achieved, or at least that was what my friends told me, and I couldn't disagree. I told Peter that I was delighted and that I had often wondered whether I was going to get the chance to join.

I should point out that you have to pay about £300 for the privilege – not a huge amount, I admit, but it is not free, and it entitles you to, well, next to nothing really, apart from being able to play in a couple of competitions at St Andrews. Nonetheless, anybody who has ever played golf wants to be a member of the R&A. It's like being a footballer and getting a call from Sepp Blatter to tell you that he wants you to join FIFA.

Peter told me that they wanted me to be involved with various committees. I guessed that they wanted to give me the opportunity to put something back into the game and I was delighted because I had always wanted to do that anyway.

'We will be in touch in due course Gary, but you can take it as read that you are going to be in,' he said. There is a book for potential members, and my name was entered at the top of it. Lots of people contacted me to tell me that they had seen my name on the list and that they were looking forward to welcoming me into the R&A clubhouse and to buying me a drink.

I didn't hear anything more on the matter, until I lost to Lloyd Saltman in the last sixteen of the Amateur Championship at Birkdale in 2005. Afterwards, Peter Dawson called me across. 'Gary,' he said. 'I've got some bad news. I am afraid that we are going to have to withdraw our invitation for you to join the R&A.'

I'd already had a bad day on the golf course, but this was really rubbing salt into the wounds.

'So why is that, Peter?' I asked.

'Well, we have had a couple of people write in to say that they don't feel you would be a suitable member for the R&A.' Peter replied.

'Really? That's quite a thing. I have had a lot of letters and phone calls of support.'

'Oh yes, lots of people were very pleased that you were going to be a member, but I really respect the opinion of one of these two people who have objected and we feel that it would not be wise for you to be put forward as a member. It doesn't necessarily mean that you can't be captain of the Walker Cup team or anything like that or that you can't be a member in the future, just not right now.'

I stood there asking myself why on earth I would now

want to be a member of an organisation that had invited me to join but had then withdrawn that invitation, just because one person thought I might not be a suitable member. Peter Dawson was the one who had approached me, presumably after discussing it with other influential people – did they not respect their own opinions more than that of one particular individual? Clearly not. The championship committee is the most important within the R&A and it was that committee that had asked me to join. Needless to say, Peter would not give me the name of the person who had objected, and nor would he tell me the specific nature of the objection to my membership, which meant that I could only speculate.

It was an extraordinary way for somebody who had won the Amateur Championship twice and who had played in six Walker Cup matches to be treated. I was especially disappointed because everybody wants to be appreciated for their efforts, and that includes me, so it troubled me that somebody out there disliked me to such an extent that they would block my membership of the R&A. It also meant that any hopes I had of influencing the way that golf was going had been shattered, so when the opportunity to turn professional eventually presented itself I didn't have to think too hard about the decision in the end.

I knew that, no matter what Peter Dawson had said, there was never now the slightest chance of me being asked to captain the Walker Cup team either, and that was a huge disappointment because it will be abundantly clear to you that this was an event that meant a huge amount to me.

To make matters worse, England were doing away with their captaincy in the classic sense – no more would somebody get the post for four years and also play an integral part in selecting and running the team. It all meant that having given my playing career and, indeed, the majority of my adult life to amateur golf in this country, there was no possibility that I could crown it in the way that other successful players such as Tony Jacklin, Bernard Gallacher, Garth McGimpsey or Peter McEvoy were able to do when they were asked to captain.

Being asked to lead a representative side is almost as great an honour as being asked to play in it, and some may argue that it is the pinnacle of one's career. I figured that this honour was going to be denied to me. At that point, I knew that my days in amateur golf were done.

CHAPTER TWENTY TWO

ROYAL FLUSH

One of the high points of my life came when I received an MBE in the 2007 New Year's Honours List. A letter dropped on the doormat, informing me of the honour and swearing me to secrecy. I didn't tell a soul, not even my mother. Then I got a phone call from a local journalist shortly after Christmas 2006, saying that he understood I was being awarded the MBE. After that, I finally told Mum, who nearly hit me. 'I can't believe you didn't tell me,' she said. 'I'm your mother.'

I collected my MBE from Buckingham Palace in May 2007, and what a day and what an honour that was. I took my mother and the owners of Kilworth Springs, Roger and Ann Vicary, to the palace with me.

Before you go in to meet the Queen you are told all about Royal etiquette and what is expected of you, and they show you how to bow. I know that she asked me two questions, but I have absolutely no recollection of what the first one was. The second was: 'So how long have you been playing at this level?'

'About twenty years at this level.'

I forgot to call her 'Ma'am' or 'Your Majesty' because you just do – it is a very nerve-racking experience.

'Very good,' she replied, shaking my hand. And that was it. I'd had my time.

It was a tremendous experience and I guarantee that everybody who is presented to Her Majesty gets a great deal of pleasure from meeting her. I was no exception. I met some wonderful people and got the opportunity to admire a large part of the Royal art collection. I am a devout royalist and regard the Queen as a heroine of the people. She does great things for our country and has sacrificed her entire life in service for us. The Queen makes this country what it is; for me, she puts the 'Great' in Britain.

After receiving my MBE I felt as high as a kite for a while, but then I started thinking about the next stage of my life.

I sometimes think that Roger believed he had me for life at Kilworth Springs, but towards the end of the year I decided that the time had to come to leave. They wanted me to become club manager, but they already had two people doing that job. Making sure the toilet rolls were changed, the doors were locked, all the light bulbs were working and that the tills balanced was not for me. Until that point my official job title was Director of Golf, but I was really in charge of the marketing and promotion of the club, and I did okay. They got a half-page spread in the *Daily Telegraph* once, as a direct result of what I had achieved in amateur golf – it was the sort of thing that would have cost them at least £20,000 if they'd had to buy the space for an advertisement.

I also fronted a digital TV programme, *Inside Golf*, which was filmed at Kilworth Springs. I never got paid for that, but it appeared two or three times a week, and gave them even more invaluable exposure. 'And now, live from Kilworth Springs, this week's episode of *Inside Golf...*' was how I began.

There were times after I announced my intention to leave that I sensed Roger wanted to sit me down and ask what it would take to keep me, but he never did. With or without me, it was a successful business then, and it will continue to be so in the future. I believe it will become one of the best golf businesses in the Midlands. When I arrived it was only three years old, so it was very new and not many people were aware of its existence, but thanks to my exploits it was mentioned on a weekly basis in the *Leicester Mercury*, one of the biggest and best regional evening newspapers in the country.

I felt that I was being given a gentle nudge by the gentleman upstairs that the time was right to start a new episode in my life, so I decided that I would sell my house, hopefully make a decent profit on it, and go home to Cumbria and live near my mum.

I had no sooner put my house on the market than the crash happened, and it took over two years to sell it. However the good news was that as soon as Cliff Heath, the Cumbria captain, heard that I had moved back into the area, he invited me to come and play for the county and I was delighted to say yes.

Lancashire phoned me a week later, but they were too late. I enjoyed the twelve months I spent playing for Cumbria and would like to believe that I had a pretty positive influence. They were going to try and get me a job, but it never materialised. I am sure they had my best interests at heart, but I am a pragmatist by nature and when somebody tells me that they are going to do something for me I always tend to believe it when it happens, and if it does, it's a bonus.

In any event, it had been my choice to up sticks and return to Cumbria and I had no right to expect anybody to do anything for me. I was just happy to be back on home soil again.

Once again, though, I wasn't making any money and was having to borrow cash just to play in tournaments. I was almost back where I had started, although at least this time I was living at home, so I didn't have too many extra bills to worry about.

CHAPTER TWENTY THREE
AMERICAN NIGHTMARE

In 2008, I entered pre-qualifying for the US Open. I had to play two rounds at Walton Heath in what is called 'international qualifying', and I was allowed to enter because of what I had achieved in winning the Amateur Championship five years earlier. It gave me a five-year exemption into final qualifying.

Two years earlier I had lost in a playoff and finished as first reserve. This needs some explanation – I was not first reserve for the entire field, but only for the players who had qualified ahead of me at Walton Heath, so if one of them had dropped out I would have been invited to play in the tournament proper, but in 2006 it didn't happen and, in any event, I wasn't in a position to fly to the United States and click my heels in the hope that one of my rivals would fall ill.

In 2008, I shot five-under par for the two rounds and found myself in another playoff. I had played with Daniel Vanscik, of Argentina, for two rounds – the distance he was capable of hitting the golf ball was amazing. He may have been a little bit off line at times, but nonetheless he was a highly impressive golfer. Daniel and I tied, and were joined in the playoff by Thomas Levet of France and Johan Edfors of Sweden. Two of the four of us were guaranteed places in the starting field, while the other two were playing for the privilege of being named as first alternate from the Walton Heath qualifiers.

So we all marched off to the first hole, a par three, where they were hitting three woods. I should have reached for my driver, but I suppose pride prevented me from doing so, and I hit a three wood too – it was never going to be enough, so I tried to hit it too hard and pulled it left of the green and made a four. Levet and Edfors parred the hole to qualify, while Daniel, like me, dropped a shot. I then birdied the second, third and fourth, to be first reserve.

From the moment I realised that I was only to be a reserve, it was a bit of a come down after doing so well to get into the playoff. I was told that I could turn up at the venue if I wanted to, but came to the conclusion that I probably wouldn't. Then, two days later, I got a phone call from the USGA in America to tell me I was now first alternate for the all-exempt players, as well as being first alternate for the Walton Heath qualifiers – I hope you are keeping up with this. I was now first reserve for seventy-nine players and not just for the seven qualifiers from Walton Heath.

I was faced with the ultimate dilemma. Did I go? I knew that I really couldn't afford to do so. I could just about scrape together the plane fares, but the tournament was being played at Torrey Pines, near San Diego in California, and there would also be the expense of finding accommodation. My friends told me I had no option. Of course, I had to go. It was the US Open, and I had a genuine chance of making the field, but how was I going to afford it? Then Peter Matsson at the EGU offered to pay for the flights, which was fantastic of him.

A friend in the States even said he could arrange a free caddy and accommodation. And when I had explained to the USGA that I was worried about the cost of the trip, they offered some positive advice, and not to worry.

So I arrived at San Diego, but when I got myself to the tournament desk they didn't know who I was. Not the most promising of starts, I am sure you will agree. I was taken to another office at the course, where I was told that my contact was not available and that I would have to go to the nearby players' hotel. Somebody dropped me off, assuming that that was where I had to book in. But then I was told at reception that there 'must have been some mistake', and was promptly directed to another office back at the course.

At Torrey Pines it was explained to me that the main hotel was going to cost $240 per night, and I told them I really couldn't afford it. So then they gave me the details of another hotel which, I was told, cost just over $100 a night. But the problem was that it was a 45 minute drive away, which would cost $60 each way in a taxi. You will not be surprised to learn that by now I was beginning to think that I had made a mistake in coming.

I started doing my sums: taxi journey to the course and back – $120 per day; and hotel – $100 plus per day. And that was without spending any money at all on food or other expenses. I might as well have stayed in the $240 hotel because at least that was within walking distance of the golf course. So the following day I duly packed all my gear from the Quality Inn and headed back to Torrey Pines, only to discover that there were now no vacancies at the main players' hotel at the course. It was frustrating because the day before, there had been dozens of rooms. I now had to go back to the Quality Inn and check back in. I was having kittens as I saw what little money I had was haemorrhaging fast.

To make matters worse, because I wasn't in the field at this stage, I wasn't able to play the golf course. I could use the practice ground, but not the course. I was, of course, allowed to walk round the holes but that doesn't really give you a feel of how to play it. Because money was tight I saved on food expenses by going to the players' lounge and stocking up on complimentary sandwiches and snacks for my dinner. I later also discovered that there was a courtesy shuttle service, but I couldn't use it as it was only for the use of families of the players in the tournament. I was getting desperate and asked if there was any chance that somebody could drive me back to my hotel. Fortunately a USGA volunteer said that the Quality Inn was on his route home, and he could drop me off and pick me up the following morning, if I could be ready to leave by 7am the following morning, not ideal but beggars can't be choosers.

I was finding it all a bit of a nightmare until, on the Wednesday afternoon, I was approached by Danny Cink, a USGA official, who told me to get myself suited up.

'What do you mean?' I asked.

'You're in the tournament,' he said. Sean O'Hair had dropped out and I was to take his place. I should have been elated, but I still had a lot on my mind, and after everything that had happened it was hard to get myself up for the experience.

They told me that they had arranged a practise round

for me with Paul Casey, Lee Westwood and Nick Dougherty (although Westwood decided to sit it out). It took us three hours to play nine holes, but that is all these guys do – they play nine holes, hitting shots to the green from all over the place as they had played the other nine holes the previous day.

Casey had heard about my financial plight through the media and, to his eternal credit, offered to give me some money, as did Justin Rose, but I couldn't possibly have accepted. People think that because you are playing in the US Open you must be rolling in money. I provided proof positive that this was not the case, but I wasn't asking for charity either. I guess I'm just too proud for that.

At 5.30pm, my illustrious playing partners walked in from the 9th, leaving me with ninety minutes to play the second nine because I had been told I had to be off the course by 7pm so that the green keepers could get it prepared for the first round the next day. I ended up running round with my Radio Five Live celebrity caddie Andrew Cotter, until I was spotted by a marshall who had a buggy. 'I will buggy you round the last few holes to get you round,' he said. At 7.01pm I was walking off the course and already the staff were getting things ready – they even raked the rough round the greens. The attention to detail is truly amazing in America.

Suddenly, as a player, I was given a courtesy car. In an instant, it seemed that the USGA's attitude towards me had changed completely. While I was still an alternate, I felt like I was something of a nuisance, but now it was all smiles. That didn't impress me too much, I can tell you.

If they had been more frank with me right from the start and told me that they couldn't help me with transport and accommodation, then I could at least have weighed up the options much more effectively. When players take part in The Open, they are offered the services of courtesy drivers who will take them just about anywhere they want to go, and they get help with finding accommodation, even if it is only with a local member. Surely the USGA could have done something like that for me?

It did all end up with me living happily ever after, inasmuch as I was going to be able to play in the US Open, and not many people can say they have done that.

But there was still further confusion is store for me. When you compete in a major such as the US Open, players are given a memento. I had seen this beautiful piece of coloured glass that had the Torrey Pines logo within it, and I got the impression that each player would receive one. I assumed that, as it was so heavy, I did not have to worry about picking it up and that it would be sent to me at home. It was a lovely thing. But then I heard that I wouldn't get one as I was an alternate. In the end, I wasn't really an alternate, so I felt that I had as much right to expect to receive this beautiful piece of glass as Tiger Woods or any other competitor. When my player gift eventually arrived though, it was a ceramic tile measuring twelve inches by twelve inches.

So to the US Open. I played with Hunter Mahan and Richard Sternie and although I hit the ball pretty well, Torrey Pines was too long for me. I failed to break 80 in either round. The greens were small and very, very fast and they were surrounded by thick rough. Because of my lack of length, I found myself hitting three-, five- and seven-wood approach shots to twelve of the greens, and there was little or no chance of stopping the ball on those surfaces with clubs like that. It was an incredibly difficult course on which to make a decent score and, to be honest, if they had given me ten attempts I still wouldn't have made the cut. You have to be able to bomb the golf ball to have a chance of winning there, yet Woods ended up doing so while playing with a broken leg. With the playoff, he carried that injury for five rounds. It was a mind-boggling achievement.

Westwood just missed out on joining Tiger and Rocco Mediate in a playoff, and I have often wondered if he would have done better had he not withdrawn from that practise round when he was scheduled to play with me.

I watched some of the play on Saturday, but then had to catch a plane because I wanted to get back home to take part in the Amateur Championship, which began at Turnberry on the Monday. I somehow managed to get to Turnberry for 6.45pm on the Sunday night, ready to play the following day. I felt like a zombie and, not surprisingly, failed to make the cut.

CHAPTER TWENTY FOUR

FANCY MEETING YOU HERE

I have had some weird and wonderful experiences because of golf. In 1993, I was invited to play in both the Hong Kong and Chinese amateur championships, along with David Fisher, another fine amateur golfer who'd won back-to-back English Amateur titles. I couldn't play in Hong Kong because I couldn't get the time off work, so on the Saturday I arrived in Hong Kong and hooked up with David, who was leading the tournament.

Peter McEvoy was also playing, so the three of us ended up in an Irish bar in Hong Kong, as you do. The next day I watched David win the tournament on a golf course that would have been right up my street – it was tight and short and I was gutted not to have been playing too.

We then had to get to Honichi Golf Club, where the Chinese amateur championship was being played, so we caught the ferry from Hong Kong to China. There were at least 500 people on the boat, and David and I were the only non-Chinese passengers. You can imagine what these people were thinking as the two of us sat there with our golf bags and other luggage. They are incredibly polite people and did everything they could not to make eye contact with us – what made it even more bizarre was that I was so much taller than everybody else on board. I guess you could say that we stuck out like a sore thumb.

When we got to the ferry terminal we realised pretty quickly that nobody spoke English, and that there were no signs in English. Now here we were in mainland China and we hadn't the foggiest idea in which direction we had to go. We wandered around for a while until David spotted a bus with the word 'golf' written on the side of it. It was clearly a tourist bus, and David announced that we were going to get on it, his theory being that when we reached the end of the line there would be a golf course or a golf tournament and that we would be able to make ourselves understood and get directions. Now I know what you are thinking – it was a long shot.

We remained on the bus for more than an hour and discovered a woman on board who spoke English. We told her where we wanted to go and, amazingly, she said that she was certain that she would be able to arrange some transport for us to Honichi. When the bus reached the end of its journey we realised that we were at a brand new golf course that had been designed by Jack Nicklaus and, unbelievably, he was there to open it.

'Gary, what on earth are you doing here?' he said. 'We meet in some funny places.' I wondered just what were the chances of getting on a bus to goodness knows where and finding Jack Nicklaus at the end of the journey? What's more, we even got to watch him giving a golf clinic.

Sure enough, transport was arranged for us to get to Honichi Golf Club, which turned out to be owned by a

Japanese company, and when we got there we were greeted by a highly articulate Japanese man who had attended university in Britain and happened to be a fully-qualified architect, who had somehow got himself into the business of running golf courses.

Honichi was an extraordinary course with a practise ground that was completely covered in netting, but the roof wasn't quite high enough, so if you struck a wedge it would hit the ceiling. Why anybody would ever think that was a good idea I will never know. One of the requirements of being allowed to build this golf course was that the owners had to employ 350 local people, and that also meant housing and feeding them. It is all well and good, but after twenty-five years the whole thing reverts back to Chinese ownership, so I cannot quite figure out how the Japanese make their money from projects such as this, but they obviously do.

We stayed in a Swiss-owned hotel, which, on its approach road, featured a bizarre internal border system that we had to pass through each time we came and went. It was very odd. And we couldn't believe what we saw on the highways – there were four lanes of traffic but unfortunately the roads only had three lanes, so it was routine for people on bikes, or walking by the road, to be 'cleared up' by traffic. There must have been fifty deaths a day on the roads back in those days. God knows what the life expectancy was in that part of the world.

One day our driver got fed up of queuing up in the traffic, and we were running late, so he turned off the road and started driving through what appeared to be people's houses – you see it in the movies, but never believe it can actually happen, but I promise you, David Fisher and I were sitting in the back of a minibus wondering what the hell was going on. People were sitting there minding their own business as we screamed past them, entering by the front door and leaving by the back one. I could have reached out and helped myself to the food they were eating. When we weren't going through their houses we were travelling along a walkway with no room on either side – anybody emerging from a front door wouldn't have stood a chance. How we didn't kill anybody I will never know. Eventually the driver got us back on to the main road without so much as a scratch to the vehicle or anyone we'd encountered.

It was a fun trip. David had won the week before, and neither of us had ever experienced hospitality quite like this. The field comprised mainly golfers from Hong Kong and China, but David and I were far and away the best players.

There was out of bounds on every hole, which was hardly surprising since the course had been carved out of jungle. On some holes there was even out of bounds on both sides of the fairway, but it all suited me because it demanded accurate play. The next time your green keeper complains about his workload, tell him that on this golf course they had women on their hands and knees picking out weeds. The attention to detail was remarkable.

David did not take it too seriously, but I figured that if I had come all this way then I wanted to win. There was an individual prize and there was also a team competition, in which the best two scores counted each day. The problem with the team event, however, was that England were represented by two players (David and I), while China had about fifty players. I shot 67 in the first round, which was a course record. My Chinese partners said: 'Gally, you play like plo...' I then followed that up with a 69 and a 70 and was something like fifteen shots in front of the rest of the field. There were only three golfers who did not go out of bounds during the entire tournament, and I was one of them. Everybody else in a field of around 120 had gone out of bounds at least once.

In the final round it was quite difficult to motivate myself because I was so far ahead, so I spent the eighteen holes watching the two Chinese guys I was playing with battle it out for second place. They were never going to catch me, but finishing second was really important to them, to find out who was going to be the best home player; it mattered to them because the one who finished on top knew that he would be looked after by the Chinese government, and it turned out to be a golfer called Zhang Lian-Wei, who would go on to become the dominant force in Chinese golf for the next fifteen years or so. However, he was only runner-up because the other Chinese player three-putted the final green. There but for the grace of God...

David, meanwhile, shot something like an 84 in the final round and later told me: 'I couldn't stop laughing because the two guys I was playing with were so bad and all three of us spent the round crying with laughter.' We lost the team event by one shot.

I recorded the best round every day, including that course record, and we finished second in the team competition, so I left the place with a bucketful of prizes. I've still got the trophy and the medal I won, but I ended up leaving most of the rest of the things with the Japanese chap who had looked after us so well. As Peter McEvoy would later jokingly point out, I'd become the champion of a billion people.

Then, in 1995, there was a trip to the United Arab

241

Emirates where I played in the UAE Open Amateur Championship. It was played at the Emirates Golf Club, the course where the Dubai Desert Classic is staged. I was leading the tournament, ahead of Mark Murliss from South Africa, who now plays much of his golf in Asia. It was nip and tuck throughout the final round until I opened the door for him by three-putting the sixteenth; by the time we stood on the eighteenth tee he was one ahead of me.

Mark hit the ball a long way. He launched into his final drive and at the top of his voice, in front of a big crowd, he yelled: 'Eat that, Freddie!' I should explain that Fred Couples had won the Desert Classic in 1995 and that he was clearly a hero of Mark's, but it was a strange thing to say. He was obviously very pumped up, but the result was not what he would have wished for: the ball disappeared into the distance and into the trees, having passed through the fairway. I found the latter piece of ground and then hit a five wood short of the water; Mark, on the other hand, had to hack out back towards the fairway, then hit a three iron, but still didn't find the green.

I knew that if I could get my approach close I could maybe make a birdie four and it would get me into a playoff. As it turned out, I hit a sand wedge to eight feet, while he put his fourth shot ten feet from the hole and then missed the putt. I holed mine. It was a two-shot swing and I had won.

The downside was that I was probably the first UAE Open champion not to be invited to play in the Dubai Desert Classic and neither was I given the opportunity to defend my title, because the EGU sent somebody else to play in the event twelve months later.

I have been fortunate to have played golf in some

wonderful places, and there was none more so than Caracas, the capital of Venezuela, where I played in the Bolivar Cup – a two-man team event. One year I partnered Justin Rose and we finished third.

Another year we played in Venezuela's second city, Maracaibo, which was a rather different experience. The humidity was awful and the sweat flowed from every pore the second you walked out into the street. At 7pm it was still almost 90°F, and they had a thunderstorm every night, without fail. The hotel was not good either, and we had to have armed guards because we were close to the Colombian border. Whenever we got onto the team bus, police outriders accompanied us, which was all very scary. It turned out that a European family had been kidnapped in the area and held to ransom only a few weeks before.

My partner in Maracaibo was Graeme Storm and neither of us would ever forget the course – they had sewn fairway grass on the greens, so it is fair to say that the putting surfaces were not the best either of us had ever experienced. It was like putting on a shag-pile carpet and, needless to say, Graeme and I both struggled. There were lots of bonuses to playing golf in Venezuela, however, and right at the top of the list were the women, who were all drop-dead gorgeous.

I played in the Bolivar Cup several times, and finally won it in Caracus in 2001 with Graeme Clark as my partner. Ireland finished second, mainly thanks to Graeme McDowell, who won the individual competition. I always felt that McDowell always looked slightly vulnerable on the greens but he was, and is, a truly great golfer who has achieved phenomenal things – as was shown by his wonderful victory at the 2010 US Open at Pebble Beach. The organisers called the Bolivar Cup the 'world pairs' and we were more than happy to go along with that. It always ended with an amazing party when they arranged for lots of beautiful women to come along and dance with the players. I ended up doing the twist at full throttle and nearly gave myself a heart attack. We were looked after really well.

Venezuela is a country where, I was told, nine per cent of the population possess ninety-nine per cent of the wealth, but I would like to think that we made some kind of contribution, even if it was only to make people who would otherwise know nothing about golf aware of the game. One of the highlights of the trip in 2001 was our visit to the British embassy and meeting 'our man in Venezuela'. In my dad's day, the golfers frequently had to do things like clamber into a log boat and travel along a crocodile-infested river to get to a golf course in the middle of nowhere in some African country that almost nobody had ever heard of – Venezuela had that tinge of exoticness to it too.

During those trips I was effectively representing England, so my expenses were covered by the English Golf Union. To be frank, if they hadn't paid for me to go on those tours I would never have been able to make them. It was a relief not to have to worry about plane fares and hotel bills.

Representing Europe was special, too. The first time I did so was in the Bonallack Trophy, in which I played four times, visiting the likes of Perth, Madrid and Auckland in the process. The first Bonallack Trophy match was played in Perth, where there were kangaroos wandering about the course. Perth is a beautiful city. It is all too easy when you are playing golf to get trapped in a bubble and you could end up heading for home without having seen anything of the area in which you have been playing, but I always made a point of going for a walk and trying to soak it all in, especially as I got older. And I did that in Perth. What a place, and what a climate. Justin Rose was in that team, too, and we won just about every match we played.

I went to Auckland with young Oliver Fisher when he was still in secondary school. He was mature way beyond his years on the golf course and I felt lucky to see such a prodigious young talent up close. I would also like to think that he might have learnt something from playing with me too, watching the way I managed my game. I was on the winning side in three of the four matches I played in the Bonallack Trophy and that clearly left me with happy memories. The Europeans appreciated having me along because I was able to add my experience and give them some advice about foursomes, pairings and suchlike.

Outside of what would be classed as the 'major' amateur championships, one of my favourite events was the Finnish Amateur, played in Helsinki every year. The first time I took part in the tournament I went with Paul Broadhurst and another international, Bob Bardsley. It was held in August and was a mixed event, with a men's and women's tournament running alongside each other on the same course. I finished fourth or fifth the first time I took part and I loved it so much that I kept going back until eventually, in 1996, I won it. I also loved the idea of men's and women's tournaments being held together. I do not understand why so few women play golf in Great Britain – female golf seems to be dying a death. It doesn't help that most top amateurs do not want to play golf with women – they don't know what they are missing. There was something about Finland that clearly agreed with me: I also won the Finnish Amateur Nations Trophy in 1993, 1995, 1996, 1999 and 2003.

One of my most memorable journeys to an event was while I was on my way to take part in the Jones Cup, which is a seventy-two-hole strokeplay tournament played at the exclusive Ocean Forest course at Sea Island in America with a field that is comprised of potential British and American Walker Cup golfers. It was an amazing event played on a great course, and all we had to do was get there.

We were meant to be flying to Atlanta and then on to Savannah in Georgia. We were all blissfully unaware of the fact that as we were crossing the Atlantic there was a fire in the cockpit, so we had to make an emergency landing in Newfoundland, and were greeted by ambulances and fire engines in attendance on the tarmac. It was a pretty hairy moment.

We were told that we would have to stay at St Johns airport for nine hours before getting onto another flight to Atlanta, but once we got in the air were told that Atlanta was fog-bound, so we had to divert to JFK in New York before finally getting our flight to Savannah, which just about left us with enough time for a practise round before the event.

Golf has taken me all over the world – Newfoundland, the United States, Chile, Venezuela, Australia, Argentina, New Zealand, South Africa, the Philippines, China, Kazakhstan, Malaysia, Hong Kong, UAE, Finland, Sweden, Denmark, Portugal, Spain, Greece, Luxembourg, Switzerland, Italy, France, Germany, Holland and Belgium.

In 1998, I lost in a playoff to Brett Rumford in the Lake Macquarie tournament in Australia, and that was very frustrating because I holed a great putt on the eighteenth green and he came in and announced, 'I couldn't have played any better than that,' when in fact I felt as though I couldn't have played much worse.

He produced a brilliant up and down for a half on the first playoff hole, we both parred the second but on the third hole I went through the back of the green while he ended up ten feet away. I chipped back and missed my par, and he two-putted to win. It was a tournament I should have won, and I was not happy to have missed out.

But I did win in Australia: the New South Wales Centenary Open at Terry Hills, playing some wonderful golf to beat Tim Stewart, the local hero 2&1. I had lost it the year before at the 37th when my opponent Won Jun Lee hit just about the longest drive I had ever seen, threading it between two bunkers and onto the green on a par four that measured not far short of 400 yards.

My father had made his mark in this part of the world, so during the New South Wales Centenary Open the organisers arranged for a host of former winners to come along, including an eighty-seven-year-old, who was the oldest surviving winner. The problem was that they put on a lunch that took place in the middle of the final's two rounds, and it didn't do Tim any good. I also had lots of elderly Australians who had been top amateur golfers in their day, patting me on the back, telling me they had known my father, and wishing me luck against Tim. Wherever I have gone and the subject of Guy Wolstenholme has come up I have always been struck by how highly people have spoken of him.

I always grabbed with both hands the opportunity to play warm-weather golf in the winter. Nick Dougherty used to spend three months at the David Leadbetter Academy in

Florida during the non-summer months and when he came back people would comment on how well he was swinging the club. Of course he was – he hadn't had to cope with 70 mph wind and driving rain or winter greens. Before the days of the England squad sessions abroad, there were always individual players, such as Freddie George, who had friends with houses in Spain, so they would clear off and play golf in the sunshine, and it always meant they were better prepared at the start of each season. They had also come through the junior ranks, whereas I never did, so I was always at a slight disadvantage.

Luke Donald attended university in Chicago, which is usually snow-bound for three months of the year, and I could never figure out how he managed to keep his swing in shape, until I discovered that his university had an indoor facility that allowed players to strike full shots into a net 150 yards away, which gives you all the feedback a good player really needs. All I could do in England during a snowbound British winter was to pound hundreds of golf balls outdoors into a net, and I used to do that quite happily.

While winning tournaments all over the world, I have picked up some pretty unusual prizes. There are those who would question the sartorial elegance of the yellow jackets that go to the winner of the Sherry Cup, and if I hadn't won the event four times (although I only have three yellow jackets for some reason), then I might agree. I have been awarded so-called silver salvers that a) were not made of silver, b) were not salvers and c) should have been thrown straight into the nearest bin too. My motto is, if it's worth doing, do it properly.

I have won prestigious events and been given no keepsake of any kind, and have had to find a local shop where I could buy my own souvenir. I got a CD player for winning the Finnish Amateur one year – some people may look upon this as an odd prize, but at least it was something I could take home and use.

Why do so many tournament organisers give golf bags to the winners? Trust me, if you are a decent amateur golfer, you already have a good golf bag. I often think that it provides an excuse for the club pro to get rid of stock he no longer wants. Far better, surely, to give the winner some vouchers for M&S or Asda so that he or she can pick up something they actually would like to have.

I have had thirteen holes-in-one, with five of them coming in competition. My first ever such achievement was performed on the second hole at Grange-over-Sands when I was about thirteen years old and my first in competition occurred during qualifying for the Amateur Championship on the twelfth hole at Prestwick. The one that gave me greatest satisfaction, however, came at the fourteenth hole on the New Course at Sunningdale during the British Mid-Amateur Championship final. I hit a perfect four iron and my opponent, Simon Vale, watched it drop into the hole, put his ball on the tee, and said: 'So, this for a half then, Gary?'

My lowest-ever round in competition was a 62 in the Midland Mid-Amateur in 2001 played at Brampton Park, which was a tight, tricky course that I had never seen before. I had three eagles, which always helps the scorecard. At one stage I thought I might be on for a 59, but I had at least one bogey, and that put paid to that. My lowest-ever score was at the Leicestershire Golf Club in a friendly game when I shot a 60 that included a three putt bogie at the ninth and a missed putt from eight feet, straight up the hill, on the eighteenth. I knew it was for a 59, and I was gutted to miss it. I was so upset that I couldn't speak for fully twenty minutes. How many chances do you get in your entire life to break 60?

You might remember that I told you about taking the assistant professional to the cleaners in various short-game challenges. His name was Adrian Jones and he was the guy marking my card that day. I beat him by thirteen shots. A month earlier, I had gone round the same course in 62, six-under par. It may only have been a par 68, but it was still a tough course.

CHAPTER TWENTY FIVE
RHYTHM OF LIFE

For me, preparation is, and always has been, everything. It may help you to work out how I tick when I tell you that I am a great believer in the power of biorhythms, apart from having faith in other things. I heard about them for the first time from somebody in Leicester and although I could easily have dismissed it as poppycock, and you may well do the same, I decided to look into the subject and came to the conclusion that there had to be something in it.

I did some research and discovered that my personal biorhythms were at their peak during February and again in August, and those periods coincided pretty much exactly with when I tended to play my best golf. Not only would I have my best scores in early February and again in late summer, but that was always when I usually felt at my best too, and when I would always strike the ball better than at any other time of year.

I knew that it was no coincidence, and soon discovered that you could actually do something to help yourself perform better at other times too, by studying how the three rhythms interconnected. When your energy levels are low, it is imperative that you eat the right kind of food, and when you are emotionally down you should wear the right colour of clothing. In my case, power colours such as red, bright blue and yellow helped. Then, if you're on an intellectual low, you should go through things twice to make sure you are not making an unforced error.

It is possible to check your biorhythms online, and I do so on a regular basis and plan my preparation around them. Green is not a good colour for me, which was not great news when I was playing for Leicestershire, because it was the county colour, but I read a few books and soon discovered, to my absolute delight, that the traditional Leicestershire colours should actually have been red and black. Armed with that news, I mounted a campaign and lobbied every county official until eventually it was agreed that the official colours should indeed be red and black, and they still are to this day.

I also believe that, in a team environment, it is essential to identify your players' star signs and, where possible, pair together golfers whose signs are compatible. Again, some of you may think this is nonsense, but I can only speak from personal experience and I am certain that it works. The other thing, of course, is that if you believe something will work for you then it probably will.

What's more I have always collected lucky markers, fortune charms etc, and without exception have felt desolate if I lost one. I picked up a 100 peso coin in Chile when I was there with the GB&I team to play in the Eisenhower Trophy and I was devastated when I lost it. When I went abroad, I was also always a sucker for picking up lucky charms and putting them in my bag. I felt sorry for anybody who ever caddied for me, because my bag was always so heavy.

Then I would pick up a pair of scissors, because you never know when you will need a pair – at one time I must have had five pairs of scissors. It was the same with pencils. I had at least 30. And I always had problems when I knew that I was going to be travelling abroad because there are certain foodstuffs that I will not do without, so I would arrive at check-in and my luggage would be four kilos over the allowed weight, almost entirely because I had packed in energy bars and boxes of cereal, just in case I couldn't get them at the other end.

I love any gadget that might help me play the game better, so I will try special tees that claim to provide less resistance than the normal ones and which claim to give you three per cent extra distance, and I was one of the leading supporters of allowing golfers to use a laser measuring device to work out distances to the flag, because I figured that if everybody had one then it must surely speed up play. However, the problem is now that all golfers are allowed to use them, they still take until the middle of next week to make a club selection. They now know the precise distance they are from the pin, but then they have to work out the wind direction, the air temperature, and whether or not the ball will stop dead on the putting surface it seems, so perhaps we have gained nothing at all.

I picked up a Y-shaped gadget that allowed me to rest the grip of a club on it while I was practising with another club, but then I realised I could just as easily rest the club on a tee peg. Golf pros rub their hands together in delight when I walk into their shops because they know there will always be something in stock that I have not seen or tried before.

Then there were the coaches. Nobody has ever taken my swing apart and rebuilt it, but throughout my golf career a number of professionals have helped me keep my swing in tune and to change things as and when I had needed to.

The first professional I consulted was Richard Emery at Keighley Golf Club, but during those formative years I also used to go and see an old golf pro, Herbert Jolly at Branshaw GC, who always used to walk around wearing white plimsolls, and was a real character. Bert, as he liked to be known, played in the 1927 Ryder Cup matches – he showed me the medal he received to mark the achievement. Talk about being thrown a curve ball. I was gobsmacked. He was in his late seventies by the time I saw him, and he showed me the basics, plus a few useful trick shots to get me out of trouble. He was a great guy.

After a particularly poor tournament, Jennifer Prentice recommended a professional called Brian Mudge and I went to see him in 1987 and was coached by him for three years. He was very enthusiastic, but I knew the time had come for us to go our separate ways when, during the last lesson I ever had with him, he said, 'Listen Gary, other than keep working on the stuff we have been doing there is not much more we need to do.' On the way home, I reached the conclusion that there had to be more to it than that, and still felt I had more to do before reaching top level.

In August 1991 I won the Amateur Championship, and by now I was living in Bristol. The month after my victory I got a phone call from Peter Thompson, a club pro based at Farrington, not far from the town, and he said he was certain he could help me hit the ball further and better, so I went along to see him. At the time, he was in the process of building a golf course and was giving lessons in what amounted to a large barn.

Everything was done on video and he was able to analyse

every part of my golf swing in minute detail; at the time, it was really innovative and the two of us clicked. I would hit a shot, he would tape it, and we would watch it back on video, which meant I could see how I was swinging the club and it was easy for him to explain how he thought I could improve things, saying things such as: 'Try this move, Gary. Try that move.' It was ideal for me. I loved going away and working on things, hitting ball after ball until it became second nature.

It took a long while before I was able to do much of what he wanted me to, but eventually it became ingrained. And what he had told me right at the start turned out to be correct. He was able to get me hitting the ball better. Peter and I worked together for about seven years, the first five on a regular basis, and the last two as and when I could see him.

Eventually he lost his golf club business, which was very sad, and he moved to Bournemouth, which brought our relationship to an end. I then also moved back to Leicestershire and eventually hooked up with David Ridley, the England coach, who could not have been more different. Whereas Peter Thompson had been almost entirely dependent upon his video analysis, David was all about feel and touch. Between the two of them, I could find only one word that sums up what they meant to me – genius! Different types of coaching styles, yes, but they both transformed my game and taught me how to strike the ball properly. I was incredibly lucky to have worked with them.

David helped me out for the best part of eight years, but it was an on-and-off relationship and I certainly never reached the point where I was seeing him once or twice a week, fifty-two weeks of the year, as I had with Peter. David was very knowledgeable though in lots of ways, because he had been a good tour player himself and I believe that if you can find a top coach who has also been a top golfer then you are blessed. It is the perfect scenario.

Peter Cowan was a coach I saw a couple of times through the EGU, but he was too cerebral for me, and I struggled to grasp what he wanted me to do. However, he is recognised as being one of the best in the business and has worked with a host of top European Tour golfers, but you need to be on the same wavelength to have a successful relationship. So basically not everyone can work with all types of people is what I'm saying.

Latterly, I have tried to figure things out for myself. By now, I know my golf swing pretty much inside out and I know what is likely to go wrong with it. I do go and see a couple of local pros in my area, particularly Simon Fletcher at Morecambe Golf Club or Ryan Done at Heysham Golf Club, who are good friends and who both have a good eye for the swing. The problem is that top coaches are very expensive: David Ridley used to charge me almost £60 a pop, and there are coaches who charge an awful lot more than that. Peter Thompson, on the other hand, never charged me for a lesson, but I was happy for him to use me as an example of what he might be able to achieve with a semi-talented pupil. I need to get my own house, put up a net and video my swing – then I will be able to watch it back and iron out the kinks as they come along.

My father gave me a list of tips, most of which still hold good today. He was a great teacher, as well as being a highly talented player. Like me, he always kept the ball in play, hit his irons well and was great around the greens. I would have loved to have had his input on my game more in the early stages of my career.

CHAPTER TWENTY SIX

YOU CAN QUOTE ME ON THAT

I haven't always enjoyed a trouble-free relationship with the media. Ahead of The Open at Royal St George's in 2003 I was asked what I thought about my chances of making the cut and playing all four rounds.

After talking about Royal St George's, journalist Mark Reason asked me what I thought were the chances of success of the various young golfers I had played with in the Walker Cup. Did I believe that any of them could go on and win majors?

We went through a list of names and then came to Nick Dougherty. I knew the kind of golf he was capable of playing, because I had partnered him to win the Juan Carlos Talihide Cup in Argentina in 2000. We ended up in a playoff with teams from Finland and South Africa, and it was being shown live on TV. Nick played the hole first, along with the first South African and Finnish players and they all parred it. So all eyes were now on me and the other South African and Finn. I was about to play my second shot and decided to hit a six iron, but the cameraman was standing about 15 feet away from me, blocking my view to the flag, so I had to ask him to move. I hit the ball and knew immediately that it was a good shot, but even I didn't think it was going to finish six inches away. I tapped it in, we won and Nick and I enjoyed a great celebration. Nick played well all week, but he had missed a putt in regulation play to win the thing for us, so he was mightily relieved.

But I had heard that it was thought that he had perhaps lost his focus since turning professional.

I told Reason that Dougherty had always enjoyed the high life, liked to go out at night and have a drink or two and enjoyed the company of pretty girls. Nothing I said was untrue, but Nick's management company took exception to it and got Nick to write a letter, the gist of which was: 'You don't know me now. I am not like that any more. I have got a girlfriend and you have put that relationship in jeopardy.'

I thought to myself: 'The only person who could possibly jeopardise your relationship with your girlfriend is you.' But I bit my tongue. The irony was that Nick would later admit in the *Daily Mail* that he had taken his eye off the ball and that he had partied too hard.

The last thing that I ever wanted to do was to upset Nick. He was a great guy and I told him: 'Listen Nick, I am your biggest fan. Outside of your family, there is nobody who is keener than me to see you do really well. You have to remember that golf is a very jealous mistress and unless you give her your full attention you are not going to achieve the goal you outwardly set for yourself, which was to become World Number One.'

Sadly it would seem that he will never become the best player in the world because unless things change dramatically there are too many other great players in the way, including one Tiger Woods. Tiger had total focus and dedication on the job of being the best when he arrived on the scene and declared his intention to beat Jack Nicklaus's record of eighteen majors. Whether Tiger still has that total focus these days, or will ever have it again, is of course open to question.

Some players take you by surprise. I hadn't expected Lee Westwood to become as good as he has. It seems that every time he plays now he is in contention to win. Ross Fisher is another golfer who has done better than I thought he would so quickly – I always knew he possessed talent, but my gut feeling was that he turned professional too quickly and I am delighted he has proved me wrong. He should have won The Open at Turnberry in 2009, but his time will come, because not only does he hit the ball long and straight, but he is also a fabulous iron player and is becoming a decent putter too.

I took Justin Rose to see Peter Thompson, my own coach who helped me so much, when Rose was still only sixteen. Peter watched him hit a few shots and then said: 'Justin, am I right in saying that your bad shot is almost always a snap hook?' Rose confirmed that it was, and Peter told him what he needed to do to eliminate it. However, when I watch Justin playing now I still see him making the same fundamental mistakes and his bad shot remains a duck hook. Although a recent change of coach has helped him to start to take the world by storm again. As for a major I wouldn't bet against it.

Oliver Fisher could still be a world-beater, even though he lost his Tour card in 2009. When he joined the professional ranks, he was still growing and developing and probably needed a new set of clubs every six months or so.

It is interesting to note that now he has stopped growing, he has found a level of consistency that will surely take him to the top of the game – if he gets the breaks and believes in his own ability.

Forget the jokes about policemen seemingly getting younger all the time, I had to laugh when I saw Rory McIlroy being interviewed and he cut it short with the words: 'Sorry, but I have to go because I need to pick my girlfriend up from school.' McIlroy has one of the best, if not the best, golf swings I have seen, but his fallibility seems to be on the greens and he needs to find a way to work that out. As long as he can cope with the expectation on his shoulders, he could well become World Number One.

I was worried about Rhys Davies initially, because I could not understand why he didn't make his mark straight away. I am not worried about him now though. What a great all round game he has! Then there is Chris Wood, who is the tallest player on tour at 6ft 6in, but is the best putter I have ever seen. He works very hard and will get his rewards in time. Sam Hutsby is another young man I expect big things from and, yet again, he is another who has wasted no time in making a successful transition from the amateur to the professional game.

Simon Dyson and Danny Willett are hyperactive individuals who need to find a way of controlling the energy that flows through their veins. Simon has already won, and will pick up more titles, and I am convinced Danny will do the same. When these guys get in the zone they are all but unbeatable.

I saw Sergio Garcia as a teenager and, like everybody else, thought he would win ten majors. I couldn't believe that after five years he still hadn't won one, and now I wonder if he ever will. Probably not. One year I watched him playing in the Sherry Cup and he had a simple pitch and run left, but chose to take his lob wedge and toss the ball miles in the air for an up and down on the 18th green and a one-shot win. Why? Just because he could. During the Spanish Amateur Championship at Valderamma, he gave his opponent a twelve-foot putt for par and then holed an eighteen-footer for a birdie. Pretty demoralising for his opponent. Not many golfers strike the ball better than the Spaniard, but he has suffered terribly on the greens and you always get the impression that he feels the entire world is conspiring against him at times too.

Warren Bennett was the best amateur golfer I ever played with. Bar none. He had every shot in the bag. We played eleven foursomes matches together and won every single one of them. He hit the ball a long way, he was wonderful with his irons, short and long, and had a wondrous touch around the greens. He turned pro, suffered some injury problems and lost confidence. He finished as leading amateur in The Open and when Sir Michael Bonallack predicted Warren would go on to become Open champion within ten years, nobody batted an eyelid. We all agreed. He even had the perfect fifteenth club in the bag, namely an ideal temperament and a brilliant golfing brain.

I don't like the way the media starts to look for scapegoats and questions when we are next going to produce somebody who is good enough to win a major. Westwood, Fisher, Paul Casey, Ian Poulter, Justin Rose, Rory McIlroy and yes, even Nick Dougherty, are all good enough to win any of the four majors, but it doesn't mean that they will. Getting into the top fifty in the world rankings is hard enough, and you need to be there before you get into the majors and all the World Golf Championship tournaments.

Look at what happened to Colin Montgomerie (Monty). To win a major, everything needs to come together, and then you need a bit of luck as well. Westwood played brilliantly in the 2010 Masters, but he could do nothing about the amazing final round of golf produced by Phil Mickelson.

Monty did not win a major because of the constant pressure he was put under by the British media. Every time he walked into a press conference he was asked the same question: 'Monty, you have won all these European Order of Merit titles – when are you going to win a major? Monty, what was it like to lose the US Open at Pebble Beach?'

In my view, there is an element among the British press that did not want Colin to succeed, and they almost rejoiced in his failures. It makes me sad. It all built up in Monty's head, I guess, so that when he stood in the middle of the seventy-second fairway with a seven iron in his hand needing only a par four to win the 2006 US Open at Winged Foot it just all became too much for him.

Yes, he may be mentally fragile, but the press knew that, so why didn't they just leave him alone? They always knew that if he'd had a bad round he would explode if the wrong buttons were pushed, and the media knew which buttons to push to get the reaction they wanted. In this country, the media seems to take pleasure from building up sports stars and then looking for the first opportunity to knock them down. Tennis player Andy Murray is the latest target. Why?

It worries me that journalists could perhaps destroy professional golf. I know that when it became clear Tiger Woods had been having a series of affairs, it was understandable that people wanted to read all about it. He is the most instantly recognisable athlete on the planet and his reputation has been built on his supposed love and respect for family values, so it was obviously a huge story, but get it written and then move on. He has clearly suffered all sorts of mental agonies and should now be left alone to try and pick up the pieces. Let's write about his golf instead of 'killing the golden goose'.

Woods has had to live with media attention all his life. I got a small taste of what he had to put up with when I was on the practise ground at Torrey Pines before the US Open in 2008. Tiger was hitting balls a few yards away from me and the press were falling over themselves to get a better view – TV and radio crews, and newspaper and magazine journalists, all fighting with one another to get the best view, and to hear every word he exchanged with his caddie, Steve Williams. It was like the attention The Beatles got in their heyday. I found it fascinating that he wasn't put off by all the commotion surrounding him.

CHAPTER TWENTY SEVEN

TOO MANY COOKS...

There are many things wrong with the game. For a start, there are too many organisations 'in charge' of developing the sport. There should be just one or two, so as not to waste precious resources. At present we have the new English Golf Partnership, Golf England, the R&A, the Golf Foundation and Faldo Junior Series to name but a few. I was involved with the English Golf Union for more than twenty years, but they have never asked me for my help in effectively contributing to the future of the game, which is pretty disappointing. I would have thought that as I'm the most capped golfer of all time, and given the knowledge I have of the amateur game, they might have thought I had something worthwhile to contribute.

There is also a lack of understanding of the basic rules and etiquette of the game, because so many clubs are desperate for new members and do not take the time and trouble to ensure that those new members have a grasp of what is expected of them. Take their money by all means, but make sure they know how they are supposed to

behave, both on and off the course, and then everybody
will benefit.

I was very surprised that the USGA and the R&A did not
grasp the nettle properly at the start of 2010 over the
question of grooves too. They have gone from box grooves
on irons to bevelled box-grooves, but there is hardly any
difference at all, and the leading players are still getting
more than enough backspin, especially the men who hit the
ball hard. They should have decreed a return to the v-
shaped grooves of the 1960s and '70s.

I remember Mark Calcavecchia winning The Open in
1989 and Jack Nicklaus and Tom Watson leading the
protests against the Ping irons he used, claiming that they
gave him an unfair advantage; but within six months both
men were also using irons with the same box-shaped
grooves. If we are going to make changes, do it properly and
bring back control, course management, skill and nerve.

Let's get one thing straight here – for the average club
golfer, the shape of the groove in his or her iron makes
virtually no difference. The game is hard enough for them
without finding ways of making it more difficult, and that
also applies to what is being done to golf courses. Is it
necessary for every golf course to be 7,800 yards long to be
a great test? Of course not. Why not introduce new hazards
in strategic places, create more doglegs and tighter fairways
for championships? Golf courses can be defended in all sorts
of ways other than by creating 500-plus yard par fours and
300-yard par threes which ruin perfectly good holes and
perfectly good courses.

The governing bodies have perhaps something to answer
for – when the US Open was played at Bethpage in 2002 for
example, Nick Faldo couldn't reach the twelfth fairway off

the tee, and the seeming obsession with length also ultimately undid the career of Nick Price too, among others. He is a wonderful striker of the ball but a man who could not hit it into the middle of next week. When Paul McGinley was asked what shot he would most like to have in the bag, he replied: 'The 320-yard drive.' This is a fabulous golfer, a man who won the Ryder Cup for Europe in 2002. It's a sad indictment on what the powers-that-be have allowed to happen to the game.

When people go to watch The Open, they do not want to see the greatest players in the world struggling to make pars; they want to be inspired, and that will only happen if they are watching professionals hit great shots and hole putts for birdies and eagles on a fairly set course, not on some 'marathon assault course' where just getting pars is considered good on virtually every hole.

Some people argue that it's the development of the golf ball that has ruined the game, but I would say that we have gone about as far as we can with golf ball technology. To mark the centenary of Bristol and Clifton Golf Club, myself and Peter McEvoy took on Tommy Horton and Brian Barnes using ancient and modern equipment. Peter and I had modern clubs and balls while Tommy and Brian used gutta percha balls and hickory shafted clubs. After three holes they had to abandon all idea of using the gutta percha balls because they couldn't compete, even off the forward tees. As soon as they starting using a modern ball they were able to hit it almost as far as Peter and I, and they were still using wooden-shafted clubs. It made me wonder how Henry Cotton managed to shoot a 65 in The Open all those years ago with a ball that wasn't even round and went probably two thirds as far.

I believe with a passion that golf should be fun. Club memberships, generally speaking, are dwindling and some people will try to tell you that it's because it is expensive to join a club, but that isn't really true. On average it costs the equivalent of about £15 per week to join a golf club, and that represents great value for money in my opinion. So I believe we should look at the other reasons for the reduced interest.

In terms of the rules, I wouldn't change much, other than trying to stamp down on slow play. Etiquette is vital and that includes teaching people the rules, encouraging them to repair pitch marks and to rake bunkers, making sure they know that they should wave faster players through and ensuring they know they are expected to dress smartly. Ensure they know cheating in any form will not be tolerated, that they should never throw golf clubs, and need to respect their fellow players. I regret that the world's number one, Tiger Woods, has not set a great example these last few years either, in respect of the number of times he's seen to spit during a round – which should not be tolerated.

At some clubs, new members are not allowed on the course until they have had two or three lessons with the club professional to make sure they know how to 'play the game' out on the course – what a great idea that is. I have often stood on a tee watching the people in front looking for a golf ball. It is almost as if they think: 'There's no way I am letting him through.' They should just step out of the way and call me through, because you can be sure that I will not hold you up. Maybe they just don't know that's what they should do?

Golf is a unique game. How many other sports are there where you can talk to your opponent and have a laugh and a joke all the way round? I don't mean to sound sexist, but women should love golf because it gives them a chance to be with their friends for three and four hours in a lovely alfresco environment and be able to chat away to their hearts content, without a husband or boyfriend urging them to be quiet. On top of that, there's a whole host of men who also play the game at the same club, many of whom don't have wives and almost all of whom have disposable income.

Women will also almost always let a group of men through because they want to enjoy their round of golf and not feel as though they are being pushed, while with men the game is always about ultra-competitive machismo I suppose. And you will find that it is men who spend ages going through pre-shot routines that don't help them in the slightest, whereas women will generally walk up to the ball, take one practise swing and then send it on its way. This is golf as it was meant to be played, and how it should be played.

In the next five or ten years, unless the game can identify a way to attract new players to become members, I expect to see a whole host of golf clubs in trouble.

Some years ago a development company offered to build a new course for the members of Glen Gorse Golf Club near Leicester, complete with a brand new clubhouse and all the other facilities you would expect to find at a modern club, including a driving range, in return for being allowed to buy the land that the existing course stood on. The new venue would have been seven miles away, but that was nothing in the grand scheme of things. It was voted out because the senior members couldn't see any benefit to them. With most clubs having high numbers of golfers aged fifty-plus, it will always be tricky getting new ideas like this through, unless those senior guys are progressive in their thinking. On the other side of the coin, Kirby Muxloe Golf Club has been extremely clever in buying and selling prime development land, and has plenty of money in the bank.

I was disappointed with the way amateur golf was going in the end. The English Golf Union implied to me that the England team would in future be comprised of young men up to the age of twenty-five, although the truth is that most of them would probably be a lot younger than that. In other words, it would purely provide a breeding ground for young professionals who would go on the various tours. They would battle their way into the England team, play in one Walker Cup match, two at the most, and then turn pro at the first available opportunity and go in search of the millions of pounds, dollars, yen and euros on offer around the world. And who could blame them?

If that is what they want, then so be it, but it was not why I played for England, it was not why I played in all those Walker Cup matches, and it was not why I won two Amateur Championships. If somebody shows talent at thirty years of age, they should be encouraged by the English Golf Union. However the chance of a British person of thirty years plus winning a major amateur is very unlikely indeed, as the young guns in the national squad are groomed for stardom twelve months a year, and are virtually unbeatable en masse by a 'part timer' who works for a living. In this day and age 'amateur' no longer truly reflects that status in British Amateur golf.

Yes, I am outspoken, forthright and opinionated, and have always spoken my mind and perhaps that is why I was never particularly embraced by anybody. On the other hand, I have always congratulated fellow players when they have hit good form or won a major event. I know there are people within amateur golf who are not fans of Gary Wolstenholme, but perhaps if they had got to know me better they might have seen more of the good side. Because I was never the most talented of players, I had to grind and sweat blood to achieve everything I have. It was never easy, so it wasn't possible for me to swan around being chirpy and smiling all the time. It was hard work for me, pure and simple. I honestly don't think many people truly understood that.

CHAPTER TWENTY EIGHT
ENJOYING THE JOURNEY

I believe that my life has been a journey where each day I learn more about myself and what 'life' actually means, and has been a fascinating learning experience to get me to where I am at now. I turned professional late in years because amateur golf had no further use for me. However, as one door shuts, others open.

Hopefully, I can compete on the European Seniors Tour and make a decent go of it and perhaps head across the Atlantic and spend some time on the Champions Tour too – variety is the spice of life. If I can do that, who knows what I might be able to achieve? I have no intentions of making any rash predictions though because I don't want to put undue pressure on myself, and I also know how unpredictable fate can be.

You will have worked out by now that I love to compete and that I enjoy the special challenge presented by matchplay golf. Sadly, there are no opportunities for professional senior golfers to play in matchplay events, but I live in hope that somebody will eventually see that there could be a huge demand for a Senior Ryder Cup, and if it happens, and if I am really, really lucky, I may get the chance to play in it. What a mouth-watering prospect. Give Tony Jacklin the job of captaining the European team, and what a team it could be, with the likes of Bernhard Langer, Ian Woosnam, Sam Torrance, Sandy Lyle and Nick Faldo all qualified to play. Name Jack Nicklaus as captain of the American team, and what a team he would have to choose from – Tom Watson, Fred Couples, Jay Haas, Kenny Perry, Fred Funk. It's a very exciting thought, don't you think?

There is no doubt in my mind that it would capture the imagination of the golfing public and that sponsors would lap it up. I am amazed that it hasn't happened yet, but I hope that it becomes a reality and that I might get the opportunity to take part in it.

It's a cliché, I know, but I believe that everything in life happens for a reason and the important thing is the way you deal with things as they unfold. It is not the journey that is important; it is the person you become along the way.

Many people have hard journeys, don't learn from them and become bitter and twisted; whereas I hope that the opposite is true of me. I have done things I am not proud of, but I have learnt from those mistakes and tried to become a better person. I believe you cannot ask more of any human being. I am fair-minded, I am always prepared to learn and I am always prepared to listen. If I believe that something is right and somebody proves that it isn't, then I will take on the new perspective. I also believe I can give good advice to people, although individuals don't always listen. There is nothing I can do about that.

I am destined to achieve something great in my life. I don't know what it is yet, but I am pretty sure that it is something I have yet to do. Perhaps it is to help the game develop, or to assist somebody to become World Number One. I can now put something back into the game, to pass on the knowledge and skills I have picked up, but who knows except the 'big fella' up above?

I am involved with a project run through the University of Central Lancashire that helps to find people careers in golf, and I have been able to use my extensive list of contacts to point people in the right direction, both at home and abroad. It looks as though they are going to set up a base in Cyprus, complete with a golf course and practise facilities, as well as full educational requirements too. It means that students will be offered year-round opportunities to play golf and learn about the game, including course design, construction and management.

The challenge that lies ahead is a difficult one. For a start, not many new Tour cards are made available each season, which makes it very difficult for new players such as myself to make the breakthrough. The other thing is that golfers who have graduated from the main European Tour tend to start working harder as they approach their fiftieth birthday because they realise they have an opportunity to earn some serious pension money. Golfers such as Tommy Horton, Neil Coles and Carl Mason earned far more as seniors than they ever did on the European Tour.

There seems to be tremendous camaraderie among the guys on the Seniors Tour and I guess part of the reason for that is that a lot of them feel able to relax because they have already made their millions, so every putt is not a matter of life and death.

I also know that I have to be prepared to take advantage of any chances that come my way outside of playing the game, such as more commentary work, but that may not happen. I have lots of ideas about equipment, even down to things such as golf bags, but it's all a question of being given the money to develop those thoughts. I have been in and around the game all my life, so if I am not qualified to design, say, the best golf bag, I can't think who would be. Some golf clothing is atrocious – it can't be rocket science to design clothes that golfers would want to wear. In fact course design, writing or running events, there are a myriad of things I can do given the chance. It just takes the right first step to begin the next journey.

I love golf and everything about the game, and as long as I feel that I am able to continue playing to a good standard I will strive to improve, but the moment I feel my game is in decline, I will hang up the clubs for good. I have no desire to see my scores climb, and the way that I feel now, I will never want to play to a fourteen handicap. I take my hat off to Gary Player, who works as hard now as he did in his prime and still manages to find a way to score.

Like everybody else my age I suffer from various aches and pains and have a back problem that goes back to an accident I had as a child. From time to time I suffer such severe discomfort that I have had to withdraw from tournaments – I had to miss the English Amateur championship one year, and on another occasion had to pull out of the Sherry Cup. I used to hit hundreds of golf balls every day and I just can't do that anymore, but I simply have to accept that. I seldom play golf without taking painkillers first. The sad fact is that I have pushed my body too hard in pursuit of perfection.

The likes of Carlos Franco and Colin Montgomerie

practise less than I do, and it hardly did Monty any harm, did it? However that was never the case for me.

Some years ago Gary Player claimed that drug-taking was prevalent in golf. I must say that I have never seen a golfer take a performance-enhancing drug, and I have never even heard of any substance that enables you to find it easier to put the ball in the hole. Sure, there are golfers who are bulked up, but I am convinced that it has been achieved through exercise. David Duval reached the top of the world rankings without working on his physique, but then Tiger Woods came along and Duval took one look at him and decided that he had to work out, too, if he was going to compete in the future, and he promptly crashed down the world rankings. I see that now he has put on weight again, and his game is improving. Don't get me wrong: staying fit for golf is important, but should never be considered the be-all and end-all of correct preparation. Getting the ball into the hole in the fewest number of shots is far more important!

There are those who claim that a half pint of beer helps you to perform better, and there is an apocryphal tale about Jack Newton, the Australian golfer, who ran Tom Watson mighty close in the 1975 Open at Carnoustie, and who very sadly lost his arm when he was hit by an aeroplane propeller, which curtailed a glittering career. The story goes that when he won the Lake Macquarie International in his native land he drank a 'stubby' of beer on every hole of the final round. I know that Jack enjoyed a drink or two, but whether or not he ever managed to get through eighteen beers per round I don't know. It's a great story, even if it isn't true.

This was never meant to be an instruction book,

although that may come later, but there are one or two common-sense thoughts I would like to share.

Look at the ball through the strike. It may sound obvious, but so many people don't do it. What I am saying is that you should focus on the ball throughout your downswing, and particularly try to look at it during the moment of impact. Let your right shoulder, if you're right handed, pass under your chin, and concentrate on not lifting your body through impact. You will be amazed how well that simple swing thought works.

Let the club do the work, and don't try to hit at it. The second that you bring your body into an iron shot and try to help it into the air is the time when, almost without fail, you will hit the ball along the ground.

I always liked the saying that to get more distance you have to 'Hit it better, not harder!' Swing with rhythm; it sounds obvious, but most high handicappers try to hit the ball as hard as they possibly can much of the time. Swing within yourself – I have spent much of my career doing it, and it is the main reason I hit so many fairways and greens. You should try to do the same.

With little chips around the green, try practising with lots of different clubs – don't pull out your lob wedge every time. Take into account the lie of the ball, whether or not you have to carry the ball over the fringe, how much room there is between the fringe and the location of the hole, and don't forget to look at the lie of the land – it seems pretty self evident that if a putt will break from right to left, then a chip shot will react in the same way. However I'm amazed how few club players take borrow into the equation when pitching a ball onto the green.

When you are struggling with your timing, go down to

the driving range and hit golf balls with your feet together. This will encourage balance: if you fall over, it is a safe bet that you are swinging the club too hard and too fast. It also helps create good hand-to-eye co-ordination as well. Just a few shots played this way can really help your strike.

Perhaps the best advice I could give is: get your clubs customised to fit you. We are all different shapes and sizes, and we all swing the club differently. It stands to reason that a fifty-five-year-old, portly, 5ft 6in man who has a fifteen handicap would not be able to use the same clubs as Tiger Woods, for example. Would you go into Marks & Spencer, pick up the first suit you saw, hand over your money and then go home and wear it? Of course not. If your club pro tries to sell you a set of golf clubs without first ensuring that they are tailored for your game, go and buy your clubs from somebody else. Clubs are expensive, so you don't want to make a costly error. If you have never played with clubs that are customised to your game, you will be amazed how much difference it makes.

This most certainly includes putters as well. Off-the-shelf putters are almost always made too long. Most of them measure thirty-five inches – which is too long for most people. Trust me, I'm 6ft 3in and Yes! Golf fitted me with a thirty-three-inch putter. Are you left-eye dominant or right-eye dominant? It can determine whether you need a faced balanced putter or a heel toe weighted one. Find out, because it'll make a huge difference to your putting stats I promise. A lesson or two wouldn't go amiss either, of course.

Always use one more club than you think you need. Many amateur golfers drive me crazy the way they always come up short because once in their life they hit a seven iron

160 yards. Why don't they just accept that they normally hit it 140–150 yards? Most hazards are short of the green, so make sure you clear them. Try to play more percentage golf to improve your handicap.

I used to stand over putts and think: 'This one for The Masters.' Try it. Or: 'Two putts to win.' Role play is a good thing to practise, so when you actually have to make two putts to win it's easier to do so. I have always been a great believer in the power of the mind, of making things happen by willpower. It is not always easy to do, but I felt that I could sometimes make things happen in my round just by thinking I could, whether it be making a ball bounce right or left or holing a crucial long putt when I absolutely knew that I had to get it in the hole. Tiger seems to have mastered that ability.

Despite everything, I will miss amateur golf, although I am not so sure that I will miss the troubled relationship I had with the authorities. Every so often I would get a letter from the R&A on breaking amateur status rules. One year I received a letter pointing out that somebody had seen an advertisement for a company advertising laser surgery. It went on to say: 'We note that your picture has been used. Your amateur status does not allow you to endorse products in this way.'

I then got back to them to explain that the person who was responsible for the advert had not performed laser surgery on my eyes but had just taken the words I had used to describe how it had improved my sight and that I was most definitely not being paid. 'Well, you are going to have to tell him he can't do it,' they told me. So I tracked down the person in question and explained that, according to the R&A, they was not allowed to use my words in his advert.

The reaction? 'Tough'. I duly reported this to the R&A, who repeated the rules were being broken. I guessed that they wanted me to get a solicitor involved, but I refused to go down that route as it would have been very costly.

On another occasion, prior to The Masters, I went to a friend's house to use his synthetic grass green in order to keep my short game sharp – it was winter-time in England after all. I told a journalist, who asked if she could come along and watch and possibly take a few pictures and, of course, as it was a good golf story out of season, I agreed. A few photos were taken of me using the green, the journalist wrote an article, and at the bottom of it were included contact details for anybody interested in buying any synthetic grass products. I had no idea that this was going to happen, and yet again I found myself in hot water.

I told the R&A it had nothing to do with me, that the reporter had connected me with the company without my knowledge. 'Okay Gary,' they said, 'but...'

I was approached all the time to endorse this product or that, to put my name to a golf complex in Morocco or wherever, and I always had to say no. 'We'll pay you,' they would say. 'I'm sorry,' I always replied, 'but I can't let you use my name or likeness and I can't possibly accept any money from you.'

Someone once joked that my R&A file is the thickest at St Andrews.

CHAPTER TWENTY NINE
LIFE BEGINS AT FIFTY

Lots of people assumed that I was waiting until I reached fifty and that it was always in my mind to turn professional, but I had never done any more than toy with the idea. I kept telling them so, but I am sure many of them did not believe me.

Simon Fletcher, the professional at Morecambe, sat me down after Anthony Abraham had told me that my England career was over and asked me what I was going to do next. I hadn't a clue, but he sowed the seeds in my mind when he told me that he was sure I was good enough to turn professional and make a decent living on the Seniors Tour.

'You may as well turn pro,' he said. 'If they are not going to pick you, why would you remain in the amateur game? You will never become England captain or Walker Cup captain. What have you got to lose by turning pro?'

I thought about it. I thought about it long and hard, and eventually I reached a conclusion. 'Do you know what Simon? I think you might be right. I've given all these years to golf, and perhaps it is time that I now tried to earn something out of it for my retirement.'

On top of that, I had been told that Slazenger would love to have me as a front man, alongside Tony Jacklin and Andrew Murray. This meant I would be sorted out with clothing at least, as well as featuring in a TV infomercial for their latest hybrid irons and be paid for doing so.

I had qualified for the US Open championship that same year. How many other British amateur golfers have managed to do that? I will give you a clue – three including me. So they felt they had a good signing with my record as it was.

I had originally decided to retain my amateur status and enter the European Tour School, just to see how I got on. However, a company called 4Sports, which looks after several top European Tour players, courted me and persuaded me to turn pro immediately, saying that they could also get me into the Kazakhstan Open, so suddenly I was a tour pro, but without a tour on which to ply my trade. I still had no money, so I was forced to cash in a PEP I was saving for a rainy day – and it was pouring.

There is not much to say about qualifying school – so much was going on for me at that time that I did well to miss out by just one shot at Dundonald, in the wind and rain. And so it was that I arrived in Kazakhstan for my first full professional tournament.

I didn't even know exactly where Kazakhstan was, but it turned out to be located on the Chinese, Kyrgyzstan border. I guess you'd call it the link between the Fast East and the Middle East, but I never thought for one moment that it would be a thriving centre for golf. I flew into the second city, the old capital of Almaty, in the southeast of the country. I arrived on the Saturday, to be met at the airport by a driver who couldn't speak a word of English, but somehow he got me to my destination in one piece – just.

As we were heading towards the hotel I saw two cars ahead of us on the dual carriageway on which we were travelling. I did a double take because I could not believe how close together the cars were, and as we got nearer to them I could see that one of the drivers was gesticulating towards the other, and it was obvious they were not idly passing the time of day.

They were also driving very erratically, so my driver decided it would be best to overtake them; thus, we were three abreast on a two-lane road, with these other two motorists still going at it hammer and tongs. As I looked across I realised that one of the drivers was holding a gun and was threatening the other guy. I could not believe my eyes. If this guy pulled the trigger it could all get very messy. At this point, my driver also became aware of the gun and put his foot to the floor to get us past these madmen.

A few hundred yards down the road we were stopped by red traffic lights and, sure enough, a moment or two later, our friends also pulled up behind us, still arguing, and with the gun still being waved around in the air. By this time I was seriously concerned that my professional golf career was going to turn out to be the shortest on record. Thankfully, the lights changed to green and we turned left while the other drivers went right and I never did find out what became of them. They may still be shouting at each other for all I know. Welcome to Kazakhstan I thought.

Things didn't get too much better when we pulled up outside my hotel. It was part-sanatorium, part-hotel and it reminded me of Colditz Castle. It was the oddest place

I had ever stayed in. Despite my unusual introduction, I liked Kazakhstan. It was a fascinating exotic country that had a great deal of oil and gas wealth, so there wasn't any evidence of the poverty that I had perhaps expected to see. The cost of going to the tournament was not cheap, with the flights alone costing the best part of £800. On top of that, the wi-fi connection was incredibly expensive, it was impossible to use credit cards and the exchange rate was shocking so, once again, I could see my money drifting away.

I checked into my room and then I went to look at the course and was pleasantly surprised by how well prepared it was, so suddenly I found myself looking forward to playing in the Kazakhstan Open.

Then I returned to the hotel for dinner, but when I got to my table I was somewhat surprised to discover that my food had already been served. I thought it was a bit odd, but prepared to start eating when two elderly women appeared and sat down at my table. They didn't say a word to me, but began chattering away to each other in what I presumed to be Russian. I later figured that they were 'inmates' from the sanatorium and that I was sitting at their table. The food was awful, so I went up to my room as quickly as possible.

On the Sunday I had the course to myself as the rest of the players were not due to arrive until later that day, and I really enjoyed both the place and the views it afforded, with the nearby mountains providing a breathtaking backdrop.

In the evening I met up with the rest of the field and realised that I knew most of them because they were former amateur golfers I had played with or against. There were the likes of Ian Pyman, Graham Clark, Ian Garbutt and Lloyd

Saltman, and I picked up straight away that they all stick together in cliques. All the Swedes and Finns eat and drink together, as do the Italians, the French, the Scots, the Welsh, the English and suchlike. I found it strange, and I refused to conform, so one night I would socialise with the French, and on another I would mix with the Swedes and I was aware of everybody looking at me. I could feel them thinking: 'What are you doing Wolstenholme? You are meant to be with the English.' Well, I am sorry, but that was not for me. And the one night I did sit with the English, they all just wanted to take the mickey out of me anyway so no change there.

As I said, the food was very poor and it struck me that a lot of the younger players would only eat things they recognised. They simply weren't prepared to experiment.

I played a practise round with Lloyd Saltman, watched him hit the ball miles and found myself asking: 'What are you doing here, Lloyd?' This was a Challenge Tour event and there was no way he should have been anywhere but on the European Tour. In saying that, the first prize in Kazakhstan was something in the order of £60,000, so it was definitely worth winning.

When the tournament got under way, I found myself asking: 'What are you doing here Gary?' After nine holes of the first round I was six-over par, although I had four birdies on the trot on the back nine to finish on two over, but the scoring was low and I knew that I needed to be under par if I was to have any chance of making the cut. The next day I played nicely on the opening nine and was level par, knowing I still needed to make some birdies, so I started to go for shots and tried to hole long putts. I dropped another shot and ended up missing the cut by four strokes.

Gary Lockerbie won the tournament and, as a result, secured his full tour card.

While I was there I was interviewed by the Russian equivalent of *Golf World* and I did a two-and-a-half hour clinic with a group of kids too, most of whom were aged about eight, and all of whom could strike the golf ball really well. These were the children of men who had made lots of money through oil and gas I guessed. Afterwards, one of the sponsors told me that nobody had ever spent that amount of time with the children, but I always believe that if you are going to do something like that, you should do it properly.

I spoke to a number of the players about life on the Challenge Tour and, to a man, they agreed that it was a grind. The first prize in Kazakhstan might well have been £60,000, but that was pretty much far and away the best prize-money on offer, and I was told by various players that the European Tour wanted to created an environment in which players would not be comfortable, would not make the sort of money that could give them a good living. They wanted hungry golfers who were desperate to play on the main Tour – that is all well and good, but the harsh reality is that not everybody who aspires to be a Tour pro is good enough to hack it with the big boys, and I see nothing wrong with a second-tier system or third tier for that matter that allows them to be able to make ends meet.

The Kazakhstan Open and Tour School ended up costing me £5,000, which was money I could ill afford to waste. When I got home I decided that 4Sports was not for me and headed into the winter of 2008 with a hill to climb, although I did pick up bits and pieces for some work I did with Slazenger, with whom I signed a two-year contract.

I then joined the Players' Tour, which is golf's equivalent

of non-league football, but at least it gave me the opportunity to remain competitive and turned out to be a good little tour, playing some great courses. Everybody told me I was doing the right thing, and I got some help with my golf expenses, but it was never quite enough. I had no option but to borrow some money from a good friend to see me through to better times.

From day one it was mentally draining, but, with sheer hard work and pure belligerence, I made a little bit of cash on the Europro and the Players' Tour and that helped to keep me going. I was living at home with my Mum and gave her some money whenever I could and soon found that I was able to scratch a living together. For the first time in my life, I was making decisions for myself, rather than just going with the flow. Throughout my amateur career, people would come to me and offer me opportunities, such as the ones in Bristol and at Kilworth Springs, but I now feel that I have taken my destiny into my own hands.

For me, golf is like being married. At times I can't live with it, but mostly I can't live without it. I guess I am married to the game, it's part of what makes me who I am and what I am, and perhaps that is why I have never walked up the aisle. Whenever I sit down for a quiet moment, I am always thinking about golf. Even when I have spent the week at The Open commentating for the BBC, I would always make sure that I had my clubs with me so that I could practise my chipping and putting at night when I was off-air.

My obsession now is all about how I am going to get the best possible clubs in my bag; who do I approach to sort out the best golf shoes and the best golf balls and gloves?

Having resolved all my equipment issues, I knew that I

needed to find a way to keep my competitive juices flowing before reaching 50, so I decided to try to get my card to play on the EuroPro Tour. There are those who would describe it as the 'third division' of the European Tour, but they would be people who have never played on it: it is a highly competitive tour.

I managed to secure my playing privileges, and found myself going head-to-head with golfers who, almost without exception, were young enough to be my sons. They were lean, hungry and gifted. Naturally, they all hit the ball way past me, too.

I played steadily enough early on without setting the world on fire, but then I had rounds of 76, 70 and 69 in the Dawson & Sanderson Classic at Longhirst Hall Golf Club to finish fifth in tough conditions. With that came a cheque for £1,400. In the Dunlop Masters at Bovey Castle, I shot 68, 70 and 71 for a share of sixteenth position and added a further £429.17 to the bank balance. It wasn't sensational stuff but it was steady and I now realised that I could compete with these guys.

Next came the Galcorm Castle Northern Ireland PGA EuroPro Open. I played nicely once more, rounds of 71, 66 and 69 being good enough to give me a sixth-place finish and another few pounds tucked away.

I arrived at Stoke by Nayland, on the Essex-Suffolk border, feeling pretty pleased with myself, although I knew that I had to start holing some more putts. I was looking forward to testing myself on the Gainsborough course, which has hosted several European Seniors Tour events. It is a course that suited me. Without wanting to sound like a stuck record, it is another of those layouts that rewards good management. So with a change of putter, off I went.

Jamie Moul, the local favourite, was in the field. He grew up on this course, and many predict great things for him, and he set off like a train with a 64. If I am honest, I would probably have settled for finishing second before the third round started, but I shot 69, 63, 69 to win by four shots, having gone into the final round trailing by two. The 63 even included a dropped shot.

I picked up a cheque for £10,000, which was also a great confidence booster, but what mattered most was that I had won my first full-field professional tournament. If ever I'd had any doubts about whether or not I belonged out here, they were now gone. That victory propelled me to third place on the Order of Merit and gained me an invitation into the Challenge Tour event on the same course a few weeks later. Suddenly I was flying, and the world had better watch out because now I know that my dreams are realistically attainable.

There are only six European Seniors Tour cards available, because the system is tilted in favour of current tour players who reach fifty. There are insufficient full-field events with a thirty-six-hole cut, which means that more often than not, everybody plays all three rounds (most Seniors Tour tournaments are played over fifty-four holes), so everybody gets a chunk of the prize pot, and nobody ever drops out. On the European Tour, if you lose your card you have to go back to Qualifying School and prove all over again that you are still able to play with the big boys. That is the way it should be, so why doesn't it happen with the over-fifties in Europe too? Bigger fields, with more thirty-six-hole cuts, would lead to many more players getting greater opportunities to earn a living – 'the law of the jungle' I'd guess you'd call it. Before anything else happens, though, I need to secure one of those cards.

I have talked about the possibility of a Seniors Ryder Cup, but why not perhaps also a Seniors Challenge Tour, which offers a small number of tournaments that give over-fifties who can't get regularly onto the main Seniors Tour the chance to play for first prizes of, say, £5,000 to £10,000? It could even have a Pro/Am format, and, let's face it, demographically the average age of club players in Britain is now over 50, so they might like to see these guys construct a round rather than just watching young guns smashing the ball miles in all directions as in regular Pro/Ams. And they may well have more in common with them too.

APPENDIX

GOLFING ACHIEVEMENTS

'Major' individual tournament victories (International)
'Amateur' Champion of Great Britain (Ganton GC) 1991
'Amateur' Champion of Great Britain (Royal Troon GC) 2003
Chinese 'Open' Amateur Strokeplay Champion 1993
'Mid Amateur' Champion of Great Britain 1995, '96, '98
    *(playoff 1st extra hole)
United Arab Emirates 'Open' Amateur Champion 1995
Finnish 'Open' Amateur Strokeplay Champion 1996
Welsh 'Open' Amateur Strokeplay Champion 1997
Sherry Cup International Strokeplay winner (Sotogrande GC)
    2000, '01 *(playoff 1st extra hole), '03, '05
South African 'Open' Amateur Strokeplay Champion 2002
Scottish 'Open' Amateur Strokeplay Champion 2003
Georgia Cup (Golf Club of Georgia, USA) 2004
New South Wales Medal (Australia) 2005
European 'Mid Amateur' Champion (Luxembourg) 2006
    *(playoff 2nd extra hole), 2007

New South Wales Centenary Amateur Champion (Australia)
    2007
The Lakes Medal winner (The Lakes GC, NSW Australia) 2008
    *(playoff 1st extra hole)

'Major' individual tournament victories (National)

Midland 'Open' Stroke play Champion 1986 *(playoff 3rd
    extra hole), 2002
West of England 'Open' Stroke play Champion 1987
Berkshire Trophy Champion 1996, '97, 2002
English County Champion of Champions winner 1994, '96, '98,
    2001
Duncan Putter Stroke play Champion 1994, '96, '99
St.Mellion International Amateur Strokeplay Champion 1998,
    2006
Lagonda Trophy Strokeplay Champion 2002
South of England 'Open' Strokeplay Championship 2006
    *(playoff 2nd extra hole)
Keepmoat Lee Westwood Trophy Champion 2008

Individual tournament victories (Regional)

Golf Illustrated Gold Vase Strokeplay winner 1989
Midland 'Closed' Stroke play Champion 1986
L. & R. G. U. County Strokeplay Champion 1998, 2001
    *(playoff 4th extra hole)
L. & R. G. U. County Matchplay Champion 1984, '85, '86, '88
L. & R. G. U. 72 hole 'Spring' Tournament 1986
L. & R. G. U. County 'Open' Amateur Salver winner 1997
    *(playoff 2nd extra hole)
L. & R. G. U. Champion of Champions winner 2006
Leicester Mercury Scratch Cup winner 1989
Leicestershire 'Silver Fox' Strokeplay winner 1984, '85, '89

Gloucestershire County Champion (strokeplay) 1992, '93, '94, '96

Gloucestershire County Foursomes Champion 1994

Berkhamsted 'Open' Scratch Trophy 1999 *(playoff 2nd extra hole), 2002

West Midland 'Open' Stroke play Champion 1987

Charnwood Rock Invitational Strokeplay winner 1986, '88, 2005

Ealing 'Open' Strokeplay Champion 1990

City & County Strokeplay Champion (Henbury G.C.) 1994, '95

Ross-on-Wye Scratch Cup winner 1993

Long Ashton Vase Strokeplay winner 1990, '92, '93

Failand Cup 'Open' Strokeplay Champion 1989, '90, '91, '93, '97

Hampshire Hog Strokeplay Champion 1997*(playoff 1st extra hole), 2002

Selbourne Salver Strokeplay Champion 2001

Wilpshire Trophy Open Strokeplay Champion 2002

Northamptonshire County Cup 'Open' Strokeplay 2003

Individual International Major Tournament 'Misses' World-wide

Semi-finalist U.S. Mid Amateur Championship 1998

Quarter finalist U.S. Amateur Championship 2000

Tied 2nd European Amateur 'Open' Strokeplay (France) 1998

3rd   ..   ..   (England) 1991

3rd Hong Kong Amateur Championship (strokeplay) 1996

2nd Welsh Open Amateur Strokeplay Championship 2004

3rd Welsh Open Amateur Strokeplay Championship 1995

2nd Lake MacQuarie Amateur Strokeplay (Australia) 1998 *(3 hole playoff)

Tied 2nd European Mid Amateur Championship (England) 2000

2nd French Mid Amateur Strokeplay 1997

2nd La Manga Masters Strokeplay Championship (Spain) 1997

3rd   1998

Tied 3rd German Amateur Strokeplay Championship 2002

2nd Finnish Amateur Strokeplay Championship 2003
   *(play-off 1st extra hole)
Finalist Italian Amateur Championship 2005
2nd New South Wales Medal Championship (Australia) 2006
Finalist New South Wales Amateur Championship (Australia)
   2006 *(play-off 37th hole)
US Open International Final Qualifying @ Walton Heath :
   (1st Alternate) 2006 *(playoff 4th extra hole)
US Open International Final Qualifying @ Walton Heath :
   (1st Alternate) 2008 *(playoff 1st extra hole)
3rd Sotogrande Cup (Individual) - old 'Sherry Cup' - (Spain)
   2007
4th Portuguese Amateur Championship 2008

Individual Tournament 'Misses' National Events
Quarter Finalist British 'Amateur' Championship 1986, 2001, '06
2nd West of England Strokeplay Championship 1999, 2001
2nd Lagonda Trophy Strokeplay 1997
3rd   1996
2nd Midland Amateur Championship 1996
'Open' Championship : 2nd Alternate (St. Andrews)2000
     *(7 hole playoff)
2nd Berkshire Trophy Amateur Strokeplay 2001
Losing Finalist English Amateur Championship 2000
Semi-finalist English Amateur Championship 1991, 2004
Tied 3rd English Open Amateur Strokeplay Championship 1992
4th English Open Amateur Strokeplay Championship 1995, 2001
Tied 3rd Lytham Trophy Open Strokeplay Championship 2002
3rd Lytham Trophy Open Strokeplay Championship 2004
2nd Hampshire Salver (aggregate trophy) 2002
3rd Tillman Trophy Open Strokeplay Championship 2006
2nd Lee Westwood Trophy @ Rotherham GC 2006

2nd South of England Amateur @ Walton Heath 2008
2nd Silver Pheasant Trophy @ Fairhaven GC 2008

Representative Team Tournament 'Misses' World-wide

2nd European Men's Team Championship in Belgium,
   (England) 1995

..	..	..	..	in Holland (England) 2003
3rd	..	..	..	..	in Sweden (England) 2001
4th	..	..	..	..	in Italy (England) 1999
4th	..	..	..	..	in Scotland (England) 2007

3rd Simon Bolivar Trophy Strokeplay in Venezuela (England) 1997
5th Eisenhower Trophy Championship in Philippines (G.B.& I.)
   1996
2nd European Champion Club Tournament in Greece
   (Kilworth Springs) 2006
2nd Sotogrande Cup Nations Trophy, Spain (England) 2007
Losing finalist London Amateur Scratch Foursomes
   (The Berkshire) 2007

Miscellaneous victories / honours

World Team Championships (Eisenhower Trophy) winners 1998
Hong Kong International Amateur Open, Team Champions 1995
Leading Amateur, Benson & Hedges International Open 1993
Leading Amateur, British Masters International Open 2004
Leading Amateur US Open International Final Qualifying 2006,
   '08
Finnish Amateur Nations Trophy 1993, '95, '96, '99, 2003
The Phillip Scrutton Jug winner (Aggregate Trophy) winner
   1996, '97, '99, 2000, '01
Leicestershire & Rutland C.G.U., (Cameron Trophy) winner
   1984, '85, '89, '98, '99, 2001
Gloucestershire C.G.U., (Duchess Salver) winner 1990, '92, '93

Bristol 'Open' Stroke play Champion (now defunct) 1990, '93
  (Aggregate event)

English Champion Club Tournament Winners (Bristol & Clifton)
  1992

English Champion Club Tournament Winners (Kilworth Springs)
  2006

Cantrell Cup Northants P.G.A. Invitational Pro/Am Pairs 1999, 2000

Daily Telegraph National Amateur Order of Merit winner 1999

Daily Telegraph/JJB Amateur Order of Merit Winner 2001, '02,
  '03, '04

Daily Telegraph/JJB Amateur Order of Merit (3rd place) 2000

Daily Telegraph/JJB Amateur Order of Merit (4th place) 2006

Sherry Cup International European Nations Team Trophy (Spain)
  2000, '01, '03

Juan Carlos Talihide Cup 2 Man Pairs Championship, Argentina
  2000

Simon Bolivar Cup 2 Man Pairs Championship, Venezuela 2001

Hampshire Salver (Aggregate Trophy) 2001

British Golf Writers Award (G.B.& I. Walker Cup Team '01) 2001

German Amateur Championship Nations Trophy winners 2002

Lake Macquarie International Amateur Open Teams Event 2003

John Cheatle 'Open' Scratch Foursomes Champion 1987, '88,
  '89, '90

Norman Russell Salver, 'EGU Midland Group Qual' individual'
2003

English Golf Union National Order of Merit Winner 2003

English Golf Union National Order of Merit 3rd place 2006

Leicester Mercury 'Judges Special Sports Award' 2001

Honorary Master of Arts Degree from Northampton University
  2003

BBC East Midlands Amateur Sports Person of the Year Award
  2003

European Men's Team Championships winners (Hillside,
    England) 2005
Awarded MBE (For Services to Golf), New Year's Honours'
    List 2007

Miscellaneous information on golfing exploits

It is widely regarded that after the European Men's Team
Championships @ Western Gails Golf Club in Scotland, Gary
Wolstenholme unofficially* became the most capped player in
world amateur golf. It is believed that the previous record was
held by Garth McGimpsey of Ireland who had either 204 or 206
caps dependant on whom you speak to between 1978 & 1999.
Gary passed that record on the 7th July 2007.

* There are no official records which have been obtained from
the various National Unions or Associations from around the
world, and no official determination of which events are
'capped' by different countries either. However it is generally
thought that the European countries are most likely to hold the
record for most representative matches as it is widely regarded
that they play more international matches than any other region
of the world. It is therefore deemed that by surpassing the
previous known record in Europe that this then is a record for
the world also. Addendum:- England only 'cap' players for
matchplay games in the Biannual matches with France & Spain,
the European Men's Team Championships and the Home
Internationals series of matches in September each year
between England, Ireland, Scotland and Wales. Wolstenholme
has also played other matches representing England, but these
are at present are not counted in his final total as they are
regarded at this time as 'unofficial' matches by England.

Mixed Team victories (National)
Worplesdon 'Open' Scratch Mixed Foursomes Champion 1997
Worplesdon 'Open' Scratch Mixed Foursomes (Plate) winner 1996
Hoylake 'Open' Scratch Mixed Foursomes winner 1997

Mid Amateur Championship & Tournament victories
European Mid Amateur Championship 2006, '07
British Mid Amateur Championship 1995, '96, '98
Midland Mid Amateur Champion 2001
St.George's Hill 'Mid' Amateur Silver Trophy 1997
Gerald Micklem Amateur Cup (Sunningdale New) 1998, 2000
Berkhamsted Mid-Am Quaish 'Open' Strokeplay 1999

Professional tournaments competed in:
The 'Open' Championship @ Muirfield, Scotland 1992
.. .. @ Royal St. George's, England 2003
U.S. Masters @ Augusta National 1992, 2004
U.S.P.G.A. Memorial Tournament @ Muirfield Village 1992
Benson & Hedges International @ St.Mellion 1993 (made cut / leading amateur)
Australian 'Open' P.G.A. Match play @ Kingston Heath 1992
Australian Masters @ Huntingdale 1992 (made cut)
P.G.A. Scottish Open @ Glen Eagles, Scotland 1992
British Masters @ Forest of Arden, England 2004 (made cut / leading amateur)
US Open Championship @ Torrey Pines, CA, USA 2008
Kazakhstan Open 2008
Portuguese Masters 2008

Holes-in-One achieved: 13 (8 in practise, 5 in competition)

Competitive Holes-in-One achieved

The Amateur Championship Qualifier (12th Hole, Prestwick
St. Nicholas Golf Club)

Medal Competition (17th Hole, The Leicestershire Golf Club)

British Mid Amateur Championship Final (14th Hole,
Sunningdale Golf Club - New Course)

West of England Stroke play (5th Hole, Saunton Golf Club
- East Course)

Lake Macquarie International Amateur Open (3rd Hole,
Belmont Golf Club, Australia)

Honorary Memberships / Associations

Bristol & Clifton Golf Club, Gloucestershire - England

The Leicestershire Golf Club, Leicestershire - England

Berkhamsted Golf Club, Hertfordshire - England

Scarborough North Cliff Golf Club, Yorkshire - England

Grange-over-Sands Golf Club, Cumbria - England

Heysham Golf Club, Lancashire - England

Morecambe Golf Club, Lancashire - England

The Berkshire Golf Club - England

Trevose Golf & Country Club, Cornwall - England

County Sligo (Rosses Point) Golf Club, County Sligo -
Northern Ireland

Golf Club of Georgia, Georgia - United States of America

Old Giggleswickian Golfing Society, Yorkshire - England

Past Honorary Patron Silverdale Golf Club, Cumbria -
England

Regional Representations / Teams

County Representations:

Leicestershire & Rutland Golf Union 1981, '82, '83, '84, '85, '86,
'87, '88, '89, '98, '99 2000, '01, '02, '03, '04, '07

Gloucestershire Golf Union 1990, '91, '92, '93, '94, '95, '96
Cumbria County Golf Union2008

Regional Representations:
Midland Counties Golf Union 1983, '84, '85, '86, '87, '88, '89, '99,
    2000, '01, '02, '06
South Western Counties Golf Union 1991, '92, '93, '94, '95, '96

(*N.B. Only player in history of event to represent both regional
Unions)

International Representations / Teams
Full England International 1988 - 2008
Most capped international representative player in history for
    England @ 218 Caps & highest points scorer for England at
    international level with 142.5 points:- 130(W) - 25(H) - 63(L).
Eisenhower Trophy (World Team Championships): 2002, '04
Juan Carlos Tailhade Cup, Argentina (Pairs Event): 2000#, '05
Simon Bolivar Cup, Venezuela (Biannual Pairs Event): 1997, '99,
    2001#
The Spirit International - World Pairs Championship (USA): 2003
European Team Championships (Biannual Team Event): 1995,
    '97, '99, 2001, '03, '05#, '07
    (N.B. As of 2007 the European Men's Team Championships
    are to be held annually)
England - v - France International: 1988#, '90#, '92#, '94#, '98,
    2000#, '02#, '06#, '08#

England - v - Spain International: 1989#, '91#, '93#, '95#, '97#,
    '99#, 2001#, '03#, '05, '07#
England - v - South Africa: 2001#
England - v - Western Province (South Africa): 2006#

Quadrangular Home Internationals Series 1988#, '89#, '90, '91+, '92, '93#, '94#, '95#, '96#, '97#, '98#, '99#, 2000+, '01#, '02, '03+, '04#, '05, '06, '07#

Great Britain & Ireland International

St.Andrews Trophy - v - Continent of Europe: 1992#, '94#, '96#, '98, 2000#, '02#, '04#

Walker Cup - v - United States of America 1995#, '97, '99#, 2001#, 03#, '05

(Highest points scorer for G.B.& I. in history of the Championship : 19(P),10(W), 9(L), 0(H), and most individual & team wins by a Great Britain & Ireland player in Walker Cup history.)

Eisenhower Trophy (World Amateur Team Championships) 1996, '98#

(Now individual 'home' nations compete in the Eisenhower Trophy)

Hong Kong Amateur International Teams Championship 1996#

European Golf Association International Representative :-

E.G.A. - v - Pan Asia Pacific Golf Confederation (The Bonallack Trophy) : 1998# (Perth, Australia), 2000# (Madrid, Spain), 2004 (Rome, Italy), 2006# (Auckland, New Zealand)

Turned professional September 2008.

KEY :-   # = victories + = wooden spoon